French Multinationals

Studies in International Political Economy will present new work, from a multinational stable of authors, on major issues, theoretical and practical, in the international political economy.

General Editor

Susan Strange, Professor of International Relations, London School of Economics and Political Science, England

Consulting Editors

Ladd Hollist, Visiting Associate Professor, Brigham Young University, USA

Karl Kaiser, Director, Research Institute of the German Society for Foreign Affairs, Bonn, and Professor of Political Science, University of Cologne, West Germany

William Leohr, Graduate School of International Studies, University of Denver, USA

Joseph Nye, Professor of Government, Harvard University, USA

Already Published

The Political Economy of New and Old Industrial Countries
The East European Economies in the 1970s
Defence, Technology and International Integration
Japan and Western Europe
Tax Havens and Offshore Finance
The North–South Dialogue
The International Gold Standard

Forthcoming Titles

Dependency Transformed
International Political Economy

French Multinationals

Julien Savary

Foreword by François Morin

St. Martin's Press, New York

338.88
S 265

Library of Congress Cataloging in Publication Data

Savary, Julien, 1944–
    French multinationals.

    Translation of: Les multinationales françaises.
    Bibliography: p.
    Includes indexes.
    1. Corporations, French. 2. International business
enterprises. I. Title.
HD2755.5.S29413   1984   338.8'8944   83-40590
ISBN 0-312-30476-5

The Institute for Research and Information on Multinationals (IRM) is a foundation which promotes and finances independent research on multinational companies and their impact on society.

On the basis of this research, the IRM publishes books, articles and reports, organises conferences and seminars, and is building up a bank of specialised material. Facts, figures and background information are made available to the widest possible audience (in particular to academics, company directors and other executives, trade unionists, politicians, international agency officials and journalists). By providing such data the Institute aims to fuel the debate and throw light on some of the issues raised by the role of multinationals in the world today.

IRM, 45–47, rue de Lausanne, 1201 Geneva

Contents

List of Tables

List of Figures

Foreword

French Multinationals—is this just another book investigating the subject of multinationals and the many myths about them? To some people they are a power which can conveniently be used as the most effective means of economic development, while others see them as a stateless monster whose growth must be contained as far as possible.

Julien Savary's book is certainly a work which will mark an epoch because it rejects the assumptions of economic and religious ideology. It is the first study which has taken a systematic look at the multinationalisation of French companies as part of their strategic development abroad.

Developing his work with some of the most recent methods applied in Industrial Economics and Business Management, using quantitative data which it took several years to collect and process, and finally taking his inspiration directly from what, in my view, must be called the 'French theory of multinationalisation' (represented by the Centre d'Etudes et de Recherches sur les Entreprises Multinationales (CEREM) and its director C. A. Michalet), Julien Savary presents us with a complete picture of the international relocation of French firms' activities.

This work is, however, more than just a detailed map of establishments abroad or a glossary of those sectors where the location of operations has been spread on an international level. Its primary purpose is to give an account in one movement of how and why French firms have become multinational. Leaving the reader to discover the main quantitative results of this work, I would like to highlight here what I feel are the two main conclusions.

The first relates to the highly contradictory aspects of foreign investment in an open economy. There is absolutely no doubt that within an economy like that of France investment abroad plays a positive part in competitiveness and the development of exports. But what effect does it have on employment? The answer to this is twofold. Firstly, the export movement brings with it positive effects on employment in France. But there is often an opposing trend which in some branches has reduced manpower levels, though it is true that the economic crisis is partly to blame for this adverse trend.

Coupled with these particular effects are the effects of foreign investment in France. The diagnosis here is rather more alarming.

Because of its size and concentration in certain sectors, this investment creates a massive 'domination effect' relegating France to a position well down the table of international economies. As a result the French economy has become despecialised in key industrial sectors and has less control over its domestic market. The contradictory nature of this process of internationalisation is all too obvious. The expansion of foreign markets is coupled with the loss of control over strategic segments of the domestic market.

A second major conclusion can be drawn from this study. The competitiveness of French industry abroad rests increasingly with a few big international groups. The results of this trend deserve careful consideration. Firstly, it weakens the tissue of French industry by the growing dichotomy it creates between big groups and small and medium-sized firms. It then accelerates the growth of these large units and consequently reinforces the already very oligopolistic concentration of the French production system. Finally, it encourages conservatism with regard to positions won historically: this point does of course explain the relative 'under-multinationalisation' of the French economy compared with the other economic powers in the Western World.

To what extent might this process be reversed by the nationalisation of five multinational industrial groups and the industrial policy of the new government? At the end of his work, the author suggests three possible developments. The first is to continue in the same direction, which would leave some room for reconquering the domestic market, the second is to break totally with the world market, and finally the third would be to combine the first two, making a distinction between those sectors exposed to world competition and those protected from it.

To go a little further in considering future development, I personally think we have to pay particular attention to the problems of two other fundamental questions, the first of these being relations between the production system, particularly in its multinationalised part, and the new banking and financial system, and the second being the nature of the relations which have to be built up between the State and the industrial groups.

In the first place, is there any sense in *simultaneously* nationalising big industrial groups and virtually the whole of the credit system? The answer to this question should be a resounding 'yes', as the public sector would then be given a new economic status: it would be in a position effectively to coordinate the objectives and actions of the big industrial groups, the banks and the State. Industrial policy could then be defined and deployed on a national level, as well as on a regional and international level. Any other prospect, particularly if the nationalised groups were made into purely competitive entities, would run the risk of rendering nationalisation meaningless, and even making it dangerous by increasing the risk of inefficiency due to changes in structures or control.

Secondly, it is when industrial policy is being drawn up that the relation between the nationalised and multinational groups and the State will be determined. This assumes that the multi-sector character of these groups and their development will be respected, which precludes an industrial policy based solely on the concept of economic branches and vertical integration. Such a policy would not be able to preserve the complex synergies of these groups and would run the risk of destroying their efficiency. To safeguard this efficiency, it is vital that administrative autonomy be retained, and everyone is in agreement with this.

By following these principles, I feel that it will be possible to determine the objectives of industrial policy. Can this be limited to reconquering the domestic market? Julien Savary's book shows that the development and competitiveness of these groups are based on their international expansion. The new industrial policy will therefore have to incorporate within its objectives the international dimension of the development of French industrial groups. This book has the great merit of making a vital contribution to this debate.

François Morin
Professor at the University of Toulouse I

Acknowledgements

This work, which was completed in June 1981, constitutes a condensed and entirely rewritten and updated version of the second volume of my doctorate thesis. I wish to thank all the members of the examining board—MM de Cambiaire, Devillebichot, Jacquemin, Morin, Moreaux and Desmoutier—for their advice, and particularly Professors G. Devillebichot and F. Morin who gave me their advice when this thesis was being written. Professor C.-A. Michalet and the members of CEREM, whose work often inspired my own analyses, also gave me their opinions, for which I thank them. In preparing the final text, the remarks of Professor Bertin and MM Ghertman, Olivi and Bouayad of IRM were also helpful.

The computer department of the University allowed me to process the data, which would not have been possible without the help of Mme D. Galy, computer engineer. The managers of the French companies who agreed to reply to my requests for information and my survey questionnaires also contributed to the production of this study. Finally Jean-Jacques Fournié and Michel Didier helped me make the following text more readable. I am therefore indebted to a great number of people for the interesting parts of my analysis. On the other hand, I bear full responsibility for any omissions and errors of interpretation.

Preface to the English Edition

The French edition of this book, *Les Multinationales françaises*, was first published in the spring of 1981. Since that date, which coincided with the arrival of a new Leftist political power, the scene set for enterprises operating in France has undergone profound changes.

In this English edition I have added a supplementary chapter which examines both the evolution of foreign investment in France and at the same time the expansion of French multinationals abroad, notably those that were nationalised in 1982. It would seem that the French economy has remained, from the viewpoint of direct international investment, an open economy.

I have not modified the original text of *Les Multinationales françaises*, which in itself constitutes an analysis of multinationals before May 1981.

Julien Savary
Toulouse, October 1983

Preface

The French automobile industry is composed of two big industrial groups, Renault and Peugeot, which are leading exporters and also control many production subsidiaries abroad. Michelin dominates the French tyre industry and has large factories in West Germany, Great Britain, Spain, the United States and Brazil. In 1979, Saint-Gobain Pont-à-Mousson employed 85 512 people outside France, which was 58 per cent of its total staff: on this basis it is the biggest French multinational company. Bic and Rossignol, which are medium-sized companies, also hold 'blue ribands' for export achievements, and everyone recognises their multinational characteristics. We could go on to mention small and medium-sized companies such as Goupil Laboratories, Porcher, Sigma, etc. Then, Roussel-Uclaf, the big French pharmaceuticals company, is a subsidiary of Hoechst (West Germany). L'Oréal, number one in the cosmetics field, is owned by Nestlé (Switzerland); the French data-processing industry is dominated by IBM (United States) and Honeywell (United States), which up until 1980 controlled CII–Honeywell Bull, and so on.

France today does therefore have companies that are big exporters and companies that are very multinational.[1] It is also host to many foreign multinational groups. But although it is clear that this dual commercial and industrial 'opening up' to foreign markets has become essential to the functioning of the French economy, the extent and nature of this phenomenon are ill-defined: which multinational companies are of French origin? Are they solely large companies? Why do they develop? In which countries do they become established? What are the consequences of their foreign activities on the French economy? What 'weight' do they have amongst the foreign multinationals which invest in France? How do they react to the world economic crisis and today's political and economic uncertainties? We have tried to answer these questions. In sum, what does the multinational phenomenon represent in the French economy, for the period 1974–80, the 'crisis' period?

There is unfortunately very little information on French multinational companies. It is not possible to make any comparisons with what is available, not on a world level, where there are studies by the UN[2] or Harvard University;[3] nor on an American level (official reports of the US Senate,[4] regular statistics,[5] studies by Professor Vernon's team);[6] or on a European[7] or British[8] level. In addition, the American works in particular study at regular intervals the importance of the foreign operations of American companies, their location, their consequences on the foreign trade of the United States, the international flows of money and the host economies. The only documents available relating to France are statistics on the flow of French investment abroad set out in the balance of payments,[9] and the studies carried out at the request of the UN or the US Senate! As the information published by French companies is very incomplete, there are serious gaps in the statistics. As for the studies giving more detailed information on the multinational phenomenon—and some of these are very interesting—they are in all cases either incomplete, episodic or too specific. We find some essentially theoretical approaches,[10] and others relating to the causes of the multinationalisation of companies.[11] Other writers produce managerial-type analyses often for the purposes of group financial management.[12] There are also monographs concerning one firm,[13] groups of firms[14] or the activities of French firms in a particular country.[15] Finally, the recent development of university work on French industrial and financial groups,[16] which are increasingly drawn on in extensive official studies,[17] improves our knowledge of the big French groups, and hence the multinational companies, which are very often big groups. Indirectly this work provides information on the foreign control to which they are subject, and more rarely on their exports and multinationalisation.

On the other hand, the information on foreign investment in France is much more detailed. There are official studies which measure the annual rates of foreign penetration into the French economy. But this penetration is underestimated, as the notion of minority control is not used: thus the Empain Schneider group was not considered as being under foreign control in the official statistics.[18] Though there are several very interesting university studies, which do not have this shortcoming, they are incomplete,[19] out of date[20] or essentially theoretical in approach.[21]

There is, then, no overall study of French multinational companies and no official statistical source on which such a study could be based. We have therefore had to produce our own data base. By drawing at random from among all the French companies quoted on the Paris and provincial stock exchanges, belonging to all sectors (excluding banks and insurance), we have compiled a sample of 413 firms, which is representative of the French economy. It includes some small and medium-sized companies, so as not to restrict the analysis to the big multinational companies, and some non-multinational companies so that we can look at whether multinationalisation is accompanied by specific economic and financial characteristics: out of these

413 companies, in 1974, 182 controlled production operations outside France and were thus multinational companies and fifty-six were subsidiaries of foreign groups in France (see list of firms in Annexe 1). We then collected information on the economic and financial characteristics of these companies, particularly with regard to their operations abroad: exports, production abroad in the plants controlled (even in the case of minority control), geographical distribution of this production, and its organisation (flow of trade in goods between the French and foreign plants in the group, destination of foreign production, etc.). This work was based on information published by the companies, together with the existing studies, year books, and articles in the press. Then two successive questionnaires had to be sent out to all the companies to collect full information on their operations abroad.[22] Finally, we made a briefer parallel study of the operations abroad of all the big French industrial groups. In addition we made an exhaustive study of foreign investment in France on the basis of the APEF yearbooks (Opera Mundi edition). This provided us with recent data (1974 and 1978) based on a wide definition of the control of French companies.

Why does the study cover the period 1978–80? Firstly, we had to work on the most recent data available; secondly, we had to consider the data available at the time the survey started. For 1974 we 'assembled' a sort of photographic view of the structural facts resulting from previous developments. The changes that occurred between 1978 and 1980 enabled us to analyse the reactions of foreign groups and French companies during the economic crisis.

Once all these data had been computer-processed, we had a very full description of the multinationalisation of the French economy and a detailed perception of French multinational companies, their origin, their specific characteristics compared with French non-multinational companies and foreign multinational firms, and the forms of their expansion abroad. One finding slowly emerged, the principal thesis of this study: today the opening up of the French economy to foreign markets, by exporting and multinational production, plays an essential part in the equilibrium of the trade balance, employment in France, the profitability and competitiveness of companies, industrial specialisation and adaptation to the crisis.

We have stated the field of analysis, methods of investigation, and principle thesis of the study: now we come to stating the theoretical context which forms the background to our work. We rejected both the managerial-type approach, centred on the internal management decisions of companies, and a macroeconomic method,[23] limited to the trends of overall quantities, such as flows of international investment and exports. Our approach fell midway between these two: we did of course have to study firms, but a large number of them and from the point of view of an outsider, in relation to a breakdown of the economy by sectors of activity. We examined the interaction between the market structures, the behaviour of companies and the consequences of their behaviour. A study of the economic role which these firms play was to reveal certain overall structural characteristics of these phenomena: we proceeded along the lines of industrial economics. The originality of our procedure lay in applying this method of investigation to French industry, centred on the multinational phenomenon in its widest sense; that is the operation of French companies abroad and the operations of foreign companies in France. This modification of the traditional framework of industrial economics had several consequences:

— A distinction could be drawn between companies which are French multinationals and those which are not, between multinational companies and those which are only exporters and between the subsidiaries of foreign groups in France and companies under national control.

— Activity abroad is considered as a type of corporate behaviour explained by the structural characteristics of the markets in which the companies are involved, and a study is made of its consequences on the company results.

— But while industrial economics looks at companies within a national economy and studies the structures of the markets in this economy, we concentrated here on the problems of companies' operations in foreign economies: the choice of geographical location of these operations, their importance and their nature must also be explained by the structural characteristics of the foreign economies, and even by what could be called the structures of the world market. These structures must also be examined, and considered as a determinant factor of the behaviour studied. While the French economy is the main object of our study, one can understand why reference is also made to the world economy.

— Finally, while the theories explaining international investment are all too often concerned with one particular cause of the multi-nationalisation of firms, when we come to the end of this study we are able to suggest an analysis of the overall process of multi-nationalisation, which considers those factors specific to the home economy, those linked with the structures of the world economy, those arising out of the strategies of the firms and even the very interaction between these different factors.

By using this method of analysis, and based on the data collected, we were able to define the essential characteristics of the multination-alisation of the French economy, which we list briefly here to show how interesting our findings are:

— extent of the multinationalisation phenomenon, which includes small and medium-sized companies, even though it is the bigger firms which account for most of the production operations outside France (in 1974, the top twenty-two big multinational groups controlled over 70 per cent of production abroad by all French industrial companies, while they only represent 13.7 per cent of workers in France);

— the role of concentration in the French production system and the oligopolisation of domestic markets in the development of exports and production operations abroad, emphasising that this development is linked with the recent development of the structures of French industry;

— the specific character of the subsidiaries of foreign groups in France, with these companies in general being terminal units which export very little and are not very multinational, and not, as one might have supposed, relay units very much open to foreign markets;

— the nature of the foreign production strategies adopted by French companies, and in particular systematic subordination of this production to the objectives of the French group (hence explaining the paradox in the title of this book, as French multinationals, although producing in several countries, are multinationals of French origin, whose foreign subsidiaries are dependent on the French parent companies);

— the importance of the multinationalisation of French companies within the developed countries, corresponding essentially to the objective of expanding market shares, in connection with competition between French groups and foreign groups;

— the nature of the multinationalisation of French companies within the countries of the Third World and southern Europe, most frequently with the objectives of reducing production costs: this type of multinationalisation, based on the unequal development of different economies, helps perpetuate this imbalance through the international division of operations implemented by the multinationals;

— the specific importance of two areas of the world economy, very often used by French multinational companies for their production plants: Africa (Maghreb and French-speaking black Africa) and southern Europe (Spain, Portugal, Greece);

— the greater profitability of French multinational companies compared with the non-multinational companies, with this superiority resulting directly from their export and foreign production activities;

— the effects of the foreign production of companies on French exports and employment in France, with this locational spread explaining the expansion of exports between 1974 and 1977 and the reduction in employment in certain sectors;

— the reactions of French multinational companies to the world

economic crisis taking the form of accentuating multinationalisation and geographical relocation within the developed countries;
— the possibility of deducing, from a comparison of direct international investment in France and other economies, the relative
industrial specialisation and France's position in a world economic
ranking (this arises from the internationalisation of the French
economy in which both large amounts of foreign investments are
made and which is the source of big foreign investments abroad).

Finally, on reaching the end of this study, we have shown clearly
how multinationalisation is essential for French companies, both for
their competitiveness and their growth, and for the development of
France's position in the world economy. At the same time, we have
described the contradictory nature of this opening up of the economy
to foreign markets, as the investments of foreign groups in France
bring with them domination effects which offset those which French
multinational companies exert on foreign economies.

It was difficult to decide on the best framework to adopt, because
many of the analyses are interrelated. In the end we opted for a three-
part framework corresponding to the traditional division in an industrial economy analysis between structure, behaviour and performance.
So, Part I studies the influence of French economic structures on
exports and the multinationalisation of companies. Part II examines
both the role of the world economic structures and the way companies
carry out their operations abroad, in other words their strategies, and
the effect of the crisis on these strategies. Finally, Part III analyses
the consequences of foreign operation on the profitability of multinational firms, and those of multinationalisation on French exports
and employment in France. The relation between the economic crisis
and the multinationalisation of French companies is therefore described
in both Part II (effects on strategies) and Part III (effects on exports
and employment, measured over the period 1974-7).

The conclusion then goes on to stress the great opening up of the
French economy to foreign markets, the essential part which foreign
expansion plays in the competitiveness of firms, and the trade-offs
from this international opening up. We also consider the prospects
for French multinationals at a time when they are faced with a permanent world economic crisis, the outcome of which cannot be forecast: at a time, too, when political change in France is affecting some
of them directly (nationalisation) and altering the conditions under
which all the others operate.

In the preliminary chapter we give a brief history of the multinationalisation of the Western and French economies.

NOTES

1 We use the term 'multinational company' to mean a company controlling production operations in at least one foreign country, and multinationalisation, or multinational production, the corresponding action. The term 'operations abroad' covers exports plus production carried out abroad.

2 UN, 1973 and UN, 1978.

3 Vaupel and Curhan, 1969.

4 US Senate, 1973.

5 Survey of Current Business.

6 R. Vernon, 1971; Robbins and Stobaugh, 1973; Stopford and Wells, 1974.

7 L. G. Franko, 1976.

8 Many official sources, Reddaway reports, Stener report, etc. quoted for example in J. H. Dunning, 1979. This article by Dunning updates all the previous studies.

9 See the Notes bleues published by the Information Service of the Ministry of Economics.

10 C. A. Michalet, 1976 is the most interesting analysis; M. Rainelli, 1979; W. Andreff, 1976; H. Claude, 1978.

11 M. Delapierre and C. A. Michalet, 1973, from a sample of seventy-two firms who had replied to a very detailed questionnaire, with this work constituting the fullest study on the multinationalisation of French companies, with a historical analysis and an examination of the methods and areas of establishment, as well as a study of the factors of locational spread; C. A. Michalet, 1972; G. Y. Bertin, 1972.

12 B. Marois, 1979:1; B. Marois, 1979:2 for the banks, Bodinat Klein and Marois, 1978.

13 Béaud, Danjou, David, 1975 for PUK; Drugman and Eisler, 1972 for SGPM; Masini, Ikonicoff, Jedlicki and Lanzarotti, 1979 for three companies in Ivory Coast; R. Montavon, 1979 for BSN in Mexico.

14 For example the 'Analyses de groupes' published by DAFSA, testimonials of companies published by CNPF, 1979:1.

15 For French companies in the United States: H. Couffin, 1977; for French companies in the United States and Canada: R. Guir, 1980.

16 F. Morin, 1975; F. Morin, A. Alcouffe *et al.*, 1977; P. Allard, M. Béaud *et al.*, 1978; B. Bellon, 1980; J. M. Chevalier, 1980; J. P. Gilly and F. Morin, 1981; P. Jeanblanc, 1981; B. Soulage, 1981 and many articles in the journal *Economie Industrielle*.

17 M. Hannoun, 1978; INSEE, 1980; STISI, 1980.

18 STISI annual publication (figures relate to the position as at 1 January 1978).

19 Centre de recherche de géographie industrielle, 1975.

20 G. Y. Bertin, 1975.

21 M. Delapierre and C. A. Michalet, 1976.

22 A note on methodology in Annexe 2 describes the method by which the sample was compiled, its representativeness, the sources used and the choice of variables and the criteria of multinationalisation.

23 A method derived from international economics.

Introduction: Multinational Companies and Multinationalisation of the Economy

How far has the French economy now opened up to foreign countries? Is this a recent phenomenon? Does France export more or less and is it more or less multinational than other economies? We propose to answer these questions here, first examining trends through the twentieth century and then the position in the 1980s.

INTERNATIONAL INVESTMENT: GROWTH AND CHANGE

In the absence of any study on the historical development of French direct investment abroad, we have to look for information in studies on the development of international investment at world level (American and UN work) or at European level.[1]

International investment has been with us a long time.[2] It made its appearance at the end of the nineteenth century and has developed continuously throughout the twentieth century. Even though, originally, portfolio investments were more important than direct investments, by 1914 a large number of firms which are well-known multinationals today had already set up abroad: according to Franko, in 1914 American firms had 122 foreign production subsidiaries, English firms 60, and firms from Continental Europe 167 (see Table I.2). M. Wilkins has even shown that the ratio of capital invested abroad to GNP was the same for the United States in 1914 (7.3 per cent) as it was in 1968 (7.5 per cent):[3] even in 1914 its relative weight was considerable and investment abroad then developed significantly in parallel with the rapid expansion of GNP. However, the multinationalisation of French firms had scarcely begun in 1914: only one of the big firms described by Franko had industrial subsidiaries abroad—SGPM.[4]

Since 1914, multinationalisation has developed steadily although it slowed down between 1929 and 1950.[5] The world stock of international investment increased as follows (in $US billion*): 1914, 41.6; 1967, 108; 1971, 165; 1976, 287 (UN, 1978 and for 1914, estimates of W. Andreff, 1974).

But while Europe, and in particular the United Kingdom, dominated

---

*The term 'billion' is used to denote '1000 million' throughout this text.

in 1914, investment of American origin expanded very rapidly and forged ahead in 1960 to account for 59 per cent of the total investment stock. On the other hand, since then investments of European and Japanese origin have developed more rapidly, reducing the share of American investment, as shown in Table I.1.

Table I.1   Development of international investment by country of origin (book value of assets, as a percentage of the world total)

	1914	1930	1960	1967	1971	1976
United States	6.3	35.3	59.1	55.0	52.0	47.6
United Kingdom	50.4	43.8	24.5	16.2	14.5	11.2
West Germany	17.3	2.6	1.1	2.8	4.4	6.9
Japan				1.3	2.7	6.7
Switzerland				3.9	4.1	6.5
France	22.2	8.4	4.7	5.5	5.8	4.1
Canada	0.5	3.1	5.5	3.4	3.6	3.9
Netherlands	3.1	5.5	4.2	2.1	2.2	3.4
Sweden	0.3	1.3	0.9	1.4	2.1	1.7
Benelux				1.9	2.0	1.2
Italy				1.9	2.0	1.0

Source: J. D. Maurino, 1974 and H. Magdoff, 1979, for 1914, 1930, 1960 (the 1960 figures are 'very approximate estimates'): UN, 1973 for 1967 and 1971; UN, 1978 for 1976.

This trend is confirmed by the number of foreign production subsidiaries: general growth has continued since 1974, but has been irregular over this period. The main expansion of European firms has taken place since the Second World War: 'Dutch, Swiss and Swedish firms continued their international growth, German firms reconstructed their foreign assets for the second time and the big Belgian, Italian and French firms set up abroad.'[6] Table I.2 also shows that this international expansion of European firms accelerated over the 1960s.

For French multinational companies, international growth seems to have accelerated in an even more marked fashion after the Second World War. The 457 foreign production subsidiaries owned by the twenty-one French groups studied by Franko were in fact set up over the following periods (as a percentage):[7] before 1914, 2 per cent; 1914-29, 3 per cent; 1930-45, 4 per cent; 1946-55, 7 per cent; 1956-64, 18 per cent; 1965-70, 67 per cent.

This does not mean that there were no production subsidiaries before that, but they are underestimated in this study because it only covered industrial and oil groups, while before 1950 the foreign subsidiaries of French companies were mainly concerned with extraction, mining and plantation operations.

Table I.2 Development of the number of foreign production subsidiaries
set up or acquired by the biggest multinational firms by origin

Period	United States	United Kingdom	Continental Europe	Japan
Before 1914	122	60	167	0
1914–19	71	27	51	0
1920–29	299	118	249	1
1930–38	315	99	112	3
1939–45	172	34	44	40
1946–52	386	292	129	2
1953–55	283	55	117	5
1956–58	439	94	131	14
1959–61	901	333	232	44
1962–64	959	319	229	90
1965–67	889	459	532	113
1968–70	inc.	729	1030	209
Total	4836	2529	3023	521

Source: Vaupel and Curhan, used by Franko, 1976, p. 10. These are the operations of the biggest companies: 187 for the United States, 47 for the United Kingdom, 85 for Continental Europe and 67 for Japan.

Before 1958: the Search for Raw Materials

In fact, generally, the first phase of the multinationalisation of European companies up until around 1955-60 can be characterised by investment aimed at finding the agricultural, mineral and power-producing raw materials needed for the development of the European economies.[8] It has been shown that capital exports expanded in parallel with the accumulation of capital in the developed countries, following the cycles during which this capital was accumulated.[9] Investment of this type did, of course, take place in other European countries, but was concentrated in Southern Europe, the Eastern bloc countries (before 1945), the Middle East and Africa; that is, very often in areas influenced or colonised by European countries.

After the Second World War, while some countries accepted the domination of the American and British oil companies, France and Italy adopted a policy of support for their national companies (CFP, ERAP, ENI). However, this initial period also saw the development of European international investment in the manufacturing industry, especially in other European countries. These operations were due to the national customs barriers and were based on the technological advantages which certain firms gained by developing products or production processes suited to the characteristics of their own market, e.g. saving raw materials and aiming at low-income consumers (compared with the American consumer). Nationalism and the risks of conflicts did, however, limit this type of expansion.[10] It would seem that protectionism and a degree of Malthusianism, which were more pronounced in France, reduced this type of investment abroad by French firms, especially since the size of the French colonial empire made the development of these new processes less necessary than in West Germany, for example.[11]

After 1958: the Opening Up of Frontiers and Industrial Investment in Europe

The second phase of the multinationalisation of European companies, from 1955-60 until today, was characterised by a rapid growth in investment abroad (cf. Tables I.1 and I.2) and by its essentially industrial nature. The opening up of frontiers following the creation of the Common Market (in 1958), the increase in competition and the accelerated concentration of production facilities which resulted from this, were the cause of this change in operations abroad. This was particularly true for France, where the role of State economic policy, trying to set up big competitive industrial groups, was another essential factor in this trend.[12] This new investment was then located in the developed economies and particularly in Europe.

A parallel phenomenon must be mentioned: while the effects of American investment in Europe had been felt for a long time, during the years 1955-60, this American penetration was intensified. Attracted by the Common Market,[13] the US groups accelerated the change and concentration of the economies of the Old Continent. This, coupled with the developing multinationalisation of European firms, explains why foreign (American and European) investment developed very rapidly in French industry at this time.[14]

Table I.3 shows the geographic origins of foreign direct investment in recent years. For the developed European economies, and in particular for France, most foreign investment comes from the United States and other European countries. This shows both the importance of American investment in Europe and the high level of inter-penetration of the European economies resulting from reciprocal international investment. Conversely, the European economies were the source of most foreign investment in the United States (where their penetration did, however, remain low). Finally, each of the developed economies today has geograhical areas in the Third World where its international investments predominate, corresponding to the areas under their influence: Latin America and many other countries for the United States, Nigeria for Great Britain, Ivory Coast for France, etc.

The Growth of World Trade

World trade, too, has gone through a spectacular development during the twentieth century, expanding much more rapidly than world production. This development has been accompanied by a structural change because the share of food products and raw materials has been in constant decline in favour of manufactured products, while trade is increasingly being carried out between developed countries: hence, within the market economies, in 1950, the industrial countries sent 46 per cent of their exports to other industrial countries, with this rate rising to 64 per cent in 1970.[15]

In France, trade has opened up considerably over the last thirty years: the ratio of imports to the GNP climbed from 14.3 per cent in 1950 to 20.3 per cent in 1977 while, over the same period, the ratio of exports to the GNP rose from 14.3 per cent to 18.3 per cent,[16] thanks primarily to sales of manufactured products. A geographical change was taking place simultaneously as the share of exports to countries in the free trade area fell from 36 per cent in 1950 to 14.1 per cent in 1977, while that of exports to the Common Market countries increased from 20.3 per cent to 42.3 per cent.[17]

In all the developed Western economies, the twentieth century has therefore been marked by rapid growth in international trade and international investment and by a twofold development: more and more trade and international investment is being carried out between the developed economies—and this is relating increasingly to manufactured products and the corresponding industries.

THE MULTINATIONALISATION OF THE FRENCH ECONOMY TODAY

Following this general change in the Western economies, represented by a twofold opening up towards foreign countries, the French economy would, as regards the intensity of this phenomenon, seem to be in an intermediate position with respect to the other economies.

The French economy's export rate (cf. Table I.4) is certainly lower than that of the smaller European countries (Sweden, Belgium, the Netherlands, Switzerland), Italy, West Germany, the United Kingdom and Canada, but it is higher than that of the United States and Japan.

As regards international direct investment, France, which in 1976 ranked sixth by total stock of investment seems to have a rate of production abroad (cf. Table I.5) which is much lower than that of the smaller countries of Europe (Switzerland, Netherlands, Sweden), the United Kingdom and the United States, lower than that of West Germany, Belgium and Canada, similar to that of Japan, and higher than that of Italy. The multinationalisation of French companies today is,

Table I.3　Extent and geographical origins of foreign direct investment within the economies over the years 1974-8 (the geographical origins of investment are given by country of origin as a percentage of total foreign investment)

Country of origin	Host country							
	United States (*76)	Great Britain (†74)	W. Germany (‡74)	Belgium (§75)	France (‖74)	Italy (†74)	Netherlands (‡62-71)	Ireland (‡60-75)
United States		55.6	44.1	40	35	24.3	45.2	43.2
Great Britain	18.9		10.2	6	9.8	6.2	14.5	20.1
West Germany	6.6	2.6		13	10.9	3.3		9
Benelux		3.2	5.5		9.6	7.2	23	
France	5	2.5	5.3	15		3.8	(1)	
Italy		1.7	1.1	1	6.2			
Netherlands	20.5	5.1	12.8	17	12.1	3.4		12.7
Sweden		2.5	1.8	3	1.8			
Switzerland	7.6	7.5	15.4	3.4	10.5	25.1		
Japan	3	0.3	1.7		0.5	0.2	0.1	
Canada	19.2				1.2			
Other countries	19.2	19	2.1	2	2.4	16.5	17.3	15
Total	100	100	100	100	100	100	100	100
Penetration of the economy by foreign capital % — Industry	3 (§74)	10.3 (§71)	22.4 (§72)	33 (§75)	25.4 (‖74)		19 (**71)	
		14.2 (**71)	25.1 (**72)	44 (**75)	25.8 (**73)			
Total	5 (**74)				15 (‖74)			
GNP 1976 (billion $US)	1695	234	462	69	356	181	92	2.6

(1) France accounted for 0.35 per cent of the flow of foreign investment to the Netherlands in 1977 (CNPF 1979-82)
(2) Origin France in part
Basis of calculations:
* Cumulative net assets in
† Investment stock in
‡ Investment
§ Number of employees
¶ Flow of investment for the year
‖ Share capital
** Turnover
Sources:
— for origins: Great Britain to Ireland: Van den Bulcke, 1979; US and Canada to Hong Kong: CNPF, 1979-2; Brazil: Banco Central.
— for penetration: for the US all sectors: Couffin, 1977, and for industry: UN, 1978; for the European economies: Van den Bulcke, 1979 and Savary, 1980; for France: on the basis of the share capital; for Greece: Vaitsos, 1980 and for the other economies: UN 1978.

Canada (*78)	Spain (¶78)	Greece (¶76)	Brazil (‡69-77)	Argentina (*76)	Argentina (‡58-61)	Mexico (*78)	Nigeria (¶76)	Ivory Coast (¶76)	Japan (*76)	Hong Kong (¶78)
75	26	50.2	34.3	58.6	55.9	72.2	17.4		55	46
12			6.2	9.1	8.8	4.7	55.6		6.8	7
	15.1	13.5	12.1		6.6	5.8			3.4	2.3
3	11.1	12.7	3.8	6.6	2	1.8	5.2	69.3	1.2	1.1
			1	10	3.4		10.7		1.4	5
					7.2					
	16.7 (2)		9.3		9	4.2			6.1	5
			9.2			1.9	5.9			19
			6.6		2.6	2			2.5	
10	31.1	23.6	17.5	15.7	4.5	7.4	5.2	30.7	23.6	14.6
100	100	100	100	100	100	100	100	100	100	100
58 (**69)						25 (†75)	70 (*68)	Over 55 (**76)	4 (**72)	11 (§71)
52 (§73)	11 (**71)	29 (*75)	49 (**74)	31 (**72)		27 (**72)				
182	107	24	43	41	41	65	31	4.6	574	10

then, on the whole less significant than that of the other developed Western economies, which can in part be explained by the historical reasons mentioned previously.

Table I.4 Export rate for the developed Western economies in 1978 (amount of exports/GNP)

United States	6.7%	Switzerland	31.0%	Sweden	25.4%
United Kingdom	25.5%	*France*	*17.4%*	Benelux	48.0%
West Germany	24.2%	Canada	21.3%	Italy	25.7%
Japan	11.7%	Netherlands	42.8%		

Source: GNP: World Bank Atlas 1979 (forecast); exports: report of the World Bank 1980, p. 125.

Table I.5 Rate of production abroad by the developed Western economies in 1976 (billion $US)

Country of origin*	Capital invested abroad†	GNP‡	Estimates	
			International production§	Rate of production abroad
	(A)	(B)	(C)	(C)/(B) %
United States	137.2	1695	274.4	16.2
United Kingdom	32.1	234	64.2	27.4
West Germany	19.9	462	39.8	8.6
Japan	19.4	574	38.8	6.8
Switzerland	18.6	58	37.2	64.2
France	11.9	356	23.8	6.6
Canada	11.1	183	22.2	12.2
Netherlands	9.8	92	19.6	21.4
Sweden	5.0	74	10.0	13.6
Benelux	3.6	71	7.2	10.1
Italy	2.9	181	5.8	3.2

*Classified by the amount of capital invested abroad in 1976.
†Book value of assets—source: UN, 1978.
‡Source: World Bank.
§Production achieved by capital invested abroad, estimated at double the book value of the capital, as estimated by UN, 1973 (quoted by Gresi, 1976, p. 37).

Our own estimates also show that the rate of multinational production varies considerably according to the sectors of activity (Table I.6). It is very high in the oil industry, the intermediate products industries (sectors 2, 3, 4, 5 of the Table) and land transportation equipment (motor vehicles). It is low in electrical and mechanical engineering and very low in non-textile consumer goods, building, commerce and the agricultural and food industries.

The following analyses will explain both the general phenomenon

Table I.6 Rate of multinational production* for the whole French economy and by sector in 1974

		Rate
1. Primary industry		16.3
	including oil (1 A)	21.2
2. Mining, construction materials, glass		28.3
3. Iron and steel, metallurgy		10.6
4. Basic chemicals——fibres		12.1
5. Paper——rubber/plastic		14.2
6. Parachemicals——pharmaceuticals		7.8
7. Consumer goods		2.1
	including textiles (7 A)	3.6
8. Mechanical engineering		1.7
9. Electrical/electronic engineering		4.1
10. Transportation equipment		10.0
	including land transportation equipment (10 A)	12.5
11. Building and public works		3.7
12. A. Commerce (on a national basis)		0.3
12. B. International trading companies		42.0
13. Services		0.02
14. Agricultural/food industry on a national basis		1.6
Total		5.6
Total industry (excluding 11, 12 and 13)		9.8

*Ratio of production operations abroad to total production in France + abroad (production operations abroad are estimated from the turnover of production subsidiaries and establishments).

For the method of estimation, see Savary, 1980, Annexe 32.

of multinationalisation of French companies and the different situations in the various sectors.

NOTES

1 L. G. Franko, 1976, who studies the development of the eighty-five biggest firms in continental Europe, among them the twenty-one biggest French industrial groups.

2 See W. Andreff, 1974, for a critical analysis of the subject, 'The multinationals, new phenomenon'.

3 M. Wilkins, 1970.

4 The extent of international investment of French origin in 1914 (22 per cent of world investment; Table I.1) would then be explained by portfolio investments or investments in colonial-type operations (trade, plantations, etc.).

5 See C. A. Michalet, 1976, p. 29.

6 L. G. Franko, 1976, p. 11.

7 Ibid., p. 24. Delapierre and Michalet, 1973, pp. 18–29, also show that the movement of initial establishment abroad, trading or production, which had begun in 1914, increased after 1945 up until 1961 (sample of seventy-three

multinational companies), with most of the initial establishment of production being between 1961 and 1971 or later.

8   See ibid., chapter III, 'The search for raw materials'.

9   A. Capian, 1973.

10 See Ch. Tugendhat, 1973, p. 39. See also A. Baudant, 1980, for the primarily exporting strategy of Pont à Mousson from 1860 to 1940, even though this company was producing abroad from 1919.

11 See Franko, op. cit., p. 40.

12 The end of French colonisation, which occurred between 1956 and 1962, is another principal historical factor, stressed, for example, in the interesting study by B. Bellon, 1979.

13 For a historical analysis see Groupe de recherche de géographie industrielle, 1975 (period 1950-70); Bertin, 1975 (period 1962-72); Michalet and Delapierre, 1976 (period 1963-73). See also Laubier and Richemond, 1980, for an analysis of the dual sectoral and geographic reorientation of international investment between 1960 and 1980.

14 See Chapter 2, p. 32 ff., for an analysis of foreign penetration of the French economy.

15 See J. D. Maurino, 1974.

16 Source CFCE, 1979, p. 160.

17 Ibid., p. 166.

PART I

THE MAIN FACTORS OF MULTINATIONALISATION

In what ways do the structural characteristics of the French economy influence the multinationalisation of companies? To what extent, then, are they one of the principal reasons for the multinational phenomenon? There are two main characteristics which influence the ability of companies to implement a policy of expansion abroad:

— the existence of large-sized firms, and hence the concentration of production facilities, which varies depending on the operations in question;
— the existence of subsidiary companies of foreign groups—the foreign penetration of the French economy—which varies according to sector.

One can in fact assume, as supported by many authors and in the light of the facts, that the big companies are more internationally oriented. It is therefore interesting to look at whether the size of a company has any impact on its operation abroad (Chapter 1).

In addition, the subsidiaries of foreign groups in France must, of course, behave in a specific way as regards exporting and spreading the location of production. We shall investigate the extent to which these subsidiaries are open towards foreign countries compared with companies under national control. The answer to this question is not evident a priori, as everything must depend on the function assigned to the French subsidiary within the foreign group (Chapter 2).

One may object to the simplistic nature of our method and observe that we are not analysing any other explanatory factors which, for a particular company, could be its growth rate, the intensity of its exports, the nature of control of its ownership (family firm, public company, or company controlled by the directors), and the technological nature of the products it manufactures.

Similarly, for the various sectors of the economy, we do not directly analyse all the characteristics of these sectors.

In fact, during our analysis, we reintroduce two sectoral characteristics, the concentration of production and oligopolistic market structure, and foreign penetration.

In addition, the size of the company and the oligopolistic market structure are considered directly or indirectly, as we shall see, in all the theories explaining international investment. This does then seem to be an essential a priori characteristic.

Finally, we shall explain why, in an economy where foreign investments control more than 60 per cent of operations in certain sectors, foreign penetration or 'upstream' multinationalisation cannot be ignored in a study of 'downstream' multinationalisation.

Even though in our view the two factors discussed do describe the principal phenomena, the following two chapters analyse only some of the actual factors involved in multinationalisation.

1 Size and Multinationalisation

The big industrial groups are playing an important part in the current redeployment of the French economy, both as regards investment in production investment abroad and as regards exports. One might suppose that these are the only groups producing abroad, and the only ones to have at their disposal the power and organisation that permits this type of growth. On this basis, the small and medium-sized firms would be restricted to exporting. We shall devote the first part of this chapter to examining whether there is a size threshold below which companies do not become multinational or whether, on the contrary, while production abroad is more frequently carried out by big companies, there are still small and medium-sized firms which do so.

We shall also look at the reasons for the greater multinationalisation of the big companies, and how we can explain the very intense multinationalisation of certain small or medium-sized firms.

Finally, if big companies are more multinational than the others, the concentration of operations abroad must be very high. This is what we shall illustrate in the last part.

THE INCREASE OF MULTINATIONALISATION WITH SIZE

Our sample of 413 companies, including both small and medium-sized firms and large firms, enables us to study the connection between the size of companies and their multinationalisation. The size criterion used is the amount of parent company's capital in 1974, although we know that this criterion is closely correlated with the other possible criteria such as turnover or number of employees. The intensity of production abroad is measured by the turnover of the foreign direct and indirect production subsidiaries for the same year.

First Finding: the Frequency of Multinationalisation Increases with Company Size

The frequency (Table 1.1) rises from one in ten for the smallest companies to eight in ten for the biggest companies. By taking into account foreign indirect subsidiaries, which are more common for the big groups

Table 1.1 Frequency of multinational production for the 413 companies classed by size in 1974 (amount of capital in millions of francs)

Companies*	less than 20m	20 to 50m	50 to 100m	100 to 200m	200 to 500m	over 500m	Total
Total number companies	109	111	70	57	38	28	413
Total number companies producing abroad in 1974	12	42	40	38	31	23	186
Percentage of total companies in class	11%	38%	57%	67%	82%	82%	45%

*(Companies including subsidiary companies)

built up around big companies, the latter are attributed with foreign subsidiaries which can be controlled and managed by smaller French companies. What one could call the 'group effect' is more significant for the big companies and does distort this finding somewhat. The trend is, however, quite clear.

We therefore find the same thing happening for French companies, that Th. Horst had already detected for American companies.[1]

Second Finding: the Degree of Multinationalisation Also Increases with Size

As their size increases, companies more often have a number of foreign production subsidiaries. Thus, companies having more than five subsidiaries of this type account for less than 5 per cent of small companies (capital less than 50 million francs). This percentage increases with size and reaches 50 per cent for the very big companies (capital greater than 500 million francs). This finding very much confirms the hypothesis made by G. Y. Bertin, according to which the number of foreign subsidiaries is directly linked to company size.[2]

The average numbers of foreign subsidiaries and the countries in which they are established increase in line with company size: they increase gradually, for example, from 1.75 foreign production subsidiaries and 1.6 countries of establishment for small multinational companies (capital less than 20 million francs) to 11 foreign production subsidiaries and 8.7 countries of establishment for the very big companies (capital over 500 million francs). There is therefore a parallel and close development between the average number of production subsidiaries and the country of establishment: very often there is only one foreign production subsidiary in a given country, this being especially true for small and medium-sized companies.

In addition, the average rate of production abroad, estimated in terms of turnover, only increases with size for the very big multi-national companies. If one calculates this average rate of production abroad for the multinational companies, grouped by classes of increasing size,[3] we get a surprising result: for almost all the 'small' or 'medium-sized' multinational companies the average rate of production abroad in 1974 was 12-14 per cent. It is only higher than this (20.3 per cent) for the very big multinational companies.

These rates are average rates which hide great disparities between companies, some of which are able to produce as much as 60-80 per cent of their total turnover abroad. They do however show that there are *companies which are very multinational abroad in all the size classes*. Only the big companies, which are almost always big industrial and financial groups, have a higher rate of multinational production on average: most frequently these include very multinational companies. The consequence is that *multinationalisation of production facilities increases with company size.*

If we calculate for each size class the extent of production abroad as a percentage of total operations in France plus abroad for all companies, whether or not they are multinationals, the multinationalisation rates obtained relate to fractions of the production facilities accounted for by bigger and bigger companies.

These rates, calculated for our sample, vary as follows (for classes identical to those in Table 1.1): 1 per cent, 7 per cent, 7.6 per cent, 8.7 per cent, 11 per cent, 17.7 per cent, total 13.5 per cent.

In view of the previous findings, it is not surprising to find a 'global' rate of production abroad which increases with company size. The trend is marked, and it should be noted that the growth in the rates levels out for classes 2-4, then increases very rapidly for the biggest companies. As we have seen, this is primarily a result of the intensity of production abroad by multinational companies, which only increases by any substantial amount for the very big companies. This phenomenon can be confirmed by calculating, for our sample, the number of multinational firms which are 'very multinational', that is, which produce in at least five foreign countries, or whose foreign production operations account for at least 10 per cent of their total operations. This number, expressed as a percentage of the number of multinational firms, rises as their size increases (for classes identical to those in Table 1.1): 11 per cent, 46 per cent, 41 per cent, 45 per cent, 68 per cent, 83 per cent, total 53 per cent.

Multinational companies are therefore more and more frequently 'very multinational' as their size increases.

Third Finding: Exports Increase with Size

Table 1.2 provides us with two further results:[4]

— the incidence of companies with high export rates increases with company size;
— for companies of an equal size, the multinational companies more often have high export rates.

We can conclude from this that the export rate increases with size,[5] and that on the whole a high export rate does not preclude production abroad and vice versa. These two phenomena do on the contrary seem to develop in parallel. In fact we shall show further on (Chapter 6) that there are two types of link—positive and negative—between production abroad and exports, with the overall result observed here only being the outcome of two opposing trends.

Table 1.2 Incidence of high export companies within companies of an increasing size (ratio greater than or equal to 25 per cent)

	Size classes (millions of francs of capital)						
	less than 20m	20–50m	50–100m	100–200m	200–500m	over 500m	Total
Within all companies	13.7%	26%	28.6%	25.5%	42%	48%	26%
Within multinational companies	22%	32%	26%	28.6%	41.6%	50%	33.3%

(Companies excluding subsidiary companies)

Conclusion: Size Really is a Factor in Multinationalisation

All our findings do ultimately result from the two main positive links between the size of companies and their multinational production:[6]

— the incidence of production operations abroad increases as company size increases;
— the incidence of very multinational companies increases with size, and in this sense one can say that the intensity of production abroad increases with company size.

At this stage in the analysis, we can conclude that size does seem to be a positive factor in the multinationalisation of companies. Of course, size cannot be regarded as the only factor. So the position in the paper/cardboard, rubber and plastics sector in 1974 was as shown in Figure 1.1. In this case one should explain why Dunlop[7] and Arjomari-Prioux are not multinationals although they are big companies, and why Hutchinson-Mapa, a group of a similar size, is very much a multinational, considerably more so than some bigger groups.

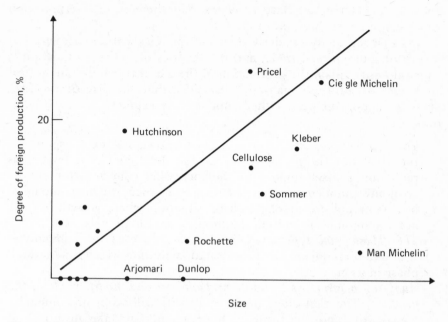

Figure 1.1 Foreign production in the paper/cardboard, rubber and plastics
sector in 1974

FROM SIZE TO OLIGOPOLISTIC MARKET STRUCTURE

Our findings tie up with those of the many statistical works which
have highlighted the specific characteristics and larger size of multinational companies compared with equivalent national firms. Vaupel
demonstrated this for American multinationals,[8] and S. Hirsch for
400 multinational firms from Denmark, the Netherlands and Israel.[9]
We shall, however, go further. There is a 'direct' link between size and
two other aspects: the existence and the intensity of multinationalisation. In this sense our work ties up with the complex econometric
tests carried out by G. Y. Bertin, which established the existence of
a close link between the size of the firm and the threshold of multinationalisation which, according to this author, shows 'that growth
abroad can scarcely be disassociated from the general growth of the
firm, and is largely conditioned by the size it has already reached. . . .'[10]

Can we deduce, as this author implicitly does, that size is a positive
factor in multinationalisation? That it is the growth of the company
which leads to its multinationalisation? There is no evidence that the
inverse is not true (that multinationalisation leads to growth) and in
particular that there are not a number of other factors behind the
two trends of size and multinationalisation. Before one can consider
that a concrete—though imperfect—measurement can reveal an

explanatory factor, we have to check that there is an interpretation which can support this hypothesis.

Apart from analyses derived from the classical or neo-classical theory of international trade, and the theories of capital or location,[11] which do not explain the production of firms abroad, all the theoretical analyses[12] of multinationalisation consider that the size of the firm plays an important part, either implicitly or explicitly. Very briefly, these are:

— *The Marxist analysis.* Exports of goods and capital are a response to the reduction in profit levels in the developed economy. This reduction is itself linked to the increasing concentration of the economy and its monopolistic nature. It is, then, the big companies, in a monopolistic or oligopolistic situation where growth in their home economies is limited, that become multinationals.

— *The 'Managerial'-type analyses.* The large size of the company is seen as a prerequisite for its multinationalisation which is a 'natural' phase in its growth.

— *Analyses in terms of technological advance and the life cycle of the product.* The first stage in the multinationalisation of companies consists of exporting from the home country to take advantage of the technological advance it has acquired on the national market. This is also done to expand the growth of total sales, which is limited on the home market by the saturation of the market, the dominant position of the firm and/or the appearance of competitors. In this sense, the firms in question are large and occupy a dominant position on their domestic market.[13] These are the firms which then spread the location of their production to protect themselves from the appearance of competitors abroad.

— *Analyses based on oligopolistic market structures.* These correspond to the work of Hymer, 1971, Kindleberger, 1979 and R. Caves, 1971, and, in France, M. Rainelli, 1979. Starting with a study of the position in the United States in particular, these authors note that it is the large firms in an oligopolistic position, whether or not their products are diversified, that become multinational in order to reduce their costs and to improve their position on their home market, or to expand on foreign markets. The major factors behind decisions to export and to produce abroad are clearly the concentration of firms in their home economy and the resultant limit to growth for large dominant firms.

Company size is therefore mentioned in all the analyses of multinationalisation, but almost always in relation to *size as an expression of a limit to growth on the national market.*[14] R. Caves, for example, stresses that oligopolistic structure and large size are two related conditions. He believes that a firm will not invest abroad while it has ample profit opportunities on the national market through economies of scale: a firm which invests abroad will therefore always be a large firm faced with a small number of competitors in the country, which is the definition of oligopolistic market structure.

Measurement of the oligopolistic market structure should therefore supplement the measurement of the relative company size to give a full picture of a principal factor in multinationalisation which we have only measured indirectly by absolute firm size.

If we are to be satisfied with a single criterion, or carry out an analysis limited to a given sector, the share of the domestic market held by a company is then a criterion that is better able to explain multinationalisation than absolute size alone. It describes the relative size of the company and, where this is large, the oligopolistic market structure at the same time. Table 1.3 provides an example.

Table 1.3 The electrical products sector in 1974

	Size (millions of francs of capital)				
	0–100m	100–200m	200–300 m	300–400m	over 400m
No production abroad	Claude* Océanic* Saxby* Lemercier	De Dietrich	Fse tél Ericsson*		La Radio-technique*
Existence of production abroad	Cipel Française Auer PM Labinal	Sagem Piles Wonder SAFT CGR Merlin Gerin Arthur-Martin	Télé-mécanique	Seb Moulinex	Thomson Group CGE Group Alsthom CIT-Alcatel

*company under foreign control.

Two big companies, in a good position on their home market, do not produce abroad: Française de téléphones Ericsson and La Radio-technique. They are in fact under foreign control, which confirms the existence of this negative factor of multinationalisation (see note 7).

Above all, we find that small or medium-sized companies which produce abroad always have a strong position in their market in France.[15] When their operations are diversified, it is always for the operation in which their position is strongest that they move their location. As an example, in 1974 Arthur-Martin produced 25 per cent of all French cookers and 50 per cent of all washing machines. P. M. Labinal accounts for a high percentage of the market for electrical cables for cars, which it produces in Spain. Cipel and Saft together control 45 per cent of the French battery market and Piles Wonder accounts for 35 per cent. Sagem is the second world producer of teleprinters, which it produces abroad. Merlin Gerin accounts for some 40-60 per cent of the French market, depending on the product. Télémécanique Electrique controls 70 per cent of the national market in industrial automatic control equipment. Seb's share of the market varies according to the product, and is 85 per cent for pressure-cookers which it produces in Iran. Moulinex accounts for 80 per cent of the food processor market, and about 60 per cent of the market in other appliances.

Another verification: which are the most multinational operations within a group? In the case of Thomson, in 1974 their most multinational operation was medical equipment through their subsidiary CGR, with 50 per cent of production staff located abroad. In this sector CGR is the leading French producer and the third producer world-wide. On the other hand, their export rates are much lower for consumer products (approximately 15 per cent in 1974) and little production is carried out abroad. Indeed, the group does not yet have a dominant position on these markets in France: as a group director put it, 'Exports are still lower than might be expected. . . . In grouping together almost all French manufacturers of household electrical appliances and becoming the only French-controlled manufacturer of radios and televisions, Thomson's first concern was to win a substantial share of the French market which is the vital base from which it can expand its position in Europe.'[16]

Relative Company Size and Oligopolistic Market Structure as Determinants of Multinationalisation

The positive link between company size and their multinationalisation, established for the 413 companies in our sample, leads us to make the following proposal:

One of the main factors in the multinationalisation of companies consists of the limit to their growth in France, tied up with the relative size of the firm in its market or markets, and more generally with the oligopolistic market structure.[17] This was the factor which our tests measured by company size.

It is involved in multinationalisation in the wide sense and also has an impact on the exports of French companies, which we have found increase with company size.

But if both exports and production abroad are two ways in which companies can expand, why one rather than the other? It is because other factors are involved in multinationalisation mainly relating to the situation of the host economies and disparities in the world economy.

THE CONCENTRATION OF OPERATIONS ABROAD

The link between size and multinational production has one direct consequence: the concentration of production operations abroad is high, higher than that of production operations in France.

This is shown by the classification of the companies in our sample by the turnover of their foreign production subsidiaries:[18] seven groups all large, had a turnover of over 3 billion francs abroad in 1974. The extent of production operations outside France then decreases very rapidly. If we look at the companies by classes of decreasing size, the concentration of production operations is found to be much higher abroad than in France (Table 1.4).

For all French companies, we have classed the top multinational groups by their total production abroad (Table 1.5). The top twenty-two groups are all large. They are among the top sixty-seven French groups, classed by *Le Nouvel Economiste* on the basis of their capital.[19] The smallest employs ten thousand people. All are leaders in their sector of activity: they include the top one or two national groups in the sectors of oil, tyres, cars, chemicals, construction materials, parachemicals and electrical engineering. Finally, they all have high levels of multinational production: their foreign employees almost always represent more than 30 per cent of their total workforce, 50 per cent in the case of L'Oréal and BSN and as much as 60 per cent for SGPM, Michelin, Imétal and Air Liquide.

The concentration of production operations abroad is also very high. In 1974 the top twenty-two French-owned multinational groups did in fact control at least 70 per cent of the production operations abroad of all French industrial companies,[20] while they only accounted for 24 per cent of the capital of these companies and 13.7 per cent of their employees in France.[21]

This concentration of production operations abroad for French multinational companies seems to be much higher than for all multinational companies throughout the world. In fact, Stopford and Dunning estimated that in 1978, 80 per cent of the total international stock of direct investment existing in the world was controlled by the top 430 multinational companies.[22]

From surveys carried out each year,[23] we know that the concentration of the export operations of French companies is very high because of the high level of exports by the big groups.[24] In 1974, the 1363 export leaders accounted for a total of 80.2 per cent of French exports, while in 1979 the 1417 leaders still represented 71 per cent (MOCI surveys). The most significant result, however, was that from 1974 to 1979 the top sixty French exporting companies accounted for more than 30 per cent of total exports, and the weight of these firms increased as time went on.[25] Finally, an analysis of groups of companies, including

Table 1.4 Concentration of the operations abroad of 413 companies classed by size in 1974 (in cumulative percentages)

Size classes (capital in millions of francs)	Number of companies	Number of foreign production subsidiaries	Number of foreign trading subsidiaries	Turnover foreign production subsidiaries	Exports	'Total' turnover of groups
28 companies over 500m	6.8	27.6	25.4	67.8	62.3	51.6
66 companies over 200m	16.0	48.4	49.8	83.9	80.0	71.3
123 companies over 100m	29.8	69.6	73.8	92.5	89.2	84.6
193 companies over 50m	46.7	86.0	91.6	96.4	94.4	91.5
304 companies over 20m	73.6	97.8	98.9	99.8	99.2	98.2
413 companies	100	100	100	100	100	100

Table 1.5 The top 22 French companies producing abroad

Rank	Group producing over one billion francs abroad	Foreign production¶ (millions of francs)	Years	Number of employees			Percentage (A)/(C)
				Abroad (A)	In France (B)	Total (C)	
1	CFP	18 000	1979	14 198	29 395	43 593	32.6
2	SGPM	7 837	1979	85 512	62 096	147 808	58.0
3	Michelin	6 932	1977	66 000	48 200	114 800	58.0
4	ERAP	6 500					
5	PUK	4 857	1979	21 244	70 682	91 926	23.1
6	Marine Wendel	3 905					
7	Compagnie Nord-Imétal*	3 861	1977	10 161	5 282	15 442	65.8
8	Rhône-Poulenc	3 827	1979	36 503	70 192	106 695	34.2
9	Renault	3 658	1979	60 521	172 887	233 408	25.9
10	BSN-GD†	3 104	1979	26 966	29 621	55 895	48.2
11	Citroën	3 000					
12	Lafarge	2 615	1978	10 337	12 472	22 809	45.3
13	Air Liquide	2 465	1979	14 000	10 000	24 000	58.3
14	Vallourec	1 876					
15	Empain Schneider	1 681	1977	28 416	115 590	144 006	19.7
16	L'Oréal (Nestlé group)	1 418	1977	9 894	10 718	20 612	48.0
17	Thomson	1 376	1979	16 000	110 300	126 300	12.7
18	CGE	1 363	1977	10 380	93 430	103 810	10.0
19	EMC	1 338	1978			10 815	
20	Automobiles Peugeot	1 262	1979	8 340	13 929	22 269	37.5
21	DMC	1 048	1979	6 428	10 613	17 041	37.7
22	Roussel-Uclaf (Hoechst group, West Germany)	1 000					
	Established after 1974						
	Elf Aquitaine‡		1979	7 610	17 410	25 020	30.4
	Peugeot§		1979	70 100	194 630	264 730	26.5

*Excluding Cie de Mokta.
†In 1980 reduction in foreign employees (disposal of glass subsidiaries).
‡Merger of Erap and SNPA. The employees here relate to only the energy sector.
§Absorption of Citroën and the European subsidiaries of Chrysler (ranked 3rd or 4th in 1979).
¶Turnover of foreign production subsidiaries.
Source: Savary, 1980. Ranking on the basis of 1974.

Table 1.6 The top 56 French exporting groups in 1979
(ranked by export turnover, in rounded billions of francs)

1.	PSA Peugeot Citroën	26.8	30.	Routière Colas	1.8
2.	Régie Renault	21.8	31.	Snecma	1.7
3.	Pechiney Ugine Kuhlman	10.0	32.	Lyonnaise des eaux et de	
4.	Cie générale d'électricité	9.8		l'éclairage	1.6
5.	Rhône-Poulenc	9.7	33.	Ford-France	1.4
6.	Thomson-Brandt	9.1	34.	Poclain	1.4
7.	Creusot-Loire (Empain-		35.	Matra	1.4
	Schneider)	7.4	36.	Moët-Hennessy	1.3
8.	IBM-France	6.0	37.	General Motors France	1.3
9.	Usinor	5.8	38.	Amrep	1.3
10.	Dassault-Breguet aviation	5.3	39.	Cnim	1.3
11.	Michelin	5.2	40.	CII–Honeywell-Bull.	1.3
12.	Alsthom-Atlantique	5.1	41.	Bouygues	1.3
13.	Aérospatiale-Snias	5.1	42.	J.-G. Durand et Cie	1.2
14.	Saint-Gobain Pont-à-Mousson	4.7	43.	Chantiers naval de la Ciotat	1.2
15.	Elf-Aquitaine	4.7	44.	Constructions métalliques de	
16.	Vallourec	4.4		Provence	1.2
17.	Sacilor	3.8	45.	Fougerolle	1.2
18.	Ato Chimie	3.6	46.	Sainrapt et Brice	1.2
19.	CDF Chimie	3.6	47.	Société Le Nickel	1.1
20.	Spie-Batignolles	3.6	48.	Kléber-Colombes	1.1
21.	Screg	2.4	49.	Valeo (ex-Ferodo)	1.1
22.	Technip	2.2	50.	L'Oréal	1.1
23.	Dumez	2.1	51.	Entreprise minière	
24.	Total-CFR	2.1		et chimique	1.1
25.	Union laitière normande	2.1	52.	Moulinex	1.1
26.	Philips France	2.0	53.	Grands Travaux de Marseille	1.1
27.	Française des pétroles-BP	1.9	54.	Kodak–Pathé	1.1
28.	Fives-Lille	1.8	55.	Heurtey Industries	1.0
29.	Unic	1.8	56.	Esso Chimie	1.0

Source: MOCI NO. 416, 15 September 1980 (for the building and public works firms, the figure used for turnover abroad corresponds to direct production outside France).

large subsidiaries with high export rates, reveals an even higher concentration: in 1979, for example, the fifty-six 'billionaire' export groups on their own accounted for a total of 42 per cent of French exports (see Table 1.6). All these groups are large: the seven top exporting groups in 1979 were, in order of importance, Peugeot-Citroën, Renault, PUK, CGE, Rhône-Poulenc, Thomson and Creusot-Loire.

These seven groups number among the top twenty companies producing abroad. They do, however, rank differently in the two classifications by foreign production and exports. Even though these groups seem to have both high export rates and to produce a lot abroad, some are primarily exporters (Peugeot, Renault, CGE, Thomson-Brandt), while others mainly produce abroad (CFP, SGPM, Michelin).

If the big French industrial groups are often both big exporters and very multinational because of direct production abroad, this is the result of different strategies, concentrating on one or other of these methods of expanding abroad.[26] But does production abroad promote exports, or does it limit their growth? To answer this question (cf. Chapter 6) we first have to examine the international organisation strategies of production abroad (Part II, Chapter 3).

To sum up: the frequency and intensity of the multinationalisation of companies increases with their size on the national market. A limit to their growth in France leads these companies to develop their operations abroad. In this sense, it is a positive factor for exports and production abroad.

In addition, the concentration of production facilities and the oligopolistic market structure constitute another factor involved in exporting and multinationalisation. The more this concentration and oligopolisation of the markets increase, the more exports and multi-nationalisation grow, provided this increasing concentration is not due to foreign investment in France, as foreign-controlled companies are not very multinational. We still have to examine this tendency and look at whether it can be explained by the very dependence of companies on the strategies of foreign groups.

NOTES

1 Th. Horst, 1972, p. 261.
2 For French companies in 1968 the author shows that beyond a threshold zone 'the average number of permanent establishments abroad increases with size' because of industrial establishment, which 'corresponds to transition to the stage of industrial expansion', G. Y. Bertin, 1972, p. 318.
3 This is the ratio between the turnover of foreign production subsidiaries and establishments and a 'total turnover' estimated from the total figures for the company and its French and foreign subsidiaries. This last figure overestimates the consolidated turnover all the more because the group nature is more pronounced. If one accepts that this nature is more marked for the big companies, then the rates of production abroad given here are underestimated for the biggest companies. This remark applies to the overall rates calculated in the following paragraph.
4 See Savary, 1980, pp. 420–6.
5 Similarly, H. Glejser, A. Jacquemin and J. Petit, 1980, when carrying out complex econometric tests for 1446 Belgium export companies, showed that exports increased proportionately more than firm size.
   A. Auquier, 1980, arrives at the same conclusion for French firms.
   J. Y. Chevalier and J. Y. Nizet, 1980, p. 225, also show for 2800 private French firms, that the average export rate increases with size.
   J. P. Dubarry and Z. Cardot, 1981 stress, again for French companies, that it is only the frequency of existence of exporting companies which increases with size. This could explain our findings and those mentioned above.
6 In all sectors, the frequency of multinational production increases with company size, cf. Savary, op. cit., p. 432.
7 Dunlop does not have any subsidiaries abroad, as it is itself the subsidiary of a foreign group, whose object is to supply the local market, and so has no

strategic autonomy. This stresses one big factor, negative this time, in production abroad which we shall call the 'foreign control' factor, and which we shall study in the next chapter.

8 Quoted by J. H. Dunning, 1972, p. 38.

9 S. Hirsch, 1972, p. 106.

10 Bertin, op. cit. This author also considers that the structure of the national market and that of the world market are explanatory variables.

11 Cf. Dunning, op. cit.

12 We only give here the references for the last type of analysis, which we feel gives the best explanation of the link studied.

13 This may be the position on a narrow market, for a very specific product, and this analysis applies above all to companies which diversify their products.

14 This limitation is found in all the surveys on the objectives of production abroad. The main objective mentioned by the directors of multinationals is very often the search for an outlet or the attraction of a big market . . . This is found in Dunning, 1972, p. 18, who summarises six different surveys, and in Michalet, 1972, for French multinationals.

15 To be precise, this analysis assumes that the share of the market is calculated at narrow branch level, and for the company's main activity. In the case of a multi-product firm, this assumes that \the study is broken down for each product.

16 J. M. Fourier, chairman and managing director of Thomson-Brandt, 'Développement d'une entreprise à vocation internationale', journal *Humanisme et Entreprise*, 1st quarter 1978. In addition, in 1977, Thomson took control of the 3rd German television producer, and decided to produce televisions and radios in Singapore.

17 R. Guir, 1980, studying seventy cases of the establishment of French firms in the United States and Canada, showed that horizontal direct investment could basically be explained by the existence of an oligopoly in the home country (cf. p. 97) and by the 'monopolistic technological advantage' held by the firm (cf. p. 96). This second characteristic would have been interesting to analyse here; we would probably have made the same finding, at least for multinational firms in developed countries. J. Metais, 1979, also stresses that the oligopolistic structure explains the multinationalisation of American and European banks. P. Jeanblanc also stresses that the multinationalisation of Rhône-Poulenc is linked with its size and its position in an oligopoly (P. Jeanblanc, 1981, p. 430).

18 See Savary, 1980, table No. 108, p. 428.

19 If we take the top twenty French groups according to the classification in this journal, nine of them are included in the top twenty-two producers abroad (in order of size, and ranked as in the classification in this journal, these are CFP No. 3, Rhône-Poulenc No. 4, SGPM No. 5, PUK No. 6, BSN No. 10, CGE No. 11, Peugeot No. 12, Imétal No. 13, Renault No. 17. Among the big groups which are not included are nationalised groups (EDF, GDF, SNCF, Seita), iron and steel groups (Denain-N.-E.-Longwy), and groups under foreign control (Shell-France, Française pétroles BP, IBM-France, Esso Saf). We again find that there is a tendency for foreign control to limit multinationalisation.

20 See Savary, 1980, Annexe No. 32, for an estimate of production operations abroad for all French companies.

21 This is industry in the wide sense (including energy, agricultural/food industry and building/public works).

22 J. M. Stopford, H. Dunning and K. O. Harerich, 1974, Introduction.

23 See MOCI (Moniteur du commerce international), annual survey published in

September; see also Payment report, 1980, for small companies, and the study by STISI, 1980, for a very full study of the concentration of exports in 1976.

24 This concentration is greater than that of operations in France, as shown, for the companies in the sample, in Table 1.4. The results of H. Glejser, A. Jacquemin and J. Petit, 1980, and A. Auquier, 1980, lead to the same conclusion for Belgium and for France.

25 Hence, in 1974, the top sixty-five exporting companies (each with over 500 million francs of exports) accounted for 30.1 per cent of French exports and, in 1979, the top sixty-one (each with over 1 billion francs of exports) accounted for 35.7 per cent of the total exports. (Source: MOCI No. 155, 15 September 1975, and No. 416, 15 October 1980.)

26 In addition, some big groups are big exporters and produce little abroad:
   — when they belong to strategic sectors (Dassault, Aérospatiale, Snias, etc.) or to the iron and steel sector (Usinor, Sacilor), etc.;
   — when they are under public control (ATO Chimie, CDF Chimie, etc.);
   — when they are under foreign control (IBM-France, Philips, Française BP, Unic, Ford, General Motors, etc.). This third case will be analysed in the following chapter.

2 Foreign Control and Multinationalisation

It may seem surprising, a priori, to analyse the operations of subsidiaries of foreign groups in France when this study is concerned with French multinationals. However, to find the reasons why companies working in France carry out operations outside France, we also have to look at companies controlled by foreign groups: they are an important force in the French economy. In addition, these subsidiaries behave in a specific way. But what effect will this have? Foreign groups are pursuing a number of different objectives when they set up in France:

— access to the French market;
— access to this market and also, from there, to neighbouring or related markets;
— production of parts or special products all of which are exported to other plants in the group.

Which is the most common objective of these groups? What is the main impact of their investment in France on foreign trade and the international expansion of the French economy? In addition, foreign investment reaches very high levels in certain sectors, which may cause problems for the formation of big national companies, which alone would be able to develop intensively as multinationals. In an economy with a high level of penetration by foreign groups, such as the French economy, an analysis of the multinationalisation of companies cannot ignore the direct role played by the presence of foreign groups.

The first part of this chapter will be devoted to an examination of the subsidiaries of foreign groups in France. We shall then consider a hypothesis: the sectoral rates of multinational production for the economy as a whole can be explained, at least in part, by the extent of foreign penetration. And after this we present some of the structural characteristics of this foreign investment in France.

LITTLE MULTINATIONALISATION 'DOWNSTREAM' AND LOW EXPORTS BY SUBSIDIARIES OF FOREIGN GROUPS IN FRANCE

The subsidiaries are not very multinational and export very little.

Not Very Multinational?

Within our sample, let us separate the fifty-nine companies under foreign control from the 354 companies under French control: in 1974, 26 per cent of companies in the first group controlled a foreign production subsidiary; this figure was 47 per cent for the second group. One in four subsidiaries of foreign groups in France is in turn a multinational, whereas one French firm in two is a multinational.

The seven studies of foreign groups in France in the *Dictionnaire des groupes industriels et financiers en France*[1] show that the big multinational groups rarely use their French subsidiaries as a base for controlling production subsidiaries in other countries. Where such subsidiaries exist, they are a result of the group's history, that is, they had been set up by the French companies when they were independent. This is the case for the Roussel-Uclaf group, a subsidiary of Hoechst (West Germany) and the L'Oréal group, controlled by Nestlé. However in 1975:

— Chrysler-France only controlled four trading subsidiaries in Europe and had an interest in an assembly plant in Morocco;
— Fiat-France and its subsidiaries did not control any subsidiaries outside France;
— IBM-France only controlled one subsidiary in Madagascar and agencies in Africa and in the DOM-TOM (Overseas Departments and Territories);
— the subsidiaries of ITT did not control any subsidiaries outside France (except for Pigier, whose activity is fairly remote from ITT's initial activities);
— the subsidiaries of Nestlé in France, in particular the big company SOPAD, did not control any subsidiaries abroad. Only Vitell, Claude Roustang and Chambourcy had subsidiaries, which were trading subsidiaries in the latter case.

Low Export Levels?

The subsidiaries of foreign groups in France in our sample on the whole export less than companies under French control.[2] The total exports of these foreign-controlled companies represent around 9.9 per cent of their turnover in France. This average export rate is 20 per cent for all the companies in the sample. These results tie up with those obtained by the Ministry of Industry:[3] in 1976, all French companies under foreign control (defined on the basis of interests greater than or equal to 20 per cent of the capital) sold 17.9 per cent of their production abroad, compared with 23.2 per cent for the other French-controlled companies. In addition, according to studies by the US Administration, all the foreign subsidiaries of American companies, in all the developed countries, export less than local companies.[4] The situation in France is not therefore a special case.

However, the top fifty-six French exporters (Table 1.6, Chapter 1) include some subsidiaries of foreign groups: IBM-France, Philips, Ford-France, General Motors, etc. Why? Foreign groups in France are organised in a special way.

Interpretation: the predominance of the strategy of access to the local market explains the low level of multinationalisation and the low exports of the subsidiaries of foreign groups in France.

By combining the characteristics of exports and the locational spread of production by the subsidiaries of foreign groups, we can establish a typology of the ways in which these subsidiaries are integrated into the groups. There are three types:

Type 1: 'Access to local market'. The objective of the foreign subsidiary is to produce for the French market, so it exports very little and does not control any trading or production subsidiaries abroad.

It is because this is the most common type that all the above statistical results are obtained. Within our sample, examples of subsidiaries of this type are the big companies (in 1974): Esso s.a.f., Applications Mécaniques SKF, Stockvis et Fils, Dunlop S.A., Française de téléphones Ericsson, Océanic and Claude. Note that these companies are all majority-controlled, and often have been for some time, by large industrial groups whose activity is similar to that of their French subsidiary and which own other production subsidiaries in a number of countries which they incorporate directly.

Type 2: 'Decentralisation by area'. The foreign subsidiary is responsible for the organisation of production and sales of a product for a geographical area bigger than France. It exports a lot, and may have foreign trading and production subsidiaries.

This type does not seem to be very common. In our sample, for example, there is Trailor S.A., which manufactures trailers and containers, and owns two production plants in West Germany and Great Britain and a sales network in Switzerland, Belgium, Luxembourg and Portugal. This company heads the division Traimobile-Europe of the group Pullman Inc. (United States). Similarly, Floquet Monopole, a subsidiary of Dana Corp. (United States) specialises in the production of pistons and piston rings, transferring its valve production to a Spanish subsidiary which it controls.

Roussel-Uclaf (Hoechst, West Germany) and L'Oréal (Nestlé, Switzerland) can also be considered as this type, as their extensive operations outside France existed before they were taken under the control of foreign groups, who have kept them going.

Type 3. 'International specialisation of production'. The subsidiary is specialised in the production of parts exported to other plants belonging to the group. It does not control any foreign subsidiaries. It forms part of an organisation based on the international division of labour, consisting of plants specialising in the production of components, located in several countries, with final assembly only being carried out by one of them. This third type can be extended to the case where the French subsidiary specialises in the manufacture of a product or a single type of product for the multinational group, which it then exports to all the plants in this group.

Some companies in the sample are of this type, such as Arthur-Martin which exports its products through the Electrolux network, La Radiotechnique which exports colour television tubes to the other plants in the Philips group, or Poclain which, since the American group Case took control of it, has specialised in the construction of top-of-the-range hydraulic shovels marketed by the whole Case world-wide network.

The high export rates of some big subsidiaries already mentioned thus correspond to a policy of 'international specialisation of production'. Hence IBM has three factories in France, Great Britain and West Germany to supply the European market. Each specialises in certain parts and the assembly of a particular model, and hence each exports large quantities of parts and finished products: IBM is the eighth biggest French exporter. Similarly, the two Ford-France plants in Bordeaux export 75 per cent of their production of automatic transmissions to the United States and gear-boxes for the Ford Fiesta to the assembly plant in Spain.

Note that this type of international organisation very often implies high imports too: the trade balance for the groups we have mentioned above is certainly only just positive, and may even be negative. In any case, it is very much less than that of national groups with roughly the same export figures.

The specific behaviour of the subsidiaries of foreign groups in France is explained by their dependence on a foreign strategy. We have verified this indirectly as often French companies which are 'legally' the subsidiaries of foreign groups do in fact have a good deal of autonomy as regards their management. Their behaviour with regard to multi-nationalisation and exports is then similar to that of French companies. This often happens when the foreign groups controlling them are financial groups (cf. Electrobel for Logabax, Générale de Belgique for SCREG, and for Arthur-Martin up until 1975), groups which are diversifying in France (cf. ITT with Pigier) or groups which are small compared with the French subsidiary (cf. Maus group for Au Printemps, Empain for Schneider S.A., etc.).[5]

More often, however, the subsidiaries of foreign groups in France do not enjoy such autonomy, and their operations as regards exporting or spreading their production locations really do depend on the strategies of the foreign groups.

In certain cases, the subsidiaries of foreign groups in France are big exporters and (or) control foreign production subsidiaries. However, with the exception of certain subsidiaries which enjoy great autonomy with regard to their foreign shareholders, these operations outside France always fit into the international organisation determined by the foreign groups.

One thing must however be stressed in conclusion: this is the pre-dominance of the strategy of access to the local French market, when foreign groups invest in France. This explains why the subsidiaries of these groups generally produce very little outside France and export very little.

The study carried out by the Ministry of Industry concludes that the overall tendency for all foreign companies in France to export very little is primarily due to the biggest of them, for which 'this corresponds to the principal objective of extending their share of the domestic market and instead of exporting, spreading their production locations'.[6]

In this sense, if we include under the term 'French companies' all those companies operating in France, whether or not they are foreign controlled, it can be considered that for French companies on the whole this foreign control is a negative factor for their exports and multinational production.

This result may seem insignificant, but it was not clear a priori, as we have shown. It contradicts the assertions of the subsidiaries of foreign groups in France, that these companies are big exporters.[7] It also refutes an over-simplified analysis, presenting France as being very dominated by foreign groups, who use their establishments in the Hexagon to penetrate markets which are under the economic and political influence of France, such as those of Black Africa. In addition, our analysis throws light on the subsequent study of the strategies of multinationals of French origin by illustrating the different strategies possible for multinational groups investing in a developed country like France.

FOREIGN PENETRATION AND MULTINATIONALISATION OF THE ECONOMY

After outlining some of the structural characteristics of foreign invest-ment in France, we shall look at whether there is any link between the degree of foreign penetration and that of sectoral multinationalisa-tion. Studies on foreign investment in France are often limited to samples of firms.[8] The official work carried out by the Ministry of Industry, for all French companies, underestimates foreign penetration.[9]

We therefore had to carry out a statistical study of foreign investment in France for the years 1974 and 1978, based on an analysis of the yearbooks of APEF, *Opera Mundi.*[10] This enabled us:

— to get the best possible grasp of the economic notion of foreign control, which is normally underestimated. In this we have taken into account the possibility of minority control;
— to analyse this foreign control from the point of view of the decision centres from which it originates, that is, the foreign groups.

We set out very briefly here some of the structural characteristics of foreign investment in France, which show that this investment can exert considerable pressure on the firms it controls in France, and can also exert great influence on the French economy.

Penetration Primarily Exerting Control

We have distinguished foreign controlling interests assumed to give economic control over companies, even where in certain cases they hold less than 50 per cent of the capital. Non-controlling interests, on the other hand, are those which do not give this control. The criterion used to measure the weight of French companies is the amount of share capital. In 1974 the situation was as shown in Table 2.1. This corresponds to 15 per cent of French production facilities, taking all sectors together, and 25.4 per cent of industry. In 1978 the position was similar.[11]

Table 2.1 Foreign investment in France in 1974

Controlling interests	
number of foreign-controlled companies	8 089
total share capital of these companies (thousands of francs)	42 608 048
Non-controlling interests	
number of interests	775
total corresponding share capital	
(in proportion to interests) (in thousands of francs)	2 644 357
Total number of branches	742

Foreign investment in France does, then, take one main form: that of interests in the capital of French companies which give economic control of these companies. The non-controlling interests either representing alliances between groups, or temporary interests, with a view to future control, or interests with purely financial objectives, are rare.

Great Concentration at Foreign Group Level

The wealth of the information we have available enables us to analyse the subsidiaries of foreign groups in France, and in particular their high concentration.[12] It also enables us to group together investments made in France in several subsidiaries by a single foreign group, and hence to measure the total weight of each foreign investor in France. Table 2.2 shows the concentration of foreign investment for the foreign investor groups.

Table 2.2 The concentration of foreign investors in France in 1978

	Amount of share capital for all controlled companies in 1978 (million francs)	Percentage with respect to all companies under foreign control
Top 5 investors	8 105.4	16
Top 10 investors	12 696.5	25
Top 88 investors (each controlling more than 100 m. fr. of share capital)	28 661.7	56.5
Top 172 investors (controlling more than 50 m. fr. share capital)	34 687.8	68.4
Total of 6 039 investors	50 717.7	100

Here 6039 investors control 9356 subsidiaries, which implies that many investors only control one subsidiary, in general a small one. On the other hand, the biggest investors are also those which control several French firms, in general large ones. They therefore have very great weight: the eighty-eight biggest, for example, on their own control 56 per cent of the total capital under foreign control.[13] In addition, the top ten account for a total of 25 per cent of this same capital. The concentration of foreign investment in France, measured from the viewpoint of the investor groups, is therefore very high.

The ranking of these foreign groups, set out in Annexe 4, stresses that these are mostly very large groups, which are national or world leaders in their field of activity.

The fact that foreign investment in France is principally in the hands of a few big multinational industrial groups indicates that this investment corresponds to clearly determined industrial strategies, which the French companies they control must strictly follow.

A High Sectoral Concentration

Foreign investment in France is very unevenly distributed between the different sectors of activity. The degrees of penetration—ratios between the size of the foreign-controlled companies and that of all French companies—vary considerably according to the sector.[14] Thus, according to our estimates in terms of share capital, we get the results as shown in Table 2.3.

Table 2.3 Degree of penetration by foreign capital in the sectors of French industry*

Low (less than 10%)	Average (10–20%)	High (over 20%)
Electricity	Constr. materials (13.1%)	Land transportation (22.9%)
Fuels	Iron and steel (16.5%)	Basic chemicals (23.3%)
Building, civil eng.	Leather, shoes (18.4%)	Meat, milk (26.3%)
Shipbuilding, aeronautics	Paper, cardboard (18.6%)	Other Agr./Food ind. (28.9%)
Armaments	Wood, furniture, misc.	Oil, gas (48.6%)
Glass	(19.8%)	Rubber, plastics-processing
Foundries, metalworking		(49.3%)
		Mechan. eng. (62.9%)
		Parachemicals, pharma-
		ceuticals (64.2%)
		Electrical and electronic
		eng. (71.2%)

* Degrees of penetration calculated on the basis of the share capital.
Source: our calculations from APEF yearbooks—base year: 1974.

Foreign penetration is even higher in certain subsectors, such as, for example, pharmaceuticals, data processing, electronic components, building and public works equipment, farm machinery, the dairy industry, etc., and is on the other hand lower in certain other subsectors.

This high concentration of foreign investment in certain sectors is important from the double viewpoint of industrial policy and the weaknesses in the French production facilities which it reveals. This concentration also gives the small number of foreign groups involved considerable 'market powers' in certain sectors.

A High Concentration of Foreign Groups in Certain Sectors

The big foreign groups investing heavily in France very often make their French establishments specialise in a single big sector, that of their own operations in their home country.[15] This is evident from the fact that the top foreign groups investing in France (Annexe 4) belong in the majority to sectors where the levels of foreign penetration are high: oil, data processing, chemicals, pharmaceuticals, agricultural and food industries, automobiles, agricultural machinery, consumer electronics, etc.

This is shown, too, by a concentration of foreign investment in France, in terms of foreign investor groups, which is very high in certain sectors. These are very often sectors with high levels of foreign penetration: hence, in 1978 the percentages of total foreign investment accounted for by the top eighty-eight foreign investor groups were:

96% for oil
80% for meat, milk
56% for chemicals
54% for mechanical engineering
67% for electrical and
    electronic engineering

82% for land transportation
    equipment
59% for parachemicals,
    pharmaceuticals
46% for financial organisations

And these percentages are even bigger for certain narrow sectors where penetration is high: 85 per cent for fats (Unilever), 70 per cent for agricultural machinery (International Harvester, Massey-Ferguson, Tenneco, etc.) and 78 per cent for data processing (IBM, Control Data, Olivetti). A few big groups are therefore responsible for almost all the foreign penetration in many sectors, often in fact those where penetration is very high.

This double concentration, at both sectoral and group level, illustrates the foreign investment made primarily by big industrial groups, who control one or more subsidiaries in France in the same sector. The extensive market powers of foreign groups are evident, and may exceed those measured at just subsidiary level. A few groups are often responsible for almost all foreign penetration. In the sectors where this level is high (Table 2.3) this implies that a large share of the French market is held by each of these groups.

It also reveals the existence, for foreign groups, of industrial strategies to penetrate industry and the French market, with specialisation in certain operations. It can then be assumed that the dependence of French subsidiaries on foreign groups, which we have shown to be the case for fifty-nine companies is very general and occurs often for all companies under foreign control. As we have shown, foreign groups frequently assign their French subsidiaries with the objective of gaining access to the market, putting few foreign subsidiaries under their control and 'ordering' few exports from them. If our sample is not too distorted, these trends should be found for all companies under foreign control. In addition, a study by STISI, already mentioned, has confirmed this as regards exports.

WHAT IS THE LINK BETWEEN THE LEVEL OF FOREIGN PENETRATION AND THE LEVEL OF MULTINATIONALISATION IN THE VARIOUS SECTORS?

According to the above results, we can, then, assume that foreign-controlled French companies on the whole are not very multinational, to the extent that they control very few production activities outside France. The sectors of activity for which the level of foreign penetration is high would then not be very multinational, and vice versa. From a comparison of the levels of foreign penetration (Table 2.3) and the levels of multinational production (Introduction, Table I.6) we have found that this link is very often confirmed.

High Level of Foreign Penetration and Low Level of Multinationalisation

The sectors with high levels of foreign penetration are in fact often sectors with a low level of multinationalisation (these two rates are given in brackets). This is the case for:

— mechanical engineering sector (62.9/1.7 per cent);
— electrical and electronic engineering sector (71.2/4.1 per cent);
— sector of fourteen agricultural/food industries (28/1.6 per cent).

There are, however, three sectors where penetration is very high which have high levels of multinationalisation:

— *Sector 6*: Parachemicals, Pharmaceuticals (64.2/7.8 per cent) as two big foreign-controlled companies, Roussel-Uclaf and L'Oréal, have retained the production operations outside France which they owned before control was taken over;
— *Sector 5*: Rubber, Plastics (49.3/14.2 per cent) as the big group Michelin is very multinational;
— *Sector 1*: Oil (48.6/21.2 per cent) as the national oil companies are very multinational.

Low Level of Foreign Penetration and High Level of Multinationalisation

The sectors with low rates of foreign penetration are often sectors with high levels of multinationalisation:

— *Sector 2*: Mining, Construction Materials, Glass (13.1/28.3 per cent);
— *Sector 3*: Iron and Steel, Metallurgy (16.5/10.6 per cent);
— *Sector 11*: Building and Public works (5.7/3.7 per cent) (as the level of multinationalisation is very much above 3.7 per cent for the big companies).

This is not true for the sectors which are not very multinational because of the strategic nature of their operations (electricity, ship-building, aeronautics, armaments) or which tend to be linked with a low concentration of national companies (building and public works), leather shoes, miscellaneous wood and furniture, other non-textile consumer goods, commerce, etc.), with the latter point referring to the size and concentration factor analysed in Chapter 1.

How Foreign Penetration Limits Multinationalisation of the Economy 'Downstream'

There are, then, trends which are intrinsic in a low level of multi-nationalisation (consumer goods, . . .) and in a high level of multi-nationalisation (oil, rubber, . . .) which distort the relation we are trying to analyse, and which are also often linked with the degree of concentration of national firms (and in the previous chapter we have seen that this is a factor in multinationalisation). The assumed link is, however, clear: a high level of foreign penetration often corresponds to sectors which are not very multinational and vice versa.

This comes directly from the low level of multinationalisation of companies under foreign control. It also comes from another pheno-menon, also linked with the relative extent of foreign penetration. When this is very high in a sector, the foreign groups then occupy a dominant position. The formation of big competitive national groups which can become multinational is then very difficult. This limits the expansion abroad of companies in the sector. So, for example, in the data processing sector in France, it is now only possible to form big groups by national shareholders buying up a company under foreign control. This is what happened in 1980 when SGPM took control of CII-Honeywell-Bull.

In terms of industrial policy, therefore, it is quite clear that the acceptance of high levels of foreign investment in a sector of the French economy:

— results in the national market being opened up to foreign industrial groups which can then compete more keenly. This may make it difficult for national groups to emerge which are large enough to withstand world-wide competition. This corresponds to the abandonment of industrial operations and the de-specialisation of the national economy, in the sense, for example, meant by André Giraud, former Minister of Industry, when he asserted, 'One should not fear foreign investment in fields where French industry has given up hope.'[16]

— very often results in a deterioration in the trade balance, either directly through the imports of the subsidiaries of foreign groups, or indirectly because their exports are lower than those which the national companies would have made.

From this point of view, one can understand how the industrial specialisations of French industry may, under certain conditions, be deduced from a comparison of foreign investment in France with French investments abroad. This proposal will in fact be set out in more detail in Chapter 3.

Summary of Part I

Multinational production, and exports, are factors involved in the growth of the company: its large size, and the oligopolistic market structure limit its growth on the French market and push it to expand abroad (Chapter 1).

In addition, multinational production, and exports, assume that the company has autonomy in decision-making. Or rather, the existence of foreign control very often leads to a lack of autonomy and subjection to a strategy of gaining access to the French market, and this reduces the operations abroad of French companies, which have become subsidiaries of foreign groups (Chapter 2).

We have therefore highlighted the existence of two factors in the multinational production (and exports) of a company:

— a positive factor: the relative size of the company and the oligopolistic market structure;
— a negative factor: the existence of foreign control over the company (trend which only comes into play on the whole as there are
   different strategies guiding the role attributed to the French subsidiary by the foreign group controlling it).

We can see how foreign investment in France modifies foreign trade and multinationalisation. These two factors can in fact be extended to the whole French economy: in simple terms, the French economy will export more and become more multinational by producing abroad the higher the concentration of production facilities, and the lower the level of foreign penetration.

The relative under-multinationalisation of the French economy, compared with other Western developed economies, as shown in Table I.5, can then be explained not only by the historical factors already mentioned in the Introduction, but in part by the extent of foreign penetration in France.

To come back to the operations abroad of French companies, in this part we have only studied two main factors relating to the situation of companies in their home economy. In particular, as we announced in the Preface, we have ignored historical factors, certain company-specific factors, and certain sectoral factors which may play a part.

On the other hand, in Part II, we shall take into account other factors involved in spreading the location of production, linked with the nature of the host economies and disparities in the world economy: the size of the markets, levels of production costs and in particular wage costs. These elements alone can explain, for example, the choice between exporting and production abroad or cases of foreign production for reimportation into France. They should therefore account for the different international organisation structures used by French companies. The following analysis will then concentrate on the structures of the world economy.

NOTES

1   P. Allard, M. Béaud, B. Bellon, A. M. Levy, S. Lienart, 1978.
2   Savary, 1980, p. 360.
3   STISI, 1980.
4   D. Frank and Mathis, 1979.
5   Cf Savary, op. cit., pp. 352–5.
6   STISI, op. cit., p. 20. This study also shows how the exports of subsidiaries of foreign groups in France are geographically polarised.
7   Cf. study by the Swiss chamber of commerce on the exports of Swiss companies established in France, which omits to calculate the balance of trade for these companies. See Keller, 1980.
8   Groupe de recherche de géographie industrielle, 1975. G. Bertin, 1976. M. Delapierre and C. A. Michalet, 1976. F. Morin and A. Alcouffe, 1977.
9   C. Hernandez, 1975. J. C. Cohen and P. Fondanaiche, 1974. B. Guibert *at al.*, 1975. STISI, 1976 and in particular STISI, 1975 to 1978 for the detailed statistical results.
10 For a detailed review of the results, see volume 1 of our thesis, Savary, 1980, and for the method of analysis, Annexe No. 2 of this book.
11 See Savary, op. cit., p. 141.
12 See Savary, op. cit., pp. 226 ff.
13 And the top seventy-six industrial investors control 61 per cent of capital under foreign control in French industry, which corresponds to an even greater concentration.
14 From F. Morin, 1975, we can estimate that the degree of penetration for the banking sector is 17.5 per cent (based on the balance sheet totals of banks registered as at 1 January 1976) and that of the insurance sector is 8 per cent (based on the total premiums for the top fifty groups as at 1 January 1976). J. Ehrsam, 1981, p. 34, quoting official sources, does, however, give lower degrees of foreign penetration for these two sectors (10.6 per cent at the end of 1979 based on the credit distributed by the banks registered and 6.6 per cent at the end of 1978 based on the turnover of the insurance companies).
15 See Savary, op. cit., p. 257, where we set out the sectoral distribution of investments in France by the big Dutch groups. See also pp. 244–86 for a fuller study of the concentration of foreign groups in France according to sector. G. Bertin, 1975, p. 59, based on a study of the investment portfolios from 1966 to 1972 also states 'In most cases the strategy used depends on the line of growth of the foreign group . . . conglomerate action does on the other hand remain the exception.'
16 *Le Monde*, 22 September 1980.

PART II

THE STRATEGIES OF THE MULTINATIONALS

How do French multinational companies behave, what are their strategies, particularly as regards their production operations abroad? While there are many complex dimensions to the strategy of a multi-national group, we shall use a very narrow definition, which will, however, enable some important results to be brought to light.

In view of the difficulties in collecting very full data, and to avoid a priori judgements which necessarily accompany this type of approach, this is not a review of the objectives and organisation methods as set out by companies in the information they issue in the normal course of events, or in response to an inquiry. Consequently, cultural or psychological factors which may explain the emergence and conduct of multinational strategies are omitted, and group-specific organisation and planning procedures are not studied.

We are only trying to identify, by means of a few significant characteristics, the existing structures of production operations abroad, so that we can set out on a factual basis the choices made by companies.

Our procedure is therefore identical to that of Michalet and Delapierre when they assert that strategies are revealed by organisation structures.[1] But while these authors carry out a very full study of the organisation structures and strategies of foreign groups investing in France, this time we are applying their methodology to French multinational companies and their foreign subsidiaries. In addition, we are only looking at a few elements of the organisation structures of French multinational firms.

We are assuming that the location of foreign production operations (cf. in a big or a small market) and the production methods (existence of French exports to these subsidiaries, production from these plants intended for the foreign local market or reimported) reveal different types of international organisation structures depending on the objectives of production abroad or strategies.

At the outset, we make a distinction between three main types, which we will then go on to explain in detail:

— *the market strategy*: production abroad, intended for the foreign local market;

— *the production strategy*: production abroad reimported into France, hence carried out with the aim of reducing production costs;

— *the supply strategy*: production abroad to provide access to an energy resource or a raw material.

We shall try to verify whether, as one might assume,[2] the market strategy applies to production in developed countries, and the production strategy to spreading the location of production to the Third World. In particular we shall study a moderately developed area very important for French multinationals, southern Europe.

We shall also highlight the specialisation of certain companies and companies in certain sectors in the use of a particular strategy.

At the same time, on a more global level, we shall describe the structural characteristics of the multinationalisation of the French economy: principal areas for production abroad, according to sector, French exports and reimportation linked with production abroad. We will then be able to analyse the consequences of production activity outside France on the profitability, exports and employment of French companies.

All of these structures and strategies will be studied on the basis of the situation at the end of 1974: this will give us a sort of photographic view of multinationalisation at this date (Chapter 3).

We shall then look at how, after 1974, the world economic crisis led French companies not to stop their expansion abroad, but to revise their international strategies, concentrating on certain geographical areas and adopting new methods of establishment (Chapter 4).

NOTES

1 Michalet and Delapierre, 1976.
2 Cf. Michalet, 1976, pp. 157 and 158.

3 Strategies of Multinationalisation

We propose to highlight *production strategies* abroad, *based on a study of the structures* set up by companies to organise this production. To be relevant, the study of these structures must be based on certain a priori strategies, which we shall try to identify, and on a breakdown of the world economy into areas, so that a distinction can be made between the different objectives.

REDEFINING STRATEGIES ON THE BASIS OF STRUCTURES

Three A Priori Strategies for Production Abroad

We shall repeat here the brief explanation given by C. A. Michalet,[1] then used by M. Rainelli.[2] It provides a dynamic outline of two types of production abroad based on different objectives and a location which very often differs according to the objective. Each type is also characterised by the specific nature of the internal organisation of multinational groups. These two types or strategies can hence be used for a concrete measurement.

The Market Strategy

We use this term to describe what M. Rainelli calls 'the commercial strategy in the national oligopoly' and C. A. Michalet calls the 'commercial strategy'. As the latter says, 'the explanatory factors involved here are national disparities, oligopolistic structures and, in part, the loss of a technological advantage. The consistent objective of the firms involved is to conquer or defend markets by a means other than that of exporting.' This corresponds to a process of multinational production by 'export-substituting', which is effected by spreading the location of production by setting up 'relay subsidiaries'. Of course, the main objective of the foreign subsidiaries is then to sell on the local markets on which they have been set up: the proportion of production exported to other countries or to the country of origin is limited.

The Production Strategy

We use this term to describe what M. Rainelli calls the 'industrial strategy' and C. A. Michalet calls the 'productive strategy'. For the latter, it is a 'process of multinationalisation guided by the concern to take advantage of the inequality of production costs from one region to another.' Wage disparities become a determinant factor, rather than the opportunities of the host market. 'In the extreme case, all the production of these subsidiaries will be re-exported to the home country or to another country, with this hypothesis becoming a fact when the subsidiary is specialised in the manufacture of part of the final product.'

Although Michalet himself considers that these two types of strategy are not enough to explain fully the spreading of production locations, we choose to use these two types as the basis for our study of the actual organisation used by French firms to produce abroad. This choice is based both on the attraction of these two strategies which constitute part of the objectives and/or some of the causes of multinationalisation, and the possibility of simply measuring the existence of each of these two strategies from flows of products within the multinational group and out of it.

We do, however, feel that the interaction of these two strategies may be much more common than Michalet leads us to suppose. For example, the 'market strategy', when production is carried out in a country with low production costs, may—as well as the search for an outlet—involve a cost saving, which is one of the objectives tied up with the 'production strategy'. An examination of the areas in which foreign production is carried out is, then, essential and will enable this typology to be expressed more precisely.

The Supply Strategy

To the extent that we are looking for a simple typology of the strategies of multinational production, accounting for all its concrete forms, we have to reintroduce a type excluded by Michalet based on the exploitation of natural surface and underground resources. The firms mainly carrying out this type of production abroad can be called 'primary' multinationals or, as C. A. Michalet terms them, 'multinationals by nature', as they move their location according to where the natural resources are. Hence we propose to call the underlying strategy the supply strategy.

Having defined three basic strategies for multinational production, linked to disparities throughout the world, we have created five areas in the world economy to describe the location of foreign subsidiaries with reference to the above strategies.

Five Areas Describe the Disparities of the World Economy

We shall break down the geographical location of the foreign production and marketing subsidiaries of French firms as follows:

— area 1: Africa (continent)
— area 2: Asia, Latin America (excluding Brazil)
— area 3: North America plus three developed countries outside Europe (Australia, New Zealand, Israel)
— area 4: Developed western Europe
— area 5: Newly industrialising countries (Brazil, Spain, Greece, Portugal, Iran, Turkey, Yugoslavia, Middle Eastern countries)

This breakdown will give a better idea of the disparities in market size and production costs, especially wage costs, between foreign economies.

National Disparities in Level of Development and Market Size

What we are interested in here is not so much in describing a hierarchy of production systems,[3] but a hierarchy in the potential markets of the world economy which French firms can enter either by exporting or by producing in the country itself (which rules out countries where it is not possible to set up subsidiaries—countries with a planned economy, particularly the Soviet Union, eastern Europe and China).[4]

We can base this on a combination of two indices: GNP and GNP per capita. The second figure illustrates the standard of living, the level of development and hence the industrialisation and existence of a solvent market for industrial goods and consumer goods.

Table 3.1 gives these two indices for all the main countries or areas. The main market area in the world economy is of course North America, both by total size and by the highest per capita income in the world.[5]

This is followed by all of developed Europe, with a market of roughly the same size and a high per capita income, though lower than that of North America.[6]

In spite of its apparent diversity, area 5, the newly industrialising countries (called NICs in the remainder of this study) is fairly uniform: these are countries with a moderate level of development, where there is a degree of industrialisation, a local market for industrial and consumer goods and a per capita income of between US$1500 and US$3000 (but wage costs lower than those in areas 3 and 4).

Asia, Latin America and Africa, which form areas 1 and 2 and which we shall call less developed countries (LDCs) hereafter, appear to have moderate GNPs, although they are continents with particularly low GNPs per capita, with a low level of development and hence poor markets for the goods produced by French companies. We could have put all the LDCs into one area, but we have kept Africa separate so that we could measure French direct investment in this continent, part of which has traditionally been 'under French influence'. It should

Table 3.1 National disparities in the development and size of markets in 1976

Country or area	GNP at market prices ($US millions)	Population (millions of inhabitants)	GNP per capita ($US)
United States	1 694	215	7 880
Canada	183	23	7 930
North America (area 3)	1 877	238	7 880
France	356	53	6 730
West Germany	462	61.5	7 510
Great Britain	233.6	55.9	4 180
Italy	180.7	56.2	3 220
Netherlands	91.6	13.8	6 650
Switzerland	58.1	6.4	9 160
Belgium	68.9	9.8	7 020
Sweden	74.2	8.2	9 030
Norway, Denmark, Finland	98.2	13.8	7 116
Austria, Ireland, Luxembourg, Iceland + 5 small countries	55	11.6	4 741
Developed Europe (area 4) (except France)	1 322.3	237.2	5 575
Brazil	143	110.1	1 300
Spain	107.2	35.8	2 990
Portugal	16.1	9.7	1 660
Greece	23.6	9.2	2 570
Turkey, Malta, Cyprus	42.8	41.9	1 021
Middle East (including Iran)	176	78	2 250
Newly Industrialising countries (area 5)	500.7	284.7	1 759
Japan	574	112.8	5 090
Asia (except Japan)	586	2 040	290
Central America + South America (except Brazil)	236	217	1 007
Asia + Central and Southern America (except Japan and Brazil) (area 2)	822	2 257	364
Africa (area 1)	180	426	420
Israel, Australia, New Zealand (area 3)	120	20.5	5 861

Source: 1978 World Bank Atlas.

also be noted that within Asia, Japan has a high level of development and constitutes a big market.[7]

National Disparities in Labour Production Costs[8]

There are very great disparities in wage costs between the different economies. To assess these accurately, they have to be measured for identical production operations.[9] A study by the United Tariff Commission (United States)[10] compares the hourly wage costs for assembling American equipment in the United States and abroad. For semiconductors, for example, the cost in around 1970 was 0.28 dollars in Hong Kong as against 2.84 dollars in the United States, and 0.61 dollars in Mexico. Other studies confirm these differences in mean wage rates between countries, in canning,[11] textiles,[12] or the car industry.[13]

Finally a study carried out by Citibank[14] gives wage costs for the NICs. These are mean wage costs for industry as a whole. It would seem that the NICs (Brazil, Spain, Portugal, Greece, Turkey, etc.) have higher costs than those of the LDCs in South East Asia, but they are much lower than those for the European countries and the United States.

Table 3.2 National disparities in wage costs (hourly costs in $US*
in industry)

	1970	1977		1975	1977
United States	4.19	7.6	Brazil	1.14	1.40
Belgium	2.08	8.4	Mexico	2.02	1.82
Great Britain	1.48	3.34	Hong Kong	0.74	1.05
Canada	3.46	7.40	Singapore	0.77	0.85
France	1.74	5.40	South Korea	0.37	0.64
West Germany	2.35	7.73	Taiwan	0.55	0.75
Italy	1.77	5.17	Greece	1.39	1.90
Japan	0.99	3.97	Portugal	1.46	1.60
Netherlands	2.14	8.21	Spain	2.33	2.62
Sweden	2.96	8.82	Turkey	0.70	

*Including wages plus social welfare costs for production workers
Source: United States Labor Statistics Bureau and calculations carried out by Citibank, loc. cit.

The differences in labour productivity between the developed countries and the NICs and LDCs seem to be small. The US Senate's Long report[15] shows that productivity per worker in the subsidiaries of American multinational firms in 1970, compared with that of the workers in the parent companies was 42 per cent in Brazil, 50 per cent in Mexico and hence lower, but much less so, than the hourly wage costs. The report of the United Tariff Commission (United States)[16] concludes also that 'the productivity of workers in the foreign subsidiaries of American firms is very close to that of workers located in the United States, with the same qualifications.' Hence for electronics assembly, the productivity of labour abroad reaches 92 per cent of that employed in the United States. This tends to be all the more true as the work carried out in the foreign subsidiaries in the Third World is simpler, because of the international specialisation of labour carried out within the multinational groups. It is precisely for the unskilled repetitive tasks, of the assembly or fitting type, that labour productivity in the LDCs can be very close to or even higher than that in the developed countries.

These two characteristics—small disparities in labour productivity and big disparities in hourly wage costs—lead us to conclude that there are great inequalities in labour production costs between countries with different levels of development. The establishment of production subsidiaries abroad, when this is carried out within a newly industrialising country (area 5) or a less developed country (areas 1 and 2) by a firm originating from a developed country in North America or western Europe, always enables unit labour costs to be reduced. Where this establishment is in a country with a similar level of development, these disparities also exist, but are much smaller.[17]

Five Areas to Illustrate Strategies

We can sum up the characteristics of the economies belonging to the five geographical areas depicted in Table 3.3. These are average characteristics which permit an overall analysis:[18] the location of the foreign production subsidiaries of French companies in a particular area will show whether a production cost saving is possible.

Table 3.3 Economies of 5 geographical areas

	Size of market	Cost of labour factor
Area 3: North America	very large	very high
Area 4: Developed Europe	large	high
Area 5: NICs (Brazil, Spain, Greece, Portugal etc.)	average	low
Area 2: Asia, Latin America	small	very low
Area 1: Africa	small	very low

Redefining Strategies on the Basis of Structures

The approach used in this chapter will consist of identifying the three types of strategy for spreading the location of production which we have defined, and of measuring their importance for French companies.

To do this, we are using as a basis a concrete study of 185 firms producing abroad. We shall examine three essential elements of foreign production:

1. Its geographical location in one of the five areas.
2. The destination of foreign production: local country itself, third country or France.

These two elements enable a distinction to be made between 'market strategies', 'production strategies' or 'supply strategies'.

Our approach will therefore be much more specific than Rainelli's[19] approach, which consists of considering that the strategy is a market strategy when foreign production takes place in developed countries and a production strategy when it takes place in newly industrialising countries 'as the commercial flows linked to monetary flows are difficult to ascertain.' Michalet[20] uses the same reasoning. An analysis of the flows will, for example, show that often there is production for the local market, even in the case of an NIC market, and that, conversely, there may be a production strategy when production is carried out in a developed country.

3. The importance of purchases by foreign production subsidiaries of semi-finished products from French companies in the group.

This third element can be used to determine the importance of exports linked to production outside France, as well as the importance of actual production abroad. This clearly indicates the international organisations and strategies used.

The strategies for the multinationalisation of French companies must, then, be 'redefined' on the basis of their structures, which will in particular lead on to the proposal of a more complex typology. In addition, the importance of each strategy for a particular company or type of company must be indicated. This will, for example, reveal the sectoral specialisations in the use of certain strategies. A simple examination of the location of production abroad shows that there are distinct geographical specialisations according to the sectors of activity.

GEOGRAPHICAL SPECIALISATIONS OF PRODUCTION ABROAD: EUROPE

In 1974, French investment in production operations was concentrated first in Europe, then in the newly industrialising countries (Table 3.4).[21] The proportion of investment in Africa was only 23 per cent. The non-industrial sectors, agriculture/food, services, commerce (with CFAO [Cie Française de l'Afrique Occidentale] and SCOA [Société Commerciale d'Ouest Africain]), oil (with Erap), building and public works, carried out production mainly in area 1. Excluding these

operations, 14 per cent of the investment of industry in the strict
sense was in Africa, 47 per cent in developed western Europe, and
68 per cent in developed Europe plus southern Europe plus Brazil
(areas 4 and 5). Industrial investment in North America was not incon-
siderable after 1974.

Table 3.4 Geographical distribution of production abroad by all French
companies (turnover of foreign production subsidiaries,
establishments or sites, direct and indirect, in 1974, by
area as a percentage of the total)

	All sectors of activity	Industry in strict sense (excluding primary ind., agr/food ind., building and public works)
Area 1: Africa	23.8	13.9
Area 2: Asia, Latin America	13.6	6.4
Area 3: North America	10.8	12.2
Area 4: Developed Europe	36.9	47.1
Area 5: NICs—Brazil, Spain, Portugal, etc.	14.9	20.7
Total	100 (120 374 m fr.)	100 (74 914 m fr.)

The geographical specialisations of production operations abroad do
in fact vary considerably depending on the sector (Annexe 5). Three
types of specialisation are, however, found which are each used by
several sectors.

Type 1: production mainly in developed Europe and important in the NICs
This type includes the biggest number of sectors, and its importance
explains the specialisation noted for the economy as a whole. It includes
the four sectors producing semi-finished products:

sector 2: mining, construction materials, glass (the only sector of this
type with a lot of production in the United States, carried out by
Lafarge)
sector 3: iron and steel, metallurgy
sector 4: basic chemicals
sector 5: paper, rubber, plastics

and the sectors producing consumer goods:

sector 6: parachemicals, pharmaceuticals
sector 7B: non-textile consumer goods

(One could include in this type the national based agricultural/food industries—14B—for which 40 per cent of production is carried out in Europe.)

Type 2: production mainly in the newly industrialising countries and important in Europe
This type includes three sectors producing capital goods:

> sector 8: mechanical engineering (also controlling significant production in North America, which makes this sector comparable with type 1)
> sector 9: electrical engineering
> sector 10: transport equipment

(The latter two also produce a considerable amount in area 2, Asia, Latin America, which confirms their tendency to produce in LDCs.)

Type 3: production mainly in Africa
This type includes:

> sector 11: building and public works
> sector 13: services
> sector 14B: agricultural/food industries with a national base (but excluding Bel and BSN)
> sector 14A: agricultural/food industries, multinationals 'by nature' (plantations, processing tropical products, etc.)
> sector 7A: textiles

(The two sectors 14A and 7A also produce a lot in area 2, Asia, Latin America.)

Two sectors yet to be analysed:

> sector 1: primary industry. This covers two types of multinational company, even though they have similar specialisations:
> (a) multinational companies 'by nature', that is, specialising in agricultural or forestry plantations in Africa and Asia;
> (b) the oil companies Erap and CFP.

> sector 12: commerce. This also covers two types of multinational company:
> (a) commerce with a national base, spreading its location to a small degree in 1974 and increasingly thereafter to Europe and Spain (cf. Radar, Carrefour, Cofradel, Nord-Ouest Alimentation), Brazil (Intermarché, Carrefour) and the United States (Casino, Nicolas, Agache Willot, Promodes, etc.);
> (b) international trading companies (CFAO, Optorg, SCOA) specialised in trade (and industrial operations) with West Africa.

Note that none of the sectors totally specialises its production abroad in a single area. In addition, type 2 only stands out because of the creation of our area 5. If, for example, Spain, where sectors 9 and 10 have high production levels, had been included in Europe this would have hidden the specialisation of these sectors in area 5, which is, however, significant.

Finally, the geographical specialisations of the big multinational groups are often enough on their own to explain the specialisations noted for a sector. To give just one example, in 1974 the operations of Lafarge in North America represented 97 per cent of the total operations of the twenty-four companies of our sample in this area.

This phenomenon is linked with the high concentration of production abroad, and it also makes the sectoral specialisations very sensitive to the decisions of the big groups (for example, recent growth of Michelin in the United States, sale of BSN in Europe). We should, however, look at how far these groups are representative of their sector: do the other firms have the same geographical specialisations? After a detailed examination we can reply that very often this is the case. There are, however, exceptions, all linked to the production figures for groups which are sector leaders, which are the only ones to expand multinationally in distant areas: in 1974, and for the 413 companies in the sample, Lafarge accounted for all the production of sector 2 in North America, and Bic and Rossignol for all that of sector 7 in the same area, Rhône-Poulenc for sector 4 in Brazil (area 5), and Thomson and CGE for sector 9 in area 2 (91 per cent). This characteristic is less obvious if we look at all French groups, and also decreases after 1974, with the increasing multinational spread of new multinationals. It is none the less still significant.

The geographical distribution of the production operations abroad of French companies, taking all sectors together, reveals three main trends:[22]

Africa: the Weight of Colonial-type Operations

Twenty-five per cent of total French production abroad is accounted for by Africa, and 14 per cent with regard to industry alone.

The sectors with a big presence in this area are: agricultural and forestry plantations, agricultural/food industries processing local products, mining and oil industries, international trading companies, services, in particular shipping, building and public works. These are the type of operations which are linked with a colonial presence: supply to France of raw materials, possibly after processing on the spot, sales of French industrial products, and infrastructures facilitating these trade flows. Heavy industry is absent (apart from PUK). The processing industries are not very well developed (drinks, textiles, cement crushing,[23] plastics processing, canning, car assembly). A study of the flows of goods exchanged between France and these subsidiaries in Africa will define these characteristics more precisely.

The weight of colonial-type operations is also underestimated here, as these are often operations carried out by small or medium-sized French companies, under family control, which are not quoted on the Stock Exchange and are hence underestimated by our method of calculation.

The nature of the French operations which have moved to Africa is related to the low economic development and low level of industrialisation in this area. However, this underdevelopment itself and the extent of French investment in Africa are of course related to the history of the colonial presence in North Africa and Black West and Equatorial Africa, the two areas in which French production operations in Africa are concentrated.[24] Note that these colonial-type operations are not very important in Asia (area 2), as decolonisation in this area in general took the form of the expropriation of French interests (Vietnam, Cambodia).

The importance of French investment in Africa and the very nature of the operations, which are very spread out through this area, reflect both the historical importance of previous colonial links and the continuing French economic and political influence in the countries of North Africa (excluding Algeria) and West and Equatorial Africa (excluding Guinea).

This is a specific character of French investment abroad which is tending to become less important as industrial investment in the developed countries increases.

J. Ehrsam[25] also points out that within French investment abroad, measured as gross flows in the balance of payments, the share of the 'overseas countries' has fallen from 14 per cent in 1973 to 5 per cent in 1978 (and this share was very probably much more than 14 per cent in the 1950s and before).

Southern Europe and Brazil: the Attraction of Countries with an Intermediate Level of Development

The second area in which French industrial investment is concentrated is the area of the newly industrialising countries (area 5) which accounts for 21 per cent of all investment. In 1974, if one excludes the Middle Eastern countries where the investment was made by building and public works companies, most French investment in this area was in Spain, while Greece, Portugal, Brazil, Yugoslavia, Turkey and Iran accounted for much smaller amounts. On the other hand, since 1974, French investment in Brazil has increased rapidly, although even before 1974 it was important for companies such as Rhône-Poulenc or Empain Schneider.

This great specialisation is a second characteristic of the multi-nationalisation of the French economy. It seems to indicate that these countries offer the following advantages for French industrialists:

— existence of a big or rapidly expanding market;
— existence of labour production costs which are lower than French costs;
— financial and social guarantees because of the authoritarian political systems.

One may add to these advantages, for the countries of southern Europe:

— geographic (and cultural) proximity;
— for Greece, Spain and Portugal, their membership or future member-ship of the Common Market, and hence the possibility of using these production bases in future to supply industrial Europe.[26]

By looking at whether or not production strategies exist in many cases, with reimportation into France of the production from these countries, we shall be able to check in the following sections on whether low wage costs and the possibility of reimportation into the Common Market are the advantages sought. For Spain, the closing of the market to French imports has been an important explanatory factor (in the case of Renault, Citroën).

Europe and North America: Multinationalisation and
Interpenetration of Industries (in Developed Countries)

The importance of developed Europe and North America, accounting for 47 per cent of total French investment abroad or 59 per cent for industry, clearly shows that in 1974 most French multinationals were located in the developed countries. This ties up with the general trend for the industries of all western developed economies.

In 1974 almost 50 per cent of French industrial investment abroad was in western Europe, with the recent expansion of French multi-nationalisation since the 1950s and 1960s[27] following a period of essentially colonial presence in the countries of the Third World. The recent investment of French industrial companies abroad since the 1950s has been aimed mainly at Europe, essentially because of the creation of the Common Market in 1958, and the consequent libera-tion of flows of goods, capital and people.

From the point of view of direct investment abroad, the fact that French industry has lagged behind that of American or German indus-try has not meant absolute domination, which would, for example, have forced the French economy to expand multinationally in only the less developed economies, and particularly the old French colonies. As French investment abroad is concentrated first in economies with a similar or higher level of development, it is only by comparing the extent of reciprocal foreign investment (which we shall do in the conclusion) that we can place the French economy in relation to its competitors.

Why are the companies in the semi-finished products sectors (sectors 2, 3, 4, 5) and certain consumer goods sectors (sectors 6, 7B, 14C) very well established in Europe and the United States, while companies in the capital goods sectors (sectors 8, 9, 10) are much less established in these countries and concentrate on the developing countries? There are three main possible interpretations for this.

One could consider that the markets for the first type of company are relatively more concentrated in the developed countries. If this proposal is true for all industrial goods, could one maintain, for example, that electrical engineering products have bigger outlets in the LDCs? Is there no international division of labour which is not related to market size?

We could also look for an explanation of these specialisations in the twofold phenomenon:

— the greater the competitiveness of French companies, which varies depending on the sector, the greater the propensity to establish in the developed countries;
— the greater the competitiveness of foreign companies, which varies depending on the sector, the lower the propensity of French companies to establish in the developed countries.

From this point of view, the strengths and weaknesses of French industrial establishments in the developed countries illustrate the strengths and weaknesses of French industry in relation to these economies, and hence the industrial specialisations.

Finally, one may ask whether those companies which develop on a more intense multinational basis in the less developed countries have a different production cost structure, with higher labour costs: or does their industrial process lend itself better to separating the different stages of production, some of which are very labour-intensive? These two characteristics would for some companies mean greater cost savings by moving the location of production to the less developed countries, which would explain the preference for this type of establishment.

In the above we have implicitly assumed that all production in a developed country was intended for the local market and hence corresponded to a 'market strategy', while all production in a less developed country was reimported into France, and corresponded to an objective of reducing costs and hence a 'production strategy'. The results of the following section will set out in detail the strategies actually used by French companies: even if it is true that these strategies seem more varied than we had assumed, the general trends which we have found are still verified, as are the hypotheses which explain them.

THE STRATEGIES OF COMPANIES: SPECIALISATION DEPENDING ON THE SECTOR AND THE AREA

For each company an examination of the destination of production abroad will show whether the production supplies the local market (market strategy) or whether it is reimported into France (production strategy, in the case of a finished product; supply strategy in the case of a raw material). The position may vary for different foreign subsidiaries of the same company, and these must then be studied separately: in Tables 3.6 and 3.7, illustrating production strategies abroad, a single French firm may be seen to use several strategies simultaneously.

Finally, the wide range of situations found has led us to talk of 'production strategy' whenever foreign production is exported from the country of origin, even if this is not to France. A distinction can be made between two different types of market strategy:

— autonomous production: the foreign subsidiaries import few or no semi-finished products from France;
— assembly production: the foreign subsidiaries import semi-finished products from the French companies in the group, and we shall see that this distinction reveals distinct specialisations according to geographical zone.

Companies in the Sectors Producing Primarily in Europe (Table 3.6)*

1. If we exclude the cases of supply strategy, which are common in sectors 2 and 3, the strategy used most is a market strategy, mostly with production in the developed countries. On the whole this verifies a hypothesis underlying this type of strategy, where market size is the chief factor involved. However, this strategy is also used to gain access to the markets of newly industrialising or less developed countries, which is our second finding.
2. According to the geographical area of establishment, the market strategy used differs:

— in developed countries production is mostly 'autonomous' or integrated with large subsidiaries[28] which have been acquired (external growth);
— in the less developed countries (areas 1, 2, 5) 'assembly production'

*In reading the following, please use the definitions in Table 3.5.

Table 3.5 Definitions of sectors and geographical areas

Sectors

1	Primary industry
1A	Oil
2	Mining, construction materials, glass
3	Iron and steel, metallurgy
4	Basic chemicals
5	Paper, rubber, plastics
6	Parachemicals, pharmaceuticals
7	Consumer goods
7A	Textiles
8	Mechanical engineering
9	Electrical and electronic engineering
10	Transportation equipment
10A	Land transportation equipment
11	Building and public works
12	Commerce
13	Services
14	Agricultural and food industries

Areas

1	Africa
2	Asia, Latin America (except Brazil)
3	North America (United States, Canada) + Australia, New Zealand, Israel
4	Developed western Europe
5	Newly industrialising countries (Brazil, Spain, Portugal, Greece, Turkey, countries of the Middle East)

is more common, with smaller subsidiaries set up for this purpose (internal growth), processing imported French products on the spot.

This fourfold specialisation (type of market strategy, geographical area, size of subsidiary, method of creating subsidiary) is clear, for example, for the cement companies. Lafarge carries out integrated production in Europe and in Canada in particular, in big subsidiaries which it has acquired while it crushes imported clinker in West Africa. Similarly, the companies in the metallurgy sector control integrated plants in Europe and the United States and have set up subsidiaries to process imported metallurgical products in Africa, Spain and Brazil. The French companies in the paper/cardboard sector process imported semi-finished products in Africa, Spain and Brazil, while since 1974 La Cellulose has taken control in Canada of a big integrated paper company.

3. The 'production strategy' is not very common (six cases) and often corresponds to subsidiaries in less developed countries (and even for iron and steel in the developed countries). The subsidiaries using this type of strategy are never important for the French group.

Table 3.6 The strategies of French multinational companies: sectors mainly multinational in Europe

Nature and destination of foreign production	Purchases of semi-finished products from French companies in the group	2 Mining, construction materials, glass	3 Iron and steel, metallurgy	4 Chemicals
I Finished products for local market (or neighbouring area) *Market strategy*	High (greater than 10% or strategic) *Production assembly*	*Lafarge, Origny-Desvroise, Lambert Frères* (Africa crushing of imported clinker)	*Vallourec* (Spain, Belgium, Ivory Coast, by processing subsids.) *Wendel* (Spain, with Mavilor, Paumellerie) *Carnaud* (Africa, Spain, Greece) *Pompey* (Africa) *Paris Outreau* (Italy, Spain) *Fichet-Bauche* (West Germany, Belgium, Spain, Brazil, Malaysia)	
	Low (less than 10%)			*Gerland* (Belgium, UK, India(?))
	Virtually nil *Autonomous production*	*Lafarge* (Canada, USA, Europe, Brazil) *Ciments français* (Luxembourg, USA, Morocco) *BSN* (Europe for glass)	*Schneider* (USA) *Imétal* (USA) *Vallourec* (Italy) (?)*Penarroya* (Spain) Greece, Italy)	*Rhône-Poulenc* (Europe, Brazil, Spain, USA, Indonesia, Thailand) *Sias* (West Germany) *Rousselot* (UK, Belgium, USA, Canada)
II Finished products exported to French (or foreign) companies in the group (even in part) *Production strategy*	*Quartz et silice* (in Switzerland, silicon tubes)		*Wendel* (in West Germany, steel from Dillinger, in Spain by Paumèllerie électrique) *Fichet-Bauche* (in Malaysia exported to Southern Asia)	
III Raw materials or unprocessed or semi-processed ore exported to France *Supply strategy*	*Placoplâtre* (Netherlands suppl. of cardboard) *Salins du Midi* (Africa* for salt) *Cie Mokta* (Africa for uranium and manganese)		*Imétal* (New Caledonia nickel, Brazil) *Penarroya* (Brazil and Morocco lead, perhaps Spain, Greece, Italy) *Usinor* (coke to Netherlands) *HF Chiers* (iron mines in Belgium)	*Rousselot* (in West Germany supply of products of animal origin)

Note: Companies in sample, situation at 31 December 1974.
(?) The percentages of products imported is uncertain.
*Exports to the USA.

5 Paper, rubber, plastics	6 Parachemicals, pharmaceuticals	7B Consumer goods (excluding textiles)	14C Agr./food industry national base
Sommer (Spain, Brazil, Ivory Coast, Italy, UK, Netherlands) *Charfa, Cellulose, Rochette-Cenpa* (Africa, Spain, West Germany) *Arjomari-Prioux* (Brazil)	*Delalande* (Europe, Brazil) *Labaz* (Belgium, Spain) (in both cases imports raw materials and active constituents)	*Skis Rossignol* (USA, Europe, Spain) (purchase of finished products)	*Bel* (Europe, USA, Spain, Morocco) (purchase of finished products) *BSN* (Africa for pasta)
Hutchinson (Europe, Spain, South Africa) *Michelin* (Europe, Spain, USA, Canada, Nigeria)	(?)*L'Oréal* (Europe, USA, Canada, Morocco, South Africa, Latin America)	*Bic* (USA, UK, Europe, Japan, Brazil)	
(?)*Michelin*	*Institut Mérieux* (Latin America for vaccinations, USA for blood)	*Hachette* (publishing, printing in Europe, USA, Canada)	*BSN* (Europe, Brazil, Mexico for milk products)
Sommer (plastic sanitary ware in Italy)	*Labaz* (Portugal and Malta, simple medical equipment marketed by Dubernard-Hôpital-France)	*Skis Rossignol* (bottom- and middle-range skis made in Spain) *Bic* (USA for America, Great Britain for Commonwealth)	
	Reti (in Italy) supplies raw materials to group sold in 1977)		

Table 3.7 The strategies of French multinational companies: sectors mainly multinational in southern Europe and the Third World

Nature and destination of foreign products	Purchases of semi-finished products from French companies in the group	8 Mechanical engineering	9 Electrical and electronic engineering
I Finished products for the local market (or neighbouring area) *Market strategy*	High (over 10% or strategic) *Assembly production*	*Ets Neu* (Belgium, USA, Spain, Brazil) *Ernault Somua* (USA) (?)*Engr. Red* (Spain) *CMP* (Italy, Netherlands, West Germany, Iran, Iraq, Saudi Arabia) *Poclain* (Mexico, USA) *Amrep* (Africa, Brazil)	*SAFT* (UK, West Germany, Spain, South Africa) *Wonder* (Madagascar, Upper Volta, Ivory Coast, Mali, Mauritania, Gabon) *Sagem* (Mexico, Venezuela, Morocco, Spain, Brazil, Australia) *Télémécanique* (UK, Belgium, Ireland, Spain, Brazil)
	Small less than 10%	*BSL* (Spain, Italy, Argentina)	(?)*Merlin Gerin* (Brazil, Morocco, Italy, Switzerland, Belgium, Spain) (?)*Moulinex* (Spain) (?)*PM Labinal* (Spain) (?)*A. Martin* (Switzerland, Argentina) *CGR* (USA,* Canada,* Italy, West Germany, Spain, Mexico, Brazil)
	Virtually nil *Autonomous production*	*CMP* (Spain,† Belgium,† Portugal†) *Nordon* (Brazil†) *Essilor* (USA,* Japan, UK)	*Cipel** (USA) *CIT-Alcatel* (Europe, USA*/Services) *Thomson* (West Germany and Spain/TV, Argentina, radio-relay systems)
II Products exported to French companies in the group (even in part) *Production strategy*	Finished product (international specialisation of production)	(?)*Transméca* (chain in Portugal) *Jaz* (mechanical alarms in Spain, radio-alarms) *Essilor* (glass in Philippines and Hong Kong to South East Asia)	*Thomson* (TV audio in Singapore) *CGR* (Belgium* to group, India to LDCs, Mexico to Latin America) (?)*Moulinex* (in Spain for Latin America, in Ireland for Commonwealth)
	Parts (international specialisation of tasks)	*Crouzet* (Spain, Italy, France) *Poclain* (Belgium, Spain, France)	*Thomson CSF* (Components in Spain, Morocco) *Thomson Brandt* (thermostats in Singapore)
III Raw materials or unprocessed or semi-processed ore exported to France *Supply Strategy*			

Note: Companies in sample, situation at 31 December 1974.

(?) Hypothesis on the percentage of products imported.

*Acquisition by external growth or common subsidiary (only for cases of autonomous production).

† Acquisition with local partner (only for cases of autonomous production).

10 Transportation equipment	14B Agr./food industry national base	7A Textiles
Peugeot (Africa, Malaysia) *Renault* (Ivory Coast, Colombia, Mexico, Venezuela) *Citroën* (Portugal, Yugoslavia, Argentina) *Motobécane* (Morocco, Central African Empire, Iran, India, Netherlands, Brazil) *Cycles Peugeot* (Morocco, Spain, S. Africa, Brazil, Iran, Turkey)	*Moët* (USA, Brazil) *GMP* (milling + sugar in Africa)	*Agache-Willot* (Niger, Central Africa, Mali)
(?)*Mavilor* and *Soulé* (Spain) (?)*Paris-Rhône* (Argentina, Belgium, Spain, Brazil) (?)*Ferodo* (West Germany, Italy, Spain, Brazil) (?)*Chausson* (Belgium, Spain, Algeria, Ivory Coast, Italy, Brazil)		
Peugeot (Argentina) *Citroën* (Spain) *Renault* (Spain, Argentina, Turkey†) *Jaeger* (Italy, Spain, Argentina, Mexico)	*Vittel** (Lebanon) *Olida* (Belgium) *Moët* (USA) *GMP* (bread in Europe, USA)	*Vitos* (Portugal, Mexico) (?)*Valisère* (Spain, Lebanon) *Lainière de Roubaix* (Brazil,* Colombia, Spain)
Citroën (2 and 3 CV in Belgium, Spain) *Renault* (R5 in Spain, R4, R5, R14 in Belgium + R18 planned in Romania) *Paris-Rhône* (regulators Morocco)	*P. Ricard* (whisky and liqueurs in UK, West Germany, Switzerland, Argentina)	*Lainière de Roubaix* (Brazil, Colombia, Spain, Tunisia, Italy, Puerto Rico) (?)*Agache-Willot* (?Tunisia and elsewhere?)
Cycles Peugeot (frames in Spain and South Africa) *Renault* (gearboxes and trans- mission sets in Romania, motors planned in Portugal)		
	Roquefort (cheese in Italy, Spain, Tunisia) *Saupiquet* (canned fish in Ivory Coast, Senegal, Portugal)	(?)*Prouvost* (combed wool in South Africa)

Companies in Sectors Producing Mainly in Southern Europe and the Third World (Table 3.7)

1. These companies mainly produce with a 'production strategy' in the countries of areas 1, 2 and 5 which are the most important for them. The foreign production exported, mostly to France, covers:

— either simple or bottom-of-the-range finished products: Citroën for the 2 CV in Spain, Renault for the R5 in Spain, R18 in Romania, Jaz, Essilor, Poclain;
— or semi-finished products or parts: Thomson with components in Spain, Morocco, Singapore, Poclain with frames and arms in Spain; Renault, Peugeot, Crouzet.

On the whole this confirms the hypothesis that this type of strategy is used for establishment in countries less developed than France.

2. But, as for the first type of company, the 'market strategy' is also used in developed countries, even though this is less common and relates to smaller subsidiaries (Thomson, CGR, Cit, Poclain, Essilor).

3. On the other hand, for this type of company, the 'market strategy' is often used for establishments in less developed countries. We then find that this is mostly 'assembly production': Renault in Mexico, Venezuela, Iran, Citroën in Yugoslavia, Portugal, Argentina; Peugeot in Africa; Saft, Wonder, Sagem and Télémécanique. However, there are cases of 'autonomous production' in the newly industrialising countries (area 5) or the bigger less developed countries (areas 1 and 2): Citroën in Spain, Renault in Argentina, Spain and Turkey, Jaeger, Nordon.

There is no doubt that for companies in these sectors, establishments in the less developed countries in areas 1, 2 and 5 are more important: they are more common and bigger.

In conclusion, an empirical analysis of ninety-three French multinational companies confirmed that market strategies do exist, that is, production abroad intended for the local market, as well as production strategies for the re-exportation of foreign production. It also showed that the attraction of big markets tended to make market strategies more common when production took place in the developed countries, and that, on the contrary, the production strategy was often used in an attempt to reduce production costs, as it was encountered more frequently when production took place outside the developed countries.

But this specialisation—market strategy in the developed countries and production strategy in the other less developed countries—was never total. In particular, market strategies often existed for production in the less developed countries, very often in the form of assembly production.

This empirical analysis of ninety-three companies also shows the sectoral specialisations in the use of different strategies, coinciding with sectoral specialisations in geographical location, which we shall interpret in the following sections, after assessing the strategies used.

AN ASSESSMENT OF THE STRATEGIES OF MULTINATIONALS

Table 3.8 sums up the three a priori strategies for production abroad and the actual strategies revealed by our study. The supply strategy has been defined as the production abroad of raw materials, which are then imported into France. This applies for the activities of Salins du Midi, Le Nickel, Penarroya, Mokta and Saupiquet, mostly, then, production outside the developed countries. A number of companies can be called multinationals 'by nature' as they have a 'colonial strategy': these are companies with no, or very few, operations in France, with almost all their production operations being carried out abroad, very often within the former French colonies in Asia or Africa (Rochefortaise de produits alimentaires, Sofical, Brasseries et Glacières Internationales).

The production strategy corresponds a priori to production abroad which is reimported into France. If this definition is extended to all

Table 3.8 Multinational production strategies

3 a priori strategies	'Actual' strategies of French multinationals		
		Production in:	
		Developed countries	NICs or LDCs
Supply strategy	supply strategy	rare	common
	colonial strategy	non-existent	common
Production strategy (foreign production exported)	production exported to developed countries	rare I international specialisation	common II 'pure production strategy'
	production exported to NICs or LDCs	rare IV international specialisation for 'access to an economic area'	sometimes III 'production strategy for the NIC and LDC market'
Market strategy (production for local market)	'autonomous production' (integrated)	common 'pure market strategy'	sometimes/rare
	'assembly production' (high imports)	rare	common 'market strategy with associated cost savings' (mixed strategy)

Notes: See Tables 3.6 and 3.7 for groups and sectors in question.
Developed countries: North America (area 3) + Developed Europe (area 4).
NICs: Brazil, Spain, Greece (area 5).
LDCs: Africa (area 1) + Asia + Latin America (area 2).

foreign production exported from the foreign country, we find four subtypes, depending on the location of this production and its geographical destination.

The most frequent type (marked II on Table 3.8) is that of production in a less developed country, exported to the developed countries. It corresponds to the implicit hypotheses of the a priori production strategy, for this type of international organisation of production most clearly shows that the objective is to reduce production costs. In this sense, we describe this type of strategy as a *'pure production strategy'*. This organisation of production abroad is relatively uncommon, although thirteen companies out of ninety-three have at least one foreign subsidiary to which this strategy applies, which is 14 per cent of the multinational companies described. These are Lainière de Roubaix (textiles), Labaz (pharmacy), Rossignol and Essilor (consumer goods) and in particular nine companies in the mechanical engineering (Jaz, Poclain, Crouzet), electrical engineering (Thomson, Moulinex) and transport (Paris-Rhône, Renault, Citroën, Cycles Peugeot) sectors.

Even though for most of these companies this type of production abroad is not very important with regard to their total operation, we should stress that we are underestimating these cases for lack of sufficient information. In addition, this method of production has developed in recent times within the French multinational companies.[29] Even though they seem to use this type of locational spread less intensively than American or Japanese companies, the trend is clear, and clearer, it would seem, than C. A. Michalet[30] indicates. Several cases of pure production strategy found here in 1974 correspond to operations in Spain. Our result comes in part from the classification of Spain among the countries with low wage costs.

One other type (marked III in Table 3.8) corresponds to production carried out in a less developed country with low wages costs and exported to other neighbouring less developed countries. This really is a production strategy as cost savings are associated with these plants: Fichet Bauche produces simple chests in Malaysia for South East Asia, CGR produces equipment which is not very complex in Mexico for Latin America and in India for Asia and Moulinex in Spain for Latin America. We call this type of strategy *'production strategy for the NIC–LDC market'*.

When production is carried out in the developed countries and is re-exported either to the developed countries or to the NICs or LDCs, there is no longer any cost advantage: a strategy of specialisation of production abroad can therefore be superimposed on our a priori typology. One can describe this strategy as the *'strategy of international specialisation of production'* (marked I and IV in Table 3.8). In fact, even though all the types of production strategy correspond to some extent to international specialisation of production, we reserve this term for this particular type: the advantages of this strategy come in fact from factors other than a reduction in unit costs related to lower average labour costs. There may either be savings from various types of aid or benefits granted by the host country (in the case of assembly work by Renault and Citroën in Belgium) or, in particular, savings arising from the specialisation of the foreign plant in a single product which is mass-produced (in the case of Sommer producing plastic products in Italy, Crouzet producing washing machine programmers in Italy, exported to the Spanish and English plants, Poclain assembling top of the range shovel-loaders in Belgium, which are then exported). Certain less developed regions in Italy or Belgium have much lower wage costs than France. If one breaks down the countries of Europe into regions which are unequally developed, this shows up these cases as *'pure production strategy'*. We are therefore very much underestimating this strategy (for French groups originating from an industrial region, the search for low production costs can also explain decisions to produce in the west and south of France). The spatial inequalities in development, labour production costs and market size do in fact determine the organisations set up by industrial groups at national and international level.

The production of Bic in the United States intended in part for Latin America, and in Great Britain for the Commonwealth, although involving an element of *'market strategy'*, is based on a *'production strategy'* in a developed country with access from this country to the less developed countries under its economic and political influence. This strategy differs in its objectives from the production strategy, though is similar to a market strategy. It could be described as a *'strategy of access to an economic area'*. This strategy is, for example, comparable to that of the American groups which use their French subsidiary as a base for access to the French-speaking African countries.

The market strategy was defined a priori as production abroad for the local market, which assumed implicitly that the market was large. On the whole this is true, as the foreign subsidiaries dependent on a market strategy, or at least the biggest of them, are mostly located in the developed countries.

However, our first finding was that the subsidiaries dependent on this strategy are also often situated in the NICs (Spain, Brazil, etc.) and in the less developed countries of Africa, Asia and Latin America. This emphasises the existence in these countries of growing markets. In the case of Africa and southern Europe, these are areas which are under French influence. This location gives savings in production costs: we have in fact shown that wage costs in these areas are very much lower than those of companies in France, while the labour productivity is around the same. This can then be called a *'market strategy with associated cost savings'* or *'Mixed strategy'*.

Second finding: there are two main methods of production abroad, *autonomous production*, with small imports from France, and *assembly production*, with the processing abroad of raw materials or semi-finished products imported from French companies in the group. This distinction is essential from the point of view of the effects of production abroad on French exports and on employment in France: these effects will be nil or very small for autonomous production, and positive for assembly production. The effects on the profitability of French plants also differ depending on the two cases (see Part III of this work on this subject). The sectoral specialisations which have appeared in the use of each of these subtypes of production abroad are therefore important.

Third finding: autonomous production is very common in the developed countries. Assembly production is, on the other hand, the main method for subsidiaries located in the other less developed countries: as the part of the production process carried out abroad is very labour-intensive, this method of international organisation of labour enables large savings to be made. Real production cost savings are associated with this strategy, hence our term, 'mixed strategy'.

One could object to the term 'strategies' attributed to these methods of organising foreign production. In fact this word implies that decisions are taken by independent firms, or at least with regard only to the two main factors, foreign market size and production cost levels. Production abroad is sometimes necessary to gain access to a market when it is difficult to export (cf. Spain and Brazil). In addition, the host countries very often limit the amount of products imported by foreign subsidiaries established in their territory, and demand that a large proportion of their production be re-exported (cf. Spain for cars). Some choices of location for production abroad, and certain methods of production, do seem to result more from constraints imposed on the firms than from strategic choices, although these constraints are not always present. None the less, depending on the geographical area of production, the French exports relating to this foreign production and the very geographical destination of this production, there is a difference in the international organisation structures as well as the specialisations for a particular company or the companies in a particular sector in adopting these structures. These are the structural characteristics and specialisations which we have highlighted.[31]

THE STRATEGIES OF MULTINATIONALISATION AND THE INTERNATIONAL DIVISION OF LABOUR

We have shown in the introduction to this chapter how the world economy is divided into areas of unequal development. The disparities in the world economy form the basis for the different types of multinationalisation adopted by French companies, which we have just studied.

But the production operations organised by French companies abroad form the basis for the international division of operations: certain production is still located in the developed countries and in France, while certain other types are moved to the less developed countries. This international division is structured to the advantage of France and the developed countries, and hence contributes to maintaining world disparities in development. This is shown on three levels:

1. On the level of the geographical specialisation of production abroad for each sector.[32] Certain highly mechanised sectors of activity which are capital-intensive and use little labour have moved principally to Europe or North Africa: integrated cement works, glass production, iron and steel, tyres, pharmaceuticals (sectors 2, 3, 4, 5, 6).

On the other hand, the textile and clothing sector (7A), which uses a lot of unskilled labour, is moving primarily to the less developed countries. The trend is similar for the three sectors of capital goods, mechanical engineering (sector 8) electrical engineering (sector 9) and transportation (sector 10). But although on the whole these sectors are more labour-intensive than the former, one notices that they only move certain production stages to the less developed countries, and these are always the most labour-intensive: boiler-making (Ets Neu, CMP, Amrep), assembly of electrical components (Télémécanique, Sagem), or electronic components (Thomson) and the assembly of cars or cycles.

2. This international division of operations does not only apply to sectors 7A, 8, 9 and 10, which we have seen produce mainly in the less developed countries. In fact, all sectors produce to a certain degree in these countries. If we look at the frequent cases where this production is intended for the market (market strategy) we have shown that this is mostly assembly production: only simple processing operations using a lot of unskilled labour are carried out in the foreign country, with the most complex and mechanised operations and the design and research stages still being located in France. As well as the assembly mentioned in (1), there is the crushing of clinker into cement, the processing of imported iron and steel products, the manufacture of paper/cardboard from imported pulp, the processing of plastics and the manufacture of batteries. Another phenomenon exists which accentuates this international division and structuring of operations: the multinational firms very often use old techniques in the less developed countries which they no longer use in their home country. For example, in Ivory Coast Carnaud produces metal cans by the old three-piece technique, while in France Carnaud is developing a modern two-piece technique. And this is a general phenomenon in this branch of activity.[33]

As autonomous production is relatively rare in the NICs and LDCs (areas 1, 2 and 5), it is not often that the whole production sequence is moved to these countries, so they virtually never gain total industrial and technical mastery. In addition, when autonomous production does exist, it often arises either out of an association with an existing local firm, or out of a political desire by the host governments. This is the case, for example, in Turkey for Renault and in Algeria for Berliet.

3. Finally, the 'pure production strategy', that is, production in less developed countries, which is re-exported to the developed countries, also applies to the international division of operations between countries. This division is structured. The production operations moved are always simple labour-intensive operations: either finished products (for example, switches in Spain for Crouzet, medical equipment in Malta and Portugal for Labaz, Rodier knitwear in Tunisia for Lainière de Roubaix, assembly of black and white televisions in Singapore for Thomson), or elements or parts (cf. assembly of thermostats in Singapore for Thomson, arms and frames for shovel-loaders in Spain for Poclain). The domination of 'workshop subsidiaries' of this type is even greater than for the market strategy with assembly production: in fact, although the majority of elements processed are imported here, too, production is also re-exported to the group. The inflow to the host country is limited to the employment created, the wages paid and the positive effect on the trade balance, as production is not supplying a local market.

Note that this international division of operations is actually carried out within the multinationals: they only relocate simple production or production stages to southern Europe and the Third World countries, keeping their strategic, complex and research operations in France or in the developed countries. Compagnie générale de radiologie carries out the integrated production of perfected radiology equipment in Europe, the United States and Canada, and only produces simple equipment in India and Mexico. Renault and Citroën only produce bottom-of-the-range models in Spain.

STRATEGIES BASED ON DISPARITIES IN THE WORLD ECONOMY

The strategies used by multinationals in their production operations outside France are based on international inequalities in development:

— the greater development of the French economy compared with the newly industrialising countries or NICs (area 5) and the less developed countries or LDCs (areas 1 and 2);

— the industrial specialisations of the French economy in certain sectors relative to the other developed economies, that is, the relative strong points in terms of industrial groups.

By their very existence, these strategies also highlight these two types of international disparity.

We have already seen in the previous paragraph how multinationalisation in the NICs and LDCs is clearly based on inequalities between the development of France and these countries and helps to maintain them through the international division of operations.

Multinationalisation in the Developed Countries and the Relative Industrial Specialisations of the Developed Countries

If one examines the strategies of the French multinationals in their production investments within the developed countries, which are the most important by volume, one can say that the extent of this investment according to sector is based on disparities in the world economy and highlights them. The term disparities is used to mean the relative strengths and weaknesses of the industries of the developed countries.

We have already assumed that the varying intensity of production in the developed countries could arise from differences in the competitiveness of French companies from sector to sector and differences in the competitiveness of foreign companies in the countries in question.

We have just seen that the production operations of French companies in the developed countries mostly relate to production for the local market: the purpose of this production is to compete directly with industrial groups from different countries, as the French groups through their investment directly control shares of the foreign market. One might have thought that this investment related to production for export to France or other markets (strategy of international specialisation of production), but it would then be less in keeping with direct competition.

The sectoral disparities in foreign production within developed countries do on their own highlight the strong and weak points of French industry (although one should also look at exports which constitute an alternative method of gaining access to foreign markets[34]). From this point of view, the strong points are the sectors producing mainly in the developed countries (sectors 2, 3, 4, 5 and to a lesser degree 6 and 7B). The weak points are the others (sectors 7A, 8, 9 and 10 in particular).

We know that foreign investment in French industry also varies in degree depending on the sector; the same reasoning can be applied to this: the sectors where their penetration is high correspond to the strong points of the foreign economies and the weak points of the French economy. So foreign penetration is high in sectors 8 (mechanical engineering) and 9 (electrical engineering). These are, then, the weak points of French industry. Finally, by comparing foreign investment from developed countries in France and French investment in these developed countries by sector, we can best show the relative industrial specialisations of the French and foreign economies.[35]

Moving the Location of Production to the Developed Countries or to the NICs and LDCs: a Sign of, or a Search for, Competitiveness

If we look at the investments of French multinationals in both the developed countries and the NICs and LDCs, that is, the specialisations and strategies of companies and sectors when producing within each of these two main areas, we find two main types of French multinationalisation: one is a sign of competitiveness and the other a search for competitiveness.

1. Production in the developed countries constitutes a sign of competitiveness.
Since the market strategy is the most common strategy, this type of production controls both a fraction of foreign production facilities and a fraction of the foreign market: it is a new way of competing, which is more efficient than exporting. In fact, production on the spot gives a better knowledge of the market, trading channels and competitors. It is also less sensitive to monetary risks and import control policies. In this sense it takes competition to the heart of the foreign economy. This penetration of foreign markets is only possible when the foreign groups in the sector are relatively undynamic while the French groups are active and competitive. As the reverse is true, we proposed to deduce the relative industrial specialisations from reciprocal foreign investment between the developed economies.

Growth abroad in the developed countries, when achieved by internal growth (setting up production plants), provides greater competitiveness than when it is achieved by external growth (taking over an existing company). We shall see in the next chapter that French companies invested heavily in the United States between 1974 and 1978. However, only Bic, Essilor and in particular Michelin set up factories, while Imétal, Schneider, Willot, CGE and Rousselot took over American companies. The first three firms have a technological and management advantage which they exploit in the United States, while the others are trying to increase their total production and to acquire new techniques and distribution channels by using their financial power. Their growth in the United States is not due to advantages which they have over their competitors, but is the result of a strategic choice to expand geographically in this country, often accompanied by sectoral diversification, although there is an underlying industrial logic.

Finally, although production in the developed countries is a sign of competitiveness, it also involves a search for competitiveness in that it facilitates the growth of the group, better knowledge of foreign markets and the acquisition of technology.

2. Production in the less developed countries (NICs and LDCs) corresponds above all to a search for competitiveness.
This proposal is of course true for all cases of 'pure production strategy': production in countries with low wage costs is reimported into France or the developed countries, and enables cost prices to be reduced and competitiveness to be improved.

It also applies to the commoner market strategies. Here foreign production is intended for the local market, and the competitiveness of the group is only increased indirectly: as production is carried out in countries with low wage costs, the profit margin is higher, and the profits repatriated increase the group's profitability. In addition, it has been shown that assembly production is the most common: exports to these foreign subsidiaries increase production in France, improve the return on investment, permit economies of scale and hence improve competitiveness.

Of course, the use of market strategies in the NICs and LDCs is also a sign of the competitiveness of companies, to the extent that there is competition between multinational industrial groups from the developed countries on the markets of the less developed countries.

A distinction can also be made for production in the NICs and LDCs between two historical phases:

— The first phase is that of the colonial presence in countries in Africa and Asia. Production in these countries improves the competitiveness of the firms involved, but there is competition with foreign firms. The competitiveness of the French industrial groups is improved indirectly because of the reduction of the price of raw materials, the industrial exports resulting from this colonisation, and in particular the drop in the price of essential consumer goods.

    This type of production operation still exists, as we have seen, but is relatively unimportant, and is located mainly in Black Western and Equatorial Africa, Tunisia and Morocco.
— In the present second phase, production in countries less developed than France is carried out in Africa, Asia, Latin America and southern Europe, with a dual objective: to reduce production costs and gain access to markets of an increasing size.

If one excludes cases of 'pure production strategy' in the less developed countries, corresponding solely to a search for competitiveness, all the types of production abroad are in fact both ways of searching for competitiveness and signs of competitiveness. It is, however, possible to classify these different types by their ability to show up the competitiveness of companies. In decreasing order we have:

— production in a developed country by internal growth;
— production in a developed country by external growth;
— production in a less developed country, NIC or LDC, with market strategy and autonomous production;
— production in a less developed country, NIC or LDC, with market strategy and assembly production;
— production in a less developed country, NIC or LDC, with pure production strategy.

Finally, it will be noted that the distinction we propose here can apply for the same company moving the location of some of its operations in the developed countries, while others are moved to NICs and LDCs. The same distinction may also be made within the same activity and then relate to products or stages of production. As Tables 3.6 and 3.7 show, only fifteen companies in our sample use a market strategy and a production strategy simultaneously. These are Penarroya, Fichet, Sommer, Labaz, Essilor, Poclain, CGR, Thomson, Citroën, Renault, Cycles Peugeot, Rossignol, Rousselot, Paris-Rhône and A. Willot. Mostly firms use only a market strategy. However, if we make a distinction between production areas and between the two types of autonomous production and assembly production, it will then be seen that they do often use several strategies (hence Renault carries out the integrated production of cars in Spain, Argentina and Turkey, and assembles them from imported parts in five other countries).

The pure production strategy is rarely used on its own (as in the case of Lainière de Roubaix, which uses it a lot, and also produces for local markets in Latin America).

On the other hand, the supply strategy is the only strategy used by some groups: Salins du Midi, Cie Mokta, Le Nickel, Saupiquet and Roquefort.

Based on a detailed study of 183 multinationals, we have just highlighted the main trends of French multinationalisation: geographical location, and links between foreign subsidiaries and parent companies. One could object to the term 'strategy' which we use to describe the different types of international organisation adopted by the firms, but the systematic framework which we have used to describe these structures will be useful, as we shall see, in analysing the performance of the French multinationals (Part III). Before this, we shall examine the reactions of these multinationals to the economic crisis.

NOTES

1   C. A. Michalet, 1976, pp. 150 ff.
2   M. Rainelli, 1979, pp. 131 ff. A. Cotta, 1972, p. 549, had already proposed this typology, which C. A. Michalet set out in detail.

3 As defined by B. Lassudrie Duchêne in the introduction to M. Rainelli's book, op. cit., p. VIII, for example.

4 In these countries, there are other forms of industrial presence which cannot be described by our method based on the setting up of subsidiaries.

5 Israel, Australia, New Zealand which in our study, together with North America, form area 3, also have high levels of development, so this comparison is justified, even though French companies have very few subsidiaries in these three countries.

6 Italy has a lower per capita income, similar to that of Spain or Greece. It will be seen that often the nature of the operations of subsidiaries in Italy is similar to that of subsidiaries in Spain. Italy could then have been included in our area 5. This remark would of course be even more justified if we could break the countries down into regional economic areas with different levels of development. Southern Italy would then clearly be included in area 5, together with Ireland (GNP per capita = $US 2260), certain regions of the Netherlands and West Germany, especially since for these different interregional levels of development, wage cost levels are also different, being lower in the less developed regions.

7 In our study, Japan is included in area 2 (Asia/Latin America) while from this point of view it would have been better to include it in area 3 (North America). Fortunately this does not have any effect on the interpretation that can be given to the results, as French firms have very few production subsidiaries in Japan.

8 See on this subject Michalet, op. cit., pp. 143-8, and in particular M. Rainelli, op. cit.,.pp. 106-23 for the fullest analysis.

9 Th. Kraseman and B. L. Barker, 1973, compare wage costs per employee within American multinationals, in the parent company and the foreign subsidiaries. However, the differences in cost also cover differences in labour qualifications, linked with different stages of production and hence the international division of operations.

10 G. K. Helleiner, 1973.

11 'Négotiations collectives, salaires et réalisations sociales dans l'industrie des emballages métalliques dans le monde.' FIOM, Geneva, 1978. Average wage rates in 1977 in US dollars: United States = 7.68; France = 3.83; Mexico = 0.9 (1976).

12 As at 1 January 1976, hourly wage rates in the textiles industry were as follows (base Sweden = 100); Great Britain = 42; West Germany = 79; United States = 70; Japan = 45; Hong Kong = 12; India = 10; quoted on p. 90 of 'Les économies industrialisées face à la concurrence du tiers monde, le cas de la filière textile', CEPII, August 1978.

13 Citibank 'Monthly Economic Letter', December 1978, p. 15.

14 Citibank 'Monthly Economic Letter', ibid., pp. 12 ff. and August 1979, p. 9ff.

15 Quoted by Rainelli, op. cit., p. 119.

16 Quoted by Michalet, op. cit., p. 145.

17 In the 1970s it could be stated, 'for American firms, the establishment of production subsidiaries abroad, whatever the host country, always enables the unit costs of labour to be reduced' (Rainelli, op. cit.). In recent years, on the other hand, the cutback in American investment in Europe can partly be explained by the rapid increase in wage costs in Europe compared with the United States, which can also be partly explained by the growth of European investment in the United States.

18 Certain countries in Asia, Latin America (e.g. Mexico, Argentina) or Africa (Nigeria) constitute markets of a considerable size. In addition, there are big differences in labour production costs between countries in the same area,

and even within a given country between regions (see note 6 and F. Vellas, 1978, for the location of Ford in Spain).

19   Rainelli, op. cit., p. 141.

20   Michalet, op. cit., p. 157.

21   These results are obtained by adding to those for the 413 companies of all sizes included in our sample those relating to the top 200 French groups and the leaders of each sector (classifications of *Le Nouvel Economiste*). This is therefore an underestimate in absolute terms (omission of small and medium-sized firms) but one which is small in view of the weight of the big groups (Chapter 1), although it is a reliable estimate of geographical specialisations.

22   Since our study is based on the operations of foreign subsidiaries, we are omitting all the operations of French firms within socialist countries, where it is generally not allowed for subsidiaries to be set up, but where the presence of French firms is increasing.

23   It is significant that Lafarge and Ciments français only have clinker-crushing subsidiaries in French-speaking Black Africa and in the French Antilles.

24   One might think that these two areas are much less important for foreign investment from the United States, Great Britain and West Germany, as shown by Table I.3 (Introduction).

25   J. Ehrsam, 1981.

26   But C. V. Vaitsos and Ph. de la Saussay, 1980, have shown that this possibility has already largely been used by French and European multinationals which have set up in these countries. P. Jeanblanc, 1981, p. 444, also shows that the European producers of synthetic fibres use their Spanish subsidiaries to export to Europe, receiving from them a 'differential income'.

27   See L. G. Franko, 1976, p. 94, and Michalet and Delapierre, 1973, pp. 18–29.

28   Hence the high weight of French production in this area, and the geographical specialisation noted for these sectors.

29   The Thomson group first manufactured radio and TV components and washing machines in Singapore, then in 1977 decided to assemble black and white televisions and radio and hi-fi equipment for the European market in this country.

30   Michalet, op. cit., p. 153.

31   As access to a foreign market can be gained either by direct production abroad or by exporting, it would be desirable also to analyse the geographical distribution of exports to give a fuller description of group strategies. We find in Savary, 1980, a study of the operations of foreign trading subsidiaries, which are mainly located in the developed countries, whatever their sector of activity.

32   We have seen that in Africa the main operations carried out by French companies related to colonial-type relations (mining, commerce, transport services, plantations, agricultural and food industries, building and public works) or light processing industries, emphasising the continuing dependence of these countries on the French economy.

33   Source R. Bennis and A. Rhiati, 1979.

34   We have studied in Savary, op. cit., the geographical distribution of foreign trading subsidiaries in 1974. For sectors 2, 3, 4, 5, 6 and 7B, producing mainly in the developed countries, trading subsidiaries are chiefly located in these countries. On the other hand, for sectors 7A, 8, 9 and 10, producing mainly in the NICs and LDCs, the trading subsidiaries are located mainly in the developed countries. This second finding somewhat alters the conclusion that these sectors are the weak points of the industry. However, this is only part of the result, as direct exports are not taken into account.

35   This analysis was carried out, for 1974, in Savary, 1980, and repeated in Savary 1981-2.

4 Crisis and Relocation

What has been the effect of the economic crisis, which hit the French economy head on, on the multinationalisation of companies between 1974 and 1979? The reduction in the growth of domestic demand and the keener competition between industrial groups should have led French companies to increase their activities abroad. But although this trend was predictable, it was more difficult to predict the geographical area to which French investment abroad would be directed: if demand falls in all developed countries, while competition becomes even keener, can these economies retain their attraction and do 'market strategies' continue to form the basis for multinationalisation in these countries? One might think that the economic crisis would, on the contrary, mean an increase in the flow of investment to the less developed countries. To understand recent trends, which have not in fact followed along these lines, it will be necessary to highlight a fundamental aspect of the economic crisis in the developed countries—the increasing demands of the NICs and LDCs, expressed as much by the price of energy and raw materials as by their desire for industrialisation with control of the operations of multinationals in their territory.

THE ACCENTUATION OF MULTINATIONALISATION

Total French investment abroad, measured by capital movements between France and abroad in the balance of payments, has increased in recent times (Table 4.1). This upward trend in investment corresponds to a small increase in their relative importance compared with the gross formation of fixed capital or investment in France, and the maintenance of their level compared with the gross domestic product (GDP) and exports.[1]

However, this measurement of investment flows underestimates the growth of French investment abroad. This may in fact be achieved by the self-financing of foreign subsidiaries, or borrowing in their own country, which does not then show up in international flows of capital. In this respect the official French statistics are very incomplete.

A study of the companies in our sample shows the source of this continued investment. We have based this study on an examination of the number of subsidiaries set up, which underestimates the actual

Table 4.1 Development of French investment abroad (total direct
investment + French loans abroad)

Millions of frs	1973	1974	1975	1976	1977	1978	1979	1980	1981
Total gross flow	5 485	6 420	7 776	11 756	10 509	11 180	12 596	18 021	38 264
Total net flow	4 256	4 216	5 883	7 702	5 965	7 383	8 414	13 260	25 079
Growth rate of gross flow*	+13.7%	+17%	+21%	+51%	−10.6%	+6.4%	+24.7%	+43.3%	+25.3%

Source: Ministry of the Economy, Studies and Balance sheets, February 1980. Note bleue,
Autumn 1981 and Note bleue No. 88, September 1982, Balance of Payments for France in
1981.
    *Compared with previous year—excluding oil.
    N.B.—the rapid growth in gross investments in 1981 is linked with big operations such as
those carried out in the USA by Elf Aquitaine, Lafarge and BSN.

growth. In three years, between the end of 1974 and the end of 1977,
the 413 companies in our sample set up 249 production subsidiaries
and 131 trading subsidiaries abroad, which is +27 per cent and +19 per
cent respectively compared with 1974: investment abroad therefore
continued at a high level in spite of the crisis.

However, only eighty-two companies, or 23 per cent of the total,
set up at least one production subsidiary abroad: the continuation of
multinationalisation, measured by this criterion, is therefore limited to
a small number of firms. Eleven companies set up production subsidiaries abroad for the first time. Multinationalisation did therefore
extend significantly to new companies. Also they often belonged to
sectors which had not been very multinational in 1974, such as commerce, building and public works.

However, most of the new subsidiaries were set up by companies
which had already been multinational in 1974: out of the eighty-two
companies which set up at least one production subsidiary, seventy-one
already had such subsidiaries. This means that one company in two
already producing abroad set up a new subsidiary. They were mostly
large companies, and included all the big groups in the sample, such
as BSN, SNPA, Rhône-Poulenc and Lafarge. Of the very big multinational firms, with a capital of over 500 million francs, one in three
set up production subsidiaries. These were often firms which were
already very multinational. So, out of the seventy-one already multinational firms that set up production subsidiaries, forty-one were
already very multinational in 1974 (that is, they produced in more
than five countries or produced more than 10 per cent abroad).

To be precise, out of the eighty-two companies which set up at
least one foreign production subsidiary, sixty-two increased the number of countries in which they were established. The extension of the
geographical area of establishment was therefore a general trend, and

was all the more pronounced since the number of countries of production was already high in 1974: 12 per cent of companies producing in a foreign country in 1974 extended their production area, with this percentage rising to 70 per cent for those already producing in more than six countries.

Our sample overrepresents the big firms and hence underestimates the spread of multinationalisation to small and medium-sized companies. We can however conclude that *investment abroad continued over the crisis period of 1974–8, and was mostly carried out by companies which were already multinational, and by big, very multinational groups.* There were not very many new multinational companies, and the crisis meant the widening of the gap between companies which were multinational and those which were not.

It is possible to measure the development of multinationalisation more accurately, by comparing for the end of 1974 and the end of 1977 the percentage of staff employed abroad compared with the total numbers of staff employed by the groups. We show in Chapter 7 that for the majority of companies already producing abroad in 1974, this percentage increased. For all the sixty-seven companies for which we know the number of employees, the trend was as shown in Table 4.2.

Table 4.2 Employees in France and abroad, 1974–7

	Total employees (1)	Employees France (2)	Employees abroad (3)	Percentage (3)/(1)
1974	1 260 082	975 892	284 190	22.5%
1977	1 427 010	1 067 548	359 462	25.2%

The rate of multinationalisation, measured by the number of employees, increases considerably for these medium and large companies, even though this is the result of different developments depending on the companies (see Chapter 7).

Two more limited studies have also given figures for this phenomenon for the big French groups. J. Cohen,[2] describing fourteen groups (Rhône-Poulenc, PUK, Michelin, SGPM, Roussel Uclaf, CGE, Thomson, Air Liquide, Creusot-Loire, L'Oréal, Peugeot, Renault, Lafarge and BSN), shows that in 1973 and 1977 'their investments abroad increased by 36.7%, the number of their employees abroad by 17.6%, while investment in France stagnated and the number of employees in France dropped by 4.4%' (falling from 71.8 per cent of the total to 69.93 per cent). Also M. Anvers,[3] covering thirteen slightly different large groups, shows that between 1972–3 and 1978 the number of staff employed by these groups abroad rose from 26 per cent to 32 per cent of the total number of staff employed.

GEOGRAPHICAL RELOCATION

In spite of the lack of official statistics, which are only available for investment flows, Table 4.3 shows a clear trend: French investment in the rest of the world, that is in the Third World, became relatively less important, in spite of the maintenance of large oil investments in the countries of the Middle East. On the whole, investment was relocated to the developed countries.

Table 4.3 Geographical distribution of gross French investment flows abroad (as a percentage of the total)

	1971	1972	1973	1974	1975	1976	1977	1978	1979	1980	1981
EEC countries	30.1	37.2	31.3	38	29	34	32	33	26	28	17
United States	15.1	9.3	14.1	8	18	15	14	14	19	23	52
Other OECD countries	16.8	15.5	17.3	22	20	19	20	25	29	18	12
Rest of the world	37.9	38	37.2	32	33	32	34	28	26	31	19
Brazil				2.1	3.3	2.8	3.1	2.1			1.4
OPEC countries				12.2	14	15.4	14.3	11.1			4
Overseas countries	13.5	11.8	14.1	8.3	7.3	5.5	4	5		8	

Note: The rapid growth in gross investments in the USA in 1981 is linked with big operations such as those carried out by Elf Aquitaine, Lafarge, BSN and Rhône-Poulenc.

Source: Ministry of the Economy. Notes bleues of September 1977, October 1980 and September 1982. Balance of Payments for France in 1981. (Balance of payments data: direct investment and loans of residents abroad.)

Investments made by French industrial companies comply with two marked trends: companies are becoming more and more multinational in the United States and Brazil, either by setting up their first establishment or extending an existing subsidiary. This phenomenon has been stressed by many authors for the United States alone,[4] whereas Brazil is also a new area of attraction. J. Cohen[5] notes, for the fourteen large groups in his study, that 'most of the recent effort to establish subsidiaries seems to have been concentrated in the United States and Brazil.' This phenomenon is also characteristic of the German economy,[6] and more generally of all the European economies.

Recent Investment in the United States

In the balance-of-payment statistics, the flow of French investment to the United States is increasing regularly.[7] In addition, the flow of European investment to the United States is growing faster than the flow of American investment to Europe.[8] H. Couffin showed that in 1975, 350 French companies controlled a subsidiary in the United States, including seventy-one production subsidiaries. These industrial establishments were recent as 82 per cent were set up after 1964 and 47 per cent after 1972.

Even though on the whole French investment in the United States is increasing rapidly, at the end of 1979 it only represented a small proportion of total foreign investment in this country: 4 per cent compared with 6 per cent for Switzerland, 7 per cent for Japan, 10 per cent for West Germany, 13 per cent for Canada, 18 per cent for the United Kingdom and 24 per cent for the Netherlands.[9]

For the firms in our sample, Table 4.4 describes the establishments in 1974 and after. Apart from nineteen companies which did not possess a trading subsidiary in 1974, twenty-one companies controlled a production subsidiary, which is approximately 11 per cent of the multinational subsidiaries in the sample. Even by adding Michelin and Cellulose du Pin, who are present in Canada, this is a poor result.

Between the end of 1974 and the end of 1979, twenty-nine companies set up for the first time via a production subsidiary, while over the same period seven companies already present there developed or set up subsidiaries. In total, at the end of 1979, forty-four companies in the sample were producing in the United States, twice as many as in 1974. Recent establishments not included in the sample are those of CEA, Air Liquide, Cie générale du Jouet, Leroy Somer, les Mutuelles Unies, Descours et Cabaud and Promodes.

One interesting fact to point out is that companies investing in the United States never consider this operation as one among others. It always corresponds to a strategic choice for long-term growth which is clearly announced but which may for the present consist only of a trading subsidiary (Jaeger, Crouzet, Manurhin, Renault), a minority interest or a technical and commercial agreement with an American firm (cf. recently Peugeot with Chrysler, Renault with AMC). For example:

— In 1975, Imétal made a take-over bid to take control of Copperweld Corp., a large producer of special steels, tubes and wire, employing 4600 people. This subsidiary represents a big force in the group; in 1977 it accounted for 35 per cent of its employees abroad and 30 per cent of its total employees. R. Loving explains that 'In 1974 De Villemejane was looking for a new stage in the growth of the Imétal group, and for a long time had wanted to expand to the United States, which he called "a country standing out by its development . . .". He wanted a company which he could then use as a base for future acquisitions, with a good profit, a large balance sheet total, and 250 to 450 million Dollars of sales. He wanted

Table 4.4 Subsidiaries recently set up in the United States by the French companies in the sample

Sector (in France)	Existing in 1974	Set up in 1975/6/7	Set up in 1978/9
(a) Production subsidiaries			
2 Mining, glass, construction materials	Lafarge (especially in Canada)	Ciments Français Lafarge (factory)	
3 Iron and steel, metallurgy	*Schneider* (Creusot-Loire)	Schneider (big take-overs) Usinor *Imétal* Vallourec* (Armosig)	
4 Basic chemicals	*Rhône-Poulenc*	Rousselot†	Rhône-Poulenc†
5 Rubber, paper, plastic	Pricel	*Michelin* Plastic omnium	Hutchinson*
6 Parachem., pharm.		Institut Mérieux†	
7 Consumer goods	Prouvost/Revillon fr. Bic/Hachette Skis Rossignol	Lainière de Roubaix/ Bic (growth) Skis Rossignol Ag. Willot† (control of Korvette, distribution chain)	Skis Rossignol† (tennis)
8 Mech. engineering	Essilor/*Amrep* Ets Neu/Poclain	Amrep H. Ernault Somua	*Essilor* (disappearance Poclain)
9 Electrical, electronic engineering	Saft *Cie gle de Radiologie* Thomson CSF	Saft (factory)/Seb Cit-Alcatel Thomson CSF†	Moulinex *Cit-Alcatel*† Cipel*/Wonder†
10 Transport			Ferodo
11 Bldg., Pub. works	Campenon-Bernard		
12 Commerce		Ets Eco. Casino Ets Nicolas	
13 Services	Pathé Cinéma	Agence Havas	Bis-Pompes Funebres générales†
14 Agr./food industries	Moët-Hennessy Gds Moulins de Paris Fromageries Bel		
(b) Trading subsidiaries			
2 Mining, glass, construction materials	Cerabati		
3 Iron and steel, metallurgy	Aciérie Paris Outreau Usinor Penarroya	*Schneider* Fichet-Bauche	
4 Basic chemicals	Rhône-Poulenc Rousselot		

Sector (in France)	Existing in 1974	Set up in 1975/6/7	Set up in 1978/9
5 Rubber, paper, plastic	Sommer Michelin‡		
6 Parachem., pharm.	Delalande		Delalande (growth)
7 Consumer goods	Lib. Hachette	Lainière Roubaix	
8 Mech. engineering	H. Ernault Somua‡	CMP‡ Manurhin	Essilor Crouzet
9 Electrical, electronic engineering	Télémécanique Sagem Seb‡/Piles Wonder‡	De Dietrich Moulinex	
10 Transport	Renault Motobécane	Cycles Peugeot	Jaeger
11 Bldg., pub. works	Forclum		
12 Commerce	Davum (SGPM) Safic Alcan		

Note: The names of the biggest subsidiaries are italicised.
*Joint venture.
†Take-over of existing company.
‡Later went into production.

a company producing metals to counterbalance Imétal's specialisation in mining and smelting. . . .'[10]
— In 1976, Schneider took control of Phoenix Steel Corp., producing sheet and tubes (1800 people), set up a mini steelworks, obtained interests in structural steelwork and metal recycling companies and carried out important iron and steel trading operations. Although the number of employees in Phoenix, the only figures known, only represents 6.3 per cent of those of the group abroad, the United States is the area in which investment is concentrated.
— In 1975 Michelin set up two car tyre factories and is planning two truck tyre factories. Between 1973 and 1977 the group invested 500 million dollars in the United States, which is 35 per cent of its total investments. The aim is to increase its share of the car tyre market from 4 per cent in 1976 to 10–14 per cent in 1985. By the end of 1979 there were already four American factories employing 7000 people, and the director of the American subsidiary anticipated that 'in the coming decade, Michelin in the United States will be as big as Michelin in France.'[11]
— Finally, there is Bic, whose big American subsidiary accounts for around half of the group's turnover, a consequence of the breakthrough of a medium-sized firm into the vast market of the United States (Rossignol is in a similar situation).

The nature of these sectors where French investment is high, as well as the nature of the big French investor groups shows that:

— they are always intermediate product sectors: cement, iron and steel, some chemicals and in particular tyres;
— they do not include parachemicals/pharmaceuticals, transportation, electrical and electronic engineering,[12] mechanical engineering[13] or banking.[14] This seems to confirm the analysis outlined in the conclusion to Chapter 3: the intermediate products sectors seem to be the strong points of French industry, while the other sectors mentioned above are the weak points.

The importance of external growth operations is a characteristic of French investment in the United States: H. Couffin[15] showed this for the period up to 1975, and here, for investments made between 1974 and 1979, we find the same trend, while before 1970 it was more common for companies to be set up directly.[16]

If we look for causes behind this investment, we find three main factors:

— the general causes of the multinationalisation of companies, in particular limited growth in France due to the oligopolistic position of firms on their own market: this easily applies to almost all investors in the United States. The economic crisis exacerbates these limits on growth;
— the characteristics of the American economy which, apart from the relatively high wage costs until recently, all constitute positive factors:
  (a) large market size, permitting rapid expansion. This factor is very often mentioned by the companies themselves;
  (b) technological level, giving access to certain types of technology, another factor mentioned by firms;
  (c) good profitability which is important when taking over companies;
  (d) considerable local competition, making exports difficult, while the take-over of a local firm immediately gives access to a share of the market, the network, etc. while local production makes it easier to adapt to demand and give a better after-sales service;
  (e) customs barriers, which make exporting difficult, and which could increase because of the economic crisis.[17]

An explanation is still needed of why French investors were not interested in the United States before. Is this a historical development, resulting partly from an increase in the multinationalisation of groups which are now interested in more distant countries? Or have they become more competitive, resulting in a reduction in American power compared with European power?[18]

There seem to be three recent developments behind this change:

— the development of wage costs: the gap to the disadvantage of the

United States is tending to narrow and even reverse, as wage costs are increasing faster in Europe than in the United States;
— the movement in exchange rates: some time ago, the falling dollar made it more difficult for France to export to the United States and made the acquisition of American firms more attractive;
— the economic and political crisis: while the economic crisis hit developed Europe head on, social movements were developing in Italy, France and Southern Europe, the Left was coming to power in France and Italy and the Third World countries were making greater economic and political demands. The United States was more and more appearing to be a large, stable and safe market: its economic power makes it self-sufficient, and its social and political stability is unique in the world. This guarantees 'financial security' for investments and led to the statement, 'The old international division of labour is now disappearing in the face of the international division of risks, hence the craze for the sanctuary of America' (*L'Expansion*, 29 November 1979).

Finally, one may wonder with regard to the future of French investment in the United States whether the increase in the dollar which followed the election of President Reagan (end of 1980) and the announcement of his economic policy will curb this investment, which has now become more expensive, and encourage French exports. However, the attraction of the American economy is at the same time reinforced by the new policy adopted and the protectionist trends which are developing and could make exporting more difficult. In addition, the factors relating to the position of the French economy, the crisis of the developed economies and the demands of the Third World, continue to play their part. One may then think that the development of French investments in the United States after the economic recession will continue for years to come. J. Desazers de Montgailhard, director general of PUK, put it this way, 'how are we not to think that the best solution for French investors consists of profiting [from the inside] from the new age of progress beginning in the United States, by developing their own business in America?'[19]

Recent Investment in Brazil

Even though, in 1978, French investment in Brazil only represented 4 per cent of total foreign investment, it showed the recent interest which French companies are expressing in this country. Even in 1974, twenty-five of the firms in our sample were producing in Brazil, which was higher than the number of firms producing in the United States (see Table 4.5). In 1979, thirteen additional firms were producing in this country, while Lafarge, Mokta, Schneider, Sommer and Lainière de Roubaix had expanded their production operations. There is then a clear trend towards the development of companies in this country[20] and the weakness of purely trading establishments should be noted, together with the main method of penetration which consists of setting up plants (and not take-overs).

We also see in Table 4.5 the trend for firms from the capital goods sectors (8, 9 and 10) to develop multinationally in the developing countries: they have a big presence in Brazil, except in the car sector, where however a recent agreement between Fiat and Peugeot could lead to Peugeot setting up in this big market. Companies in the inter-mediate products sector are also very active. It is two of these com-panies which are the most important and are creating a very high concentration of French investment in Brazil: the chemical subsidiaries of Rhône-Poulenc account for 52 per cent of total French invest-ments;[21] in recent years the subsidiaries of Schneider (Mecanica Pesada) and Imétal have been a big force.

As for the United States, the biggest establishments are still major strategic choices. The Lafarge subsidiary is the third biggest company in the group. All the subsidiaries of the Schneider group account for 6000 people, which is 21 per cent of the total foreign employees: Brazil is the top foreign country in which they are established, with the subsidiaries complementing one another to supply complex installa-tions such as a dam and its hydro-electric plant. RIQT, with 15 308 people in 1978, is also the most important foreign subsidiary of the Rhône-Poulenc group. La Lainière de Roubaix, for its part, employed 4013 people in Brazil in 1978, or 52 per cent of its foreign staff. For Sommer, Ferodo, Nordon, Michelin, Penarroya and Amrep, Brazil is also a priority in their geographical expansion.

If we also look at the reasons for French firms making these choices, we see that Brazil has the general characteristics which we attributed to the developing countries (Chapter 3): size of market and opportunities for associated cost savings, due to the low wage costs. It would seem that in the case of Brazil certain factors are particularly important:

— considerable potential growth, in view of the population size, industrialisation and natural resources;
— high customs duties limiting exports to this country;
— policy favourable to direct investment;
— high inflation, making acquisitions cheap;
— existence of an authoritarian regime, guaranteeing social and political stability.

In addition to all these factors, the French authorities have a policy to encourage firms to invest in Brazil. These incentives and French investment continued over 1980-1, even though the economic situation in Brazil was deteriorating.[22]

Table 4.5 Subsidiaries recently set up in Brazil by the French companies in the sample

Sectors		Existing in 1974	Set up in 1975/6/7	Set up in 1978/9
(a) Production subsidiaries				
2	Mining, glass, construction materials	BSN (glass) *Lafarge* Cie de Mokta	*Lafarge* (growth investment)	Mokta (mining project)
3	Iron and steel, metallurgy	Schneider Vallourec (by intermediary) Penarroya (2)	Schneider (confirmation of control and new subsidiaries†) Fichet-Bauche	
4	Basic chemicals	*Rhône-Poulenc*		
5	Rubber/paper	Sommer/ Novacel		Sommer *Michelin* (project)
6	Parachem., Pharm.	Lorilleux/ I. Mérieux Delalande/ L'Oréal		Delalande (plant)
7	Consumer goods	Bic/*Lainière de Roubaix* Orfèvrerie Christofle	*Lainière de Roubaix* (control of an interest)†	
8	Mechanical engineering	*Nordon*	Amrep/Ets Neu/ Nordon (growth)	CMP
9	Electrical, electronic engineering	Alsthom/ Thomson CSF Télémécanique elec. Merlin Gerin (Schneider)	Jaz (Schneider) Cie gle de radiologie Sagem/Merlin Gerin (growth)	
10	Transportation equipment	Paris-Rhône (Cibié)	Ferodo/Chausson Motobécane Cycles Peugeot	Ferodo (project)
11	Bldg., pub. works	SPIE Batignolles	Campenon-Bernard/ SPIE (growth)	
13	Services	SGTE		Club Méditerranée
14	Agr./food ind.	Moët-Hennesy/ BSN (fresh products)		
(b) Trading subsidiaries				
3	Iron & steel, metal.		Schneider	
7	Consumer goods	Hachette Lainière de Roubaix		
8	Mechanical engineering		CMP†	
9	Electrical, electronic engineering	Cie gle de radiologie‡ Merlin Gerin	Schneider Neyrpic instruments sa	
12	Commerce		Safic Alcan et Cie	

Note: The names of the biggest subsidiaries are italicised.
†Take-over of existing company.
‡Later went into production.

At the same time, the economic, social and political development of the countries in southern Europe (Greece, Spain, Portugal) has meant an increase in wage costs which could dissuade French companies, who have traditionally had a presence in these countries, from increasing their investments there, so making Brazil more attractive. Not to mention the risks of political expropriation as in Iran.

In conclusion, the reasons for the recent high investment in the United States and Brazil differ, as we have seen. Even though there is not one single cause in both cases, it is remarkable that the two countries in question, each within their own geo-political areas as Western developed countries or underdeveloped countries, are the most socially and politically stable economies, where the investment risks in financial terms are lowest. In addition, by investing in Brazil, an economy 'under American influence', French companies are investing in a country which has links with the United States and whose stability is assured by the United States.

The economic crisis in France and Europe underlines the reasons for the multinationalisation of French firms. Will this search for outlets and/or growth abroad, made necessary by the crisis, push firms to make more prudent choices as regards geographical areas?

THE TRANSFER OF TECHNOLOGY: A GROWING METHOD IN THE DEVELOPING COUNTRIES

In particular we have studied the production activities abroad carried out by French companies within subsidiary companies, that is, controlled by the ownership of at least part of the capital, with this control being reinforced by flows of goods between the French companies and the subsidiaries, as well as by technical links. There is another form of activity abroad which has developed in recent times. This is the transfer to a foreign firm of a technique (patent, licence, or complete plant) to be used in a company not owned or managed by the French firm. This commercial transfer, or sale of technology, corresponds to what C. A. Michalet calls 'the technology strategy',[23] which according to him will be used in the future by 'technological and financial MNCs'.[24]

This type of transfer of technology already existed in 1974 and has developed since then, although none of the firms in our sample uses this method exclusively: they always have controlled foreign subsidiaries at the same time.

The development of this new type of activity by the multinational groups has led, with regard to foreign trade, to induced growth in exchanges of technical services, personnel training services and consultancy services, accounting for a very large proportion of 'turn-key' or 'package' contracts.

In addition, it should be emphasised that this type of transfer of technology is often accompanied by a minority interest in the capital of the foreign company, considerable French exports of semi-finished products to this company or reimportation into France of all or part of production. The foreign company in question then fulfils many of the objectives assigned to production subsidiaries (related exports, production cost savings). Renault is a good example of this situation: Renault sells factories, parts and techniques to the Soviet Union, its associate in Romania manufactures cars and vans with imported Renault parts and re-exports gear-boxes and axles to France. The same happens for the associate in Yugoslavia.

An examination of the countries in the sample shows that transfer of technology, without any legal control of the foreign company, is becoming increasingly common. Examples of such companies are Ciments français (commissioning one plant abroad each year), Lorilleux Lefranc (in 1975 in Chile, South Africa, West Germany, Romania and the Soviet Union), Kleber Colombes, Grands Moulins de Paris (in Africa), Ciments d'Origny, Sagem, Ernault Somua and BSN, and, not included in the sample, the licence agreement of SNIAS in Brazil for the construction of helicopters, or, in 1981, the very large transfer of technology by PUK to India (mining, alumina plant, aluminium plant and railway development. This is a very extensive transfer covering the whole production line, with part of the aluminium being exported).[25]

The French firms may desire these situations in order to limit investments and/or risks. For all the countries in Eastern Europe and the Soviet Union, this is a need which has always existed, as their governments prohibit the setting up of subsidiaries.[26] However, this type of transfer of technology, without any control over the company, mostly arises from the wish of the developing countries, who are trying to control industrialisation by restricting the operations of multinational companies in their territory. This is true in Brazil, Morocco, Black Africa and India.[27]

One may ask if there is always a loss of real control by the foreign company, as its management may still be directed by the French group through its technology, training of personnel, and flows of imports and exports. In addition, in certain countries in Africa, for example, the authorities own the majority of the capital in these companies and this 'loose' control may permit effective control of management by the French firm. This is not the case where the local shareholder is a national industrialist.

Whatever the real degree of loss of effective control over management, legal ownership of the means of production does in any case disappear, and with it an important source of profit for the French group. In this sense, the world organisation of the economy has moved into a new phase, because of the political will of the Third World countries to restrict the power of the multinationals, and their capacity for financial growth.

In terms of the international division of labour (IDL) between developed countries and the newly industrialising countries, structured to profit the former, the new methods imposed on multinational firms tend to restrict this international division. If we accept that control is still exerted by means other than legal ownership, and in particular by the technological supervision, which on the whole is still located in the developed countries, one can then say that this is only a transformation of the forms of IDL, or 'a higher level' of IDL.

In addition to the new constraints analysed above, which are the result of an increase in the number of newly industrialising countries, some of these countries are taking control of the subsidiaries of multi-national groups with little or no compensation (Chile, Algeria, Ethiopia, Madagascar and Iran, for example). For the companies in the sample between 1974 and 1977: in 1972 Labaz handed over control of its subsidiary Pharmal in Algeria, which was large (24 million in 1974 out of a total turnover of 132 million for its foreign subsidiaries). In 1974, Lyonnaise des Eaux lost control of its Malagassy subsidiary, which employed 2113 people. In 1975, the Ethiopian subsidiary of Salins du Midi was nationalised. In 1976, the Algerian subsidiary of Wanner Isofi was put under trust. As for Iran, following the revolution in February 1979, some big French projects were halted. The most important included the construction of two nuclear power stations by Framatome, Creusot-Loire and Spie, the electrification of the railway by Spie, the Tehran metro by Ratp-Sofretu, motorways for Jean Lefebvre and housing construction for Bouygues, SAE.[28] The operations of 200 French groups engaged in industrial or commercial activities (especially after 1974) were disrupted or totally suspended, and the 8000 French residents in Iran had fallen to 1000 by the end of 1979.[29] Coface, a public institution insuring export risks, paid out 1552 billion francs for claims made in Iran[30] (at the end of 1980, the American banks and industrial groups had claims of 7 million dollars for contracts not respected, loans not repaid or assets expropriated[31]).

From the point of view of the multinational firms, it is then better to have a minority interest in a 'safe' country such as Brazil than a controlled subsidiary in an 'unstable' country. This explains the 'deliberate' choices of certain groups in favour of these minority interests coupled with other indirect means of control, principally through technology.

THE TWOFOLD MANIFESTATION OF THE CRISIS AND THE RELOCATION OF FRENCH MULTINATIONALS

The above analyses reveal one essential aspect of the world economic crisis: the new demands of the newly industrialising countries as regards the control of the operations of multinationals, which may go as far as pure and simple expropriation. The production plants of French companies abroad are restricted by this and the risks incurred increase. CNPF recently asked for better guarantees from the State against the political risks of investment abroad.[32] This explains the methods being used increasingly today, consisting of the transfer of technology, without legally controlling the foreign company using the technology.[33]

These new demands also help to explain the geographical relocation to the developed countries, and in particular to the most stable of them, the United States, as well as the attraction of Brazil, a big potential market characterised by social and political stability.

We have already noted the specific attractions of the United States and Brazil for French investors, and these characteristics also explain recent developments. However, the economic crisis within the developed countries, France and Europe in particular, restricts the operations of French companies and increases competition between them and foreign groups. It is therefore pushing companies to develop their operations abroad by exporting or direct production. In this sense the economic crisis in the developed countries is another principal factor behind recent developments. As this crisis is partly a result of the new demands of the newly industrialising countries, for example as regards the prices of raw materials and oil, these countries are then the originators of a multinationalisation movement which they are also trying to restrict and control, at the same time accepting it because they need the technological and industrial input of the multinational groups. The new international development strategies adopted by the French multinationals are therefore a result of a complex development of the world situation, involving frequently conflicting forces.

We have seen that one essential factor in this new international situation is the growth of the economic and political power of the newly industrialising countries, tending to restrict the multinationals' room for manœuvre and their power.

In addition, one consequence of this development must be pointed out, as it could threaten the big Western industrial groups: within the Third World countries, competitive industrial groups are gradually being set up which will compete more and more with the multinationals on the world markets. Some Brazilian, Korean and Indian companies are already competing with French companies on the markets in other newly industrialising countries.[34]

All these international developments are increasing the risks incurred

by multinational firms. The economic crisis, the new economic and
political demands of the Third World, the increased political risks
in these countries, the unknown quantity relating to the trend in
the price of raw materials and the very great international monetary
instability are all factors contributing to a *very uncertain world* for
French multinationals. Compared with the period before 1974-5,
these companies are facing a new age characterised by very high economic and political risks.

In this chapter we have concentrated on the economic data of this
new situation. From this point of view, it could be said that the world
economic crisis embraces two essential and connected aspects: the
crisis in the developed countries, and the new demands of the newly
industrialising countries. It is these two aspects of the economic crisis
which are leading the multinationals to relocate towards the developed
countries, with more and more production investment in subsidiaries
being made there, while this is tending to be reduced in the Third
World countries.

The overall statistics confirm this phenomenon. G. Tardy[35] shows
that the share of French investment abroad aimed at the EEC rose
from 32.2 per cent of the total over the period 1969-73 to 40 per
cent over the period 1974-7. There is a general trend among the European economies to redistribute towards the developed countries: for
the other countries of Europe, the share of foreign investment in
Europe is falling, but G. Tardy adds, 'This is the result of the more
rapid growth of investment in North America.'

The companies themselves are increasingly admitting to this new
strategic objective of relocating to Europe and North America. In the
summary to the 'Journées de l'investissement français à l'étranger',
organised by the CNPF in 1979, G. Perebeau concluded, 'What we have
to do is to divide our establishment effort as best we can, giving a certain amount of priority to the industrialised countries.'[36]

In the first part we showed the existence of two main factors in the
multinationalisation of companies, which were company-specific
and connected with the situation of the French economy (relative
company size and concentration of production facilities, existence
of foreign control of companies and foreign penetration of French
industry).

In this second part, we have just shown how the structural characteristics of the foreign economies (size, production costs, proximity,
historical links) explain the methods of production abroad, and to
some extent the very decisions to become multinational. The breakdown into strategy factors does then correspond to a breakdown
between those factors relating to the situation of the French economy
and those relating to the disparities in the world economy. We have

shown that the world economic crisis took a different form in the Third World countries, and had conflicting effects on the multinationalisation of French companies.

As we have already stressed, we have used a very narrow definition of the strategies of multinational companies. We have however obtained some interesting results. The second part has thus highlighted the actual structures used for production abroad by French companies and in particular the specialisations that use a specific type of structure according to the country of establishment and the sector of activities. Having established these structures we can now go on to study the different consequences of production abroad on the performance of multinational companies.

NOTES

1 Cf. M. C. Kaplan, 1979, volume 1, pp. 17 ff., and J. Ehrsam, 1981, pp. 47 ff. (according to this author the gross annual investment rose from 3.2 per cent of the gross formation of fixed capital to 4 per cent in 1979).

2 J. Cohen, 1979.

3 M. Anvers, 1979.

4 See, for example, the work of H. Couffin, 1977.

5 J. Cohen, op. cit.

6 See J. Roussel, 1979, and F. Frobel, 1978.

7 See Ministry of the Economy, 1979.

8 See, for example, the interesting study of D. de Laubier and A. Richemond, 1980, the doctoral thesis of J. P. Thuillier, 1979, and L. G. Franko, 1976, p. 161.

9 Source: W. K. Chung and G. G. Fouch, 'Foreign direct investment in the United States in 1979', *Survey of Current Business*, August 1980, p. 39. These figures underestimate French establishment via Canadian subsidiaries (case of Lafarge).

10 Rush Loving, 'Get a US Wing', *Fortune* magazine, July 1976.

11 Hugh D. Menzies, 'It pays to brave the New World', *Fortune* magazine, 30 July 1979.

12 There is no big French investment in strategic activities. J. M. Quatrepoint stressed (*Le Monde*, 11 December 1979) that, out of twenty American companies producing semi-conductors which had changed hands over the last few years, none had been taken over by a French group, while this had been done by firms from West Germany, Great Britain, Japan, the Netherlands and Canada. See also M. Rolant, 1981, p. 471.

13 No French investment in the United States is comparable with that of the Americans in France. (In addition, Poclain's operations in the United States ceased in 1977 following the take-over of this group by Case USA!).

14 Of the eighteen principal banks in the United States under foreign control, in 1977 there were no subsidiaries of French banks (see *Business Week*, special report on major business problems, 1979, p. 158). All the big financial groups (Paribas, Suez, etc.) and all the big French banks are however represented in the United States by agencies and subsidiaries. Minority holdings and associations with American banks are also very common, such as, for example, the cooperation agreement between the Suez group and Morgan bank.

15 H. Couffin, 1977.

16   Cf. Michalet and Delapierre, 1973, p. 70.
17   The last two arguments lead many authors to consider that the American market can only be entered by production on the spot. We could point out to these authors that the Japanese export heavily to the United States, and so intrinsic competitiveness does come into play.
18   See on this subject the analyses of L. G. Franko, op. cit.
19   *Les Echos*, 20 February 1981.
20   Outside the sample, we can mention the recent establishments of ATO chimie, Sodexho, Legrand, Turbomeca, Intermarché and Carrefour.
21   *Le Monde*, 9 October 1979. However, Rhône-Poulenc's operations are very capital-intensive in terms of number of employees, hence the weight of this group must be less.
22   See, for example, *Le Monde*, 29 January 1981.
23   C. A. Michalet, 1976, p. 154.
24   C. A. Michalet, 1979, p. 10. (MNC: multinational corporation.)
25   See *Les Echos*, 12 January 1981.
26   See A. Tirapolsky, article, p. 17, *Les Cahiers Français*, No. 190; see also C. Adam, 1973, p. 263. This author mentions the agreement of CII, Sagem and Ratier Forest in Hungary.
27   See, for example, in CNPF, 1979-1, p. 259, the study of the policy of Brazil, which led the BFCE to advise small and medium-sized French companies wanting to set up in this country to find a local associate and only to hold a minority interest in the company set up.
28   *Financial Times*, 5 June 1979.
29   *Le Monde*, 23 July 1979, and *Le Nouvel Economiste*, 14 December 1978.
30   *Le Monde*, 2 November 1980.
31   *Fortune* magazine, 5 December 1980.
32   CPNF, 1979-3, p. 150. Note also that in the United States there is a development of companies specialising in forecasting political risks. See *Fortune* magazine, 24 March 1980.
33   For an overall analysis of these demands and the new forms of the IDL, see the file compiled by the journal *Economie et Humanisme*, No. 256, November 1980, p. 26. P. Judet stresses that the measures to control the operations of multinationals are accompanied by the desire of the Third World for industrialisation, with technological inputs being necessary for this industrialisation: the majority of the newly industrialising countries would therefore like this input from the multinational firms, while at the same time wanting to control them. But would the multinationals not prefer to invest elsewhere?
34   See on this subject the article by J. Perrin, 1980, relating to 'the new exporters of technology' and that of J. Ch. Monateri, 1980, for 'the new cast in the chemical industry'.
35   G. Tardy, 1979.
36   CNPF, 1979-3, p. 143.

PART III

THE PERFORMANCE OF THE MULTINATIONALS

In Part III we examine the performance of French multinationals.[1] This performance is taken in the wide sense, to include the profitability of companies, essential to their performance and exports and employment in France, which are essential to national performance.

Does multinational production, its intensity and the methods by which it is achieved have any impact, and in what sense, on the profitability, exports and employment of companies in France? Our research is based on an examination of these characteristics for the 413 companies in the sample.

The results obtained give us a better knowledge of the French industrial apparatus, as they will show us how the multinationalisation of firms gives them big advantages over firms that do not spread the location of their production. These results will also be essential for an analysis of French economic policy, one of the basic objectives of which is to develop exports which, as we shall see, may conflict with support for the big multinational groups. Finally, at a time when industrial employment is falling, while unemployment is rising, these analyses will throw some light on the debate on the role of the multinationalisation of French companies on employment in France.

5 Activity Abroad and Profitability

First of all we shall establish that the multinational companies in our sample have a higher profitability than non-multinational companies, a characteristic already established for French industrial groups.

We shall then look at whether this specific characteristic can be explained by the higher profitability of production abroad and, more generally, by the positive effect of this production outside France as well as of exports on the profitability of these companies.

MULTINATIONAL COMPANIES: MORE PROFITABLE COMPANIES

We shall first give the results for the French companies in our sample, that is 155 multinational companies and 216 non-multinationals. We shall then look at other works already existing: although they rarely study the direct effect of multinationalisation on profitability, they do suggest that it has a positive effect.

Higher Profitability and More Stability

Profitability is measured at parent company level, as consolidated data are rarely available. We do not therefore take into account the direct effect of the high profitability of foreign subsidiaries on the consolidated results of the group. Only the indirect effects are taken into account, either those resulting from dividends received, royalties, interest and various methods of transferring funds,[2] or those resulting from the greater profitability of metropolitan operations made possible by international operation.

Table 5.1 shows that on the whole the profitability of multinational companies is higher:

— this is very marked in 1974 for the overall net and gross rates of return (difference of 2.2 per cent and 5.1 per cent);
— this is marked for the average rates (1971–4) of net return (deviation of 1:7.7/6.7 per cent). We give the mean of the average company rates of return calculated for the four years 1971–4. For sector 8, Mechanical Engineering, the comparison of the two mean figures for multinationals and companies with no foreign subsidiaries

Table 5.1 Profitability of multinational companies and other companies in 1974 and between 1971 and 1974 (371 companies in the sample)

		Multinationals		Non-multinationals	Total French companies
		very multi-national	overall		
Overall rates 1974	Net rate of return:	8.26	7.6	5.4	7.1
	Gross rate of return:	24.5	26.6*	19.3	25.2
Mean of average rates 1971–4	Net rate of return:	8.0	7.7	6.7	7.1
	Gross rate of return:	24.7	24.9	24.5	24.6
Number of companies		75	155	216	371

Notes: Multinationals: producing in at least one foreign country.
Very multinational: producing in at least five foreign countries or producing over 10 per cent abroad.
Net rate of return: net result/equity.   ⎫ Mostly calculated at
Gross rate of return: self-financing/equity. ⎬ parent company level.
The overall rates are calculated as the sum of the companies' results divided by the sum of the capital.
We have excluded four companies whose very negative rates of return distorted the mean figures: Arthur-Martin, Chantiers de France Dunkerque, Hachette and Campenon-Bernard.
*24.4 per cent excluding Usinor (rate = 72 per cent).

(either production or commercial), using the Student's T test shows that there is a less than a five per cent chance that the deviation of 5.39 per cent is due only to accident: the deviation is then significant. On average, it must be admitted that multinationalisation has a positive effect on the profitability of companies. There is also a significant deviation, from a statistical point of view, for sectors 7B (consumer goods, excluding textiles) and for a group of six sectors (3, 4, 5, 6, 7B and 8). The deviation is not significant for the sectors on their own, as the number of observations is not sufficient, often because of the wide spread in profitability rates for non-multinational companies.

The mean figures for the standard deviations in the average company rates of return (1971–4) is 2.63 per cent for multinational companies and 3.3 per cent for non-multinationals: the results of the multi-nationals are therefore more stable. We can also see that the 'very multinational' companies have even higher net rates of return, which leads us to assume that multinationalisation is the reason for this high rate of return.

The results are even more remarkable as the non-multinational category includes companies under foreign control, whose net rate of return is almost as high as that of the multinationals. This latter characteristic has been verified for both the companies in our sample[3] and for all French industrial groups.[4]

It has also been shown that for the companies in our sample, exports contributed to maintaining profitability in 1974. In fact, out of the non-multinational firms the net and gross rates of return did not drop in 1974 for the big exporters (exporting over 25 per cent) as they did for those companies exporting very little.[5]

As multinational companies, and in particular the 'very multinational' companies, are often very big exporters, (cf. Chapter 1), it could be said that the high exports of these companies, in addition to foreign production, also contributed to maintaining profitability in 1974.

Finally, if we look at the companies by sector of activity, we find that for most of them, the multinational companies do have high rates of return, especially in 1974. In some sectors, for example sector 8, we can even establish a positive link between the average level of the net rate of return and, rather than the existence of production outside France, the importance of this production (see Figure 5.1).

Verification of the important part played by multinationalisation in the rate of return is due to the fact that, for the companies in our sample, size itself has little impact on the profitability of companies. If companies are grouped by way of increasing size and if we calculate the mean rate of return for these groups of companies, size is only found to have a positive relation to the rate of return for non-multinational companies as a group. On the other hand, big non-multinational companies are not on the whole any more profitable than small or medium-sized companies. Similarly, a joint study, at individual company level, of profitability, size and multinationalisation shows that, for a given sector, the profitability of multinationals mostly increases with their rate of multinationalisation while, conversely, profitability does not always increase with size.[6]

This is not surprising. Many works have tried to measure the effect of size on company profitability: they have arrived at conflicting results as they have often shown that the big companies are neither more profitable nor more efficient. A. Jacquemin, when assisting European empirical studies on the relations between size and performance of companies, and quoting the works of Jenny and Weber, Morvan, Jacquemin, Samuels and Smyth, concluded, 'European statistical research rejects the hypothesis that large firm size significantly promotes higher profitability.'[7] On the contrary, he adds that 'Most studies confirm the existence of a negative and significant relation between size and profit variability', due to the diversification strategy often adopted by big firms.[8] He also quotes the many works which show that, on the other hand, concentration has a positive effect on profits.[9]

Hence, even though we indicated in Chapter 1 how size and a

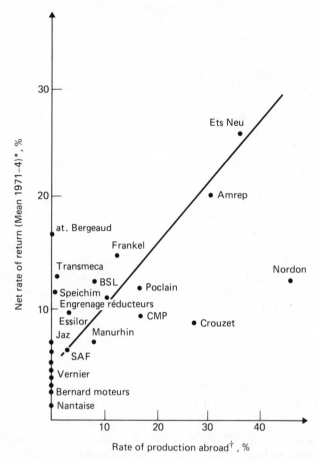

*Net rate of return: net result/equity (for the parent company).

†Rate of production abroad: turnover of foreign production subsidiaries/'total' turnover of groups (for 1974).

Figure 5.1 Production operations abroad and company rates of return: the mechanical engineering sector

dominant position on the national market were positive factors in the multinationalisation of companies, it would seem that the higher profitability of multinational companies cannot be attributed solely to their frequently greater size. At most the good level of their results is partly explained by their often dominant position on concentrated markets.

Partial Confirmation in Other Statistical Studies

Other works have noted the higher profitability of French exporting and/or multinational companies, but very indirectly, as generally the object of the four studies mentioned here was not to measure this property.

Only B. Marois[10] compares, for 1974, 1975 and 1976, nineteen very large French multinational groups and nineteen similar non-multinational groups of similar size and in the same sector. He found a slightly higher rate of return on equity (gross self-financing margin/equity) for the multinationals (20.8/17.1 per cent), and an operating return (gross trading profit/turnover) for this same group which was much higher (7.8 per cent compared with 4.8 per cent) and more stable (lower standard deviation). Note that the non-multinationals included are non-multinational by reference to a very restrictive definition and might be considered multinational in accordance with our definition. The data are consolidated, hence the profitability figure given is for the group, while we are mostly studying that of the parent company. Even though in general non-multinationals are smaller, which might distort the result, the two groups of companies compared by B. Marois are more similar in size than those in our study. The results obtained confirm that multinationalisation is a factor contributing to a high profitability.

One very important study carried out by researchers from the university of Paris I and INSEE for 1974 aimed to compare companies belonging to groups (319 groups) with independent companies. It covered 34 600 companies with more than fifty employees, taken from all sectors.[11]

The profitability, measured by the return on capital invested (gross operating profit/net fixed assets + stocks) or the return on fixed assets (gross trading profit/gross fixed assets) varied considerably depending on the type of company. The mean rates of return fall into the following order:[12]

— independent companies;
— companies belonging to foreign groups;
— companies belonging to private French groups;
— companies belonging to public groups.

This result may be surprising, but it does not contradict our own conclusions. In fact, companies belonging to private groups include both multinational companies and non-multinational companies and it is quite possible that if this study had isolated the multinational groups these would have been found to have a higher profitability.

The high profitability of companies belonging to foreign groups, which we found for the fifty-seven companies under foreign control in our sample,[13] suggests that our conclusions can be extended: multi-nationalisation in the wide sense would seem to be a factor contributing to high profitability, both for foreign subsidiaries and for the national groups becoming multinational.

In a recent survey, *Crédit national* examined a selection of ninety-four French companies which 'occupied a significant position in one or more sectors at European or world level', that is companies belonging to the top six or seven firms in the market for their production.[14] These companies, which perform very well compared with their foreign competitors, have a higher profitability and more solid financial structure than other French companies. We find that these firms are very often big exporters, they have a large commercial network abroad and one in two of them are multinationals. In comparing these two types of characteristics, can we not assume that international expansion is one of the factors contributing to high profitability?

Finally, going back to the data base on which the INSEE study already mentioned was founded, Encaoua, Franck and Jacquemin have recently carried out complex econometric tests on the influence of groups within 270 sectors of the French economy.[15] They show that the sectors where groups are the most important are the sectors which export most, and that the apportionment of value added in favour of profits is higher as the sectoral export rate rises. They make the hypothesis that the groups can make use of export trade flows to increase their profits.

After carrying out statistical tests based on very full data, these authors again found that exports have a positive effect on profitability.[16] In the theoretical justification for the higher profitability of groups, they stress that by 'benefiting from economies of scale in the production process, by internationalising their research operations and coordinating their national operations with those abroad, by vertically integrating their operations throughout the branches of production and by participating, finally, in setting up an internal capital market by the centralised reallocation of overall profits, industrial groups are able to reduce their production costs, and to benefit from substantial productivity gains. . . .' Multinational companies are mostly groups, and production abroad is an organisation structure stressed by the authors themselves: if this variable had been tested, multinationalisation would without doubt have been found also to have a positive effect on profitability.

Our own results, confirmed to some extent by the studies we have just quoted, enable us to conclude that exports and production outside France have a positive and statistically significant effect on the profitability of French companies. This property is all the more important as it seems to be a specific national characteristic.[17]

There are, of course, other factors which contribute to explaining the higher profitability of multinational companies, such as internal organisation or the variables relating to technology and the oligopolistic market structure, and all of these are used in the econometric tests.

Our statistical verifications, and some of those we quote, date from 1974. If one considers that their operations abroad give multinational groups the means to withstand the crisis, then in recent years, the difference in profitability compared with non-multinational groups would have become more marked.

To assure ourselves that this statistical correspondence, imperfect though it is, between multinationalisation and profitability has a causal link, we propose that production abroad actually is in itself more profitable than production in France, or that it leads to this higher profitability. We shall do this in the next two sections.

PRODUCTION ABROAD: OFTEN MORE PROFITABLE
THAN PRODUCTION IN FRANCE

The companies themselves often indicate that production abroad is very profitable, more profitable than French production. Seventy testimonials regarding establishments abroad were collected by the CNPF.[18] In this work, Rhône-Poulenc for example mentions its subsidiary in South Korea, set up between 1975 and 1977, which in 1978 distributed a dividend of 30 per cent of the capital and royalties relating to the licence granted. Vitos, too, explains that its industrial subsidiary in Mexico pays 1 million francs of dividends each year, while the initial investment in 1955 was 1 million francs. Studying the biggest French industrial groups, DAFSA[19] gives for 1977 a gross margin (cash flow over turnover) for Michelin of 15 per cent worldwide and 6 per cent in France, for PUK 17.7 per cent and 3.2 per cent, for SGPM 7.4 per cent and 2.5 per cent and for Rhône-Poulenc 4.6 per cent and 3.4 per cent. The margin for sales abroad, either by exporting or direct production, is therefore found to be higher than that for sales in France. M. C. Kaplan has also pointed out this phenomenon and has shown that certain big French multinational groups, such as DMC, SGPM or Rhône-Poulenc, only achieved positive financial results in recent years thanks to the inflow of income repatriated from their foreign subsidiaries.[20]

We are trying to verify here whether the higher profitability for production abroad is a general trend. As the information published on the operations of foreign subsidiaries is very incomplete, we have to be content with a number of estimates, which will all reveal the same trend. In these estimates we cannot take into account the distortion introduced by 'transfer pricing' which, as we know, may result in transfers of profits between units of multinational groups through under- or overcharging for the products transferred. This is why we talk about 'apparent rate of return'.

For 154 multinational firms in the sample we have measured the apparent rate of return on foreign investments: dividends received in 1974 from subsidiaries and direct foreign investments/inventory value of foreign investments. Our source comes from Tables of subsidiaries and trade investments. This index of the rate of return on capital invested abroad is high, higher than the net rate of return on equity in France: the mean of these indices is 9.3 per cent compared with 7.7 per cent for the mean of the average net rates of return on equity for parent companies between 1971 and 1974. In spite of the imperfections in this measurement and in particular the omission of foreign subsidiaries indirectly controlled by French subsidiaries, there would seem to be a higher financial rate of return on foreign investments.

The net rate of return on equity for foreign production subsidiaries can be measured, but only for direct subsidiaries and where they are listed, using the Tables of subsidiaries and trade investments published by their parent companies. It is then directly comparable with that of the French parent companies or their main French subsidiaries. Table 5.2 describes the main cases for which it has been possible to establish this comparison for 1974. The net rate of return for production abroad is always found to be higher than for production in France, and it is often much higher, with rates of return in excess of 30 per cent. This seems to apply whatever the country of establishment.

In certain cases, the operations of foreign subsidiaries are very different from those of the French parent companies, for example when they only concern a production stage, very often the final stage. This is the case for the foreign subsidiaries of cement companies, which crush clinker, an imported self-finished product, into cement. The same applies to car assembly subsidiaries. It is difficult to compare profitability as the operations are different. Added to this is the fact that semi-finished products may be sold to these foreign production subsidiaries at low prices, making the subsidiaries more profitable. In many cases, however, foreign production operations are of the same type as the operations in France: Rhône-Poulenc (but different operations), Lafarge in Canada, Vallourec in Europe, Carnaud in Africa and Southern Europe etc.

There is then a clear trend towards a higher productivity for production abroad. However, this result is distorted as operations in France and outside France may be different. It is then interesting to present two cases where operations in France and abroad are identical, and hence comparable, where there is no exchange of products between the parent company and its subsidiary and the latter carries out all the production stages under similar conditions to those in France.

For example, the subsidiary of Bouygues in Ivory Coast, Setao,

Table 5.2 Rate of return on capital invested in production in France and abroad (net rate of return on the equity of foreign production subsidiaries and French companies in 1974)

Companies and main foreign direct production subsidiaries for which data are known (% interest)	(Net return/ equity 1974) × 100	Companies and main foreign direct production subsidiaries for which data are known (% interest)	(Net return/ equity 1974) × 100
Lafarge		*J. J. Carnaud*	
— Group (consolidated)	13.2	— Parent company (France)	6.16
— Ciments Lafarge France		— SIEM (Ivory Coast) (85%)	15.2
(main French subsidiary)	7.65	— S. malgache emb. met.	
— Canada Cements Lafarge		(87%)	83.9
(Canada)	10.3	— Envases Carnaud (Spain)	
— Sococim (Senegal)	11.33	(53%)	10.45
— Ciments antillais	22.5	— Stumetal (Tunisia)	
		(36.6%)	49.2
Carbonisation, enterprise		— Licet metals (Lebanon)	
et céramique		(2.5%)	21.5
— Parent company (France)	4.8	— Hellas can (Greece) (10%)	18.1
— Nv Gouda Vuurvast			
(Netherlands)	4.5	*Charfa*	
		— Parent company (France)	11.6
Origny Desvroise		— Cochepa (Morocco)	
— Group (consolidated)	4.5	(45.9%)	35.4
— Ciments d'Origny (France)	3.5	— Sivem (Ivory Coast)	
— SICM (Ivory Coast)	35.4	(in 1978)	36.8
— Ciments Numbo			
(New Caledonia)	50.1	*Crouzet*	
		— Parent company (France)	5.3
Vallourec		— Crouzet Ltd (GB) (99%)	15.5
— Parent company (France)	8.6	— Crouzet espanola (Spain)	
— Tubes de Nimy (Belgium)	26.7	(79%)	42.1
— Tubes de Haren (Belgium)	46.1	— Crouzet Milan (Italy)	
— Fit ferrotubi (Italy)		(20%)	19.3
(10.6%)	7.2		
		Renault	
		— Parent company (France)	1.4
		— Renault ind. Belgique	
		(Belgium) (99%)	12.2
		— IKA Renault (Argentina)	
		(31%)	−75
		— OYAK Renault (Turkey)	
		(40%)	10.5
	Net margin/ turnover in 1978		Net profit/ turnover in 1978
Rhône-Poulenc		*Essilor*	
(all operations together)		— Parent company (France)	3.06
— France	3.92	— Milroy silor	
— Europe less France	6.08	(United States)	11.8
— Brazil	17.07	— Essels Hoya (Japan)	9.2
		— Orma Optical (GB)	6.3

Source: Annual reports and Tables of subsidiaries and trade investments.

employed 1287 people in 1977, and its operations are of the same type as those of the group (building: 50 per cent, civil engineering, road and port structures). In addition to an increase in the turnover which was not affected by the economic crisis in 1977, Setao had a net rate of return on equity of 46 per cent, double that of Bouygues, and a trading margin of 11.6 per cent, six times higher than that of Bouygues in France.[21]

Armosig, the joint subsidiary of Rhône-Poulenc and Vallourec, manufactures rigid PVC tubes from PVC supplied by Rhône-Poulenc. Its subsidiary in Ivory Coast, Sotici, carries out the same operation. Its trading margin in 1977 was five times higher (8/1.6 per cent) and its net rate of return on equity was also five times higher (47/9.6 per cent).[22] The detailed studies of these two subsidiaries in Ivory Coast show that in spite of a slightly lower labour productivity, their higher profitability is achieved thanks to higher selling prices, and above all very much lower wage costs.

Production abroad in countries less developed than France, at lower labour production costs, would therefore seem to be *intrinsically* more profitable than production in France. This is true when the production and technology are identical in France and in these countries, and this is even more marked when the stages which have been relocated are the very labour-intensive stages. We therefore confirm a hypothesis on which the analysis of strategies was based (Chapter 3). However, we also stress a logical foundation for the higher profitability of multinational companies.

Production in the developed countries was also often found to be more profitable than production in France. It can be assumed that in these cases there is another factor involved in the high profitability: the opportunity for the French group to choose a more profitable operation and/or a more modern technique than in France. This cannot, however, be regarded as the sole cause for the higher profitability of production abroad in all countries, as J. Cohen confirms.[23]

Finally, of course, in certain cases production abroad may be less profitable or not profitable at all, particularly during the start-up phase for the plant. Our analysis is based on a medium-term view here, and we are comparing the 'tendential' profitability for French and foreign operations.

HOW PRODUCTION ABROAD AND EXPORTS IMPROVE PROFITABILITY: A TYPOLOGY

How Exports Increase Profitability

It is difficult to measure whether, because of the higher trading margins, exports are more profitable than sales in France. It would seem that this is often the case in less developed countries where there is little (or no) local competition.

On the other hand, whatever their country of destination, exports increase the profitability of French operations by the simple fact that they increase production: they may permit an extension of production capacities, and economies of scale. They increase financial power, self-financing resources, and hence research and innovation capacities. In a period of crisis and falling domestic demand, they permit full employment of production facilities to be maintained or at least they limit their under-employment: they therefore minimise the fall in profitability compared with that suffered by non-exporting companies. This is also true for the exports of semi-finished products to foreign production subsidiaries.

Finally, when exports go to the developed countries, they provide knowledge of industrial and consumer needs, which may in the long term be to the company's advantage on the French market.

How Production Abroad Increases Profitability: First Typology Depending on the Geographical Area of Establishment

We have pointed out above, with the cases of Bouygues and Armosig in Ivory Coast, that the higher profitability of production in this country arose essentially from the lower wage costs. We have also shown already (Chapter 3, p. 47, Table 3.2) how labour production costs were lower in the less developed countries than in France, which is a factor in increasing profitability specific to production located in these countries.

Other characteristics of the host economies affect the opportunities for financial gain. The first is the intensity of local competition, which can be considered to relate to the level of industrial development: keen competition in the developed countries limits the possible gains, whereas lack of competition in the less developed countries enables higher gains to be made. One can also mention the size and growth of the market, its proximity (transport costs), the legal and statutory environment, aid and incentives to foreign investment, customs duties, the level of worker organisation and social stability, and the relative value of the currency. Each country is a special case for which the advantages of its location must be examined one by one. There is, however, a general trend.

The opportunities for short-term gains arising out of production abroad are found be be much higher when production is carried out in a newly industrialising or less developed country: the lower labour production costs and the less keen industrial competition, for example, are two permanent factors behind this specific character (one could add the more favourable legal environment, social stability, and weakness of the currency).

On the other hand, there are fewer opportunities for short-term gains from producing in the developed countries, as production costs are similar or higher and competition is always keen. Production in these countries mainly increases the long-term profitability of the group, by improving its market shares, its position with regard to world competition and its financial, technical and research capabilities, as well as a better awareness of needs.

In general, then, there are specific methods for making profits by producing abroad, depending on the geographical area. We now have to determine this precisely by looking at related exports.

How Production Abroad and Related Exports Increase Profitability: a Typology Deduced from the Organisation Structures of Production Abroad

The examination of geographical specialisations in adopting a particular organisation structure for production, carried out in Chapter 3, enables us to confirm here the specific methods for making profits related to the area in which foreign production is established.

In the developed countries we know that market strategies with autonomous production are the most common: in this case there are no related exports, and no immediate effect on profitability as a result. In all such cases, the advantages of production in these countries are long-term advantages: improving technical and commercial know-how, increasing overall growth, financial power and research potential. Finally, assembly production with related exports has the added immediate effect of improving profitability.

In countries less developed than France, we know that market strategies often take the form of assembly production: in addition to the production cost savings of foreign operations, there is the improvement in profitability for French operations. Spreading the location of production to the less developed countries is found directly or indirectly to increase short-term profitability. Finally, when production strategies are used in these countries, this still applies. In addition, the profitability of French production can be improved by reimporting semi-finished products at low cost prices.

These are the main trends regarding the different methods of improving profitability according to the location of foreign production.[24] All the findings of Chapter 3, which revealed specialisations in the adoption of a particular organisation for foreign production, for sectors and companies, can also be interpreted in terms of methods of making profits. The analysis pattern proposed here is a sufficient basis for this.

HIGH PROFITABILITY FOR FOREIGN PRODUCTION:
CONSTRAINT AND OBJECTIVE

The multinationals therefore have a higher and more stable profitability than non-multinational companies. We have confirmed that often foreign production is more profitable than French production, which is the first explanation. Then, on a wider basis, we have established a typology of the ways in which foreign production, and related exports, improve the profitability of French companies. In this sense, we can say that the higher profitability of multinational companies is a consequence of their multinationalisation, even though other factors may be involved, such as, for example, the size of these firms, or rather their often dominant position on the national market (see Chapter 2).

If one looks at this from the point of view of the company management and in particular their financial policy, one can consider, as B. Marois does,[25] that they will, when choosing to set up abroad, 'concentrate their efforts on two often conflicting objectives: maximising the profitability of their operations abroad, and minimising the foreign risk.' Before making any investment decisions, the multinationals compare the anticipated returns on the different possible projects with one another. They use classic criteria for this, mainly the internal rate of return or the net present value of future returns. They do, however, incorporate in these calculations a high economic risk factor, to take into account the special nature of production operations outside France. B. Marois mentions the case of a company which laid down the following figures as the minimum rate of return, including risks, '12% for investment in France, 14% for investment in Canada, 18% for investment in Italy, and 30% for investment in Argentina.' 'In the minds of the directors of this firm, the figures are considered to take into account the depreciation of the local currency, the possibility of funds being frozen and the risk of expropriation.'

B. Marois's survey related to twenty-three large French multinational groups. If one assumes that all French multinational companies, whatever their size, behave in the same way, one can accept the existence of a general constraint relating to the rate of return on capital invested. This constraint will be more severe for companies investing abroad who have to take into account specific economic risks. The choice of production operations abroad and the countries in which they are located should then be made for operations:

— with a high rate of return, and
— which permit the rapid recovery of the capital invested, thanks to the revenue transferred.

Our results confirm this hypothesis, especially since Table 5.2 shows that rates of return are very often higher in the less developed countries than they are in the developed countries.

It looks as if the order of precedence mentioned by B. Marois determining a rate of return according to the risks incurred is in fact applied. We have, however, also shown that the choices of companies are limited by the structural characteristics of the world economy: they are not made with complete freedom with respect to criteria of internal rationality, as an analysis in terms of company management would lead us to believe.

Although multinationalisation permits a high rate of return, it is clear that the analysis can be reversed: the search for a high rate of return, made possible by exports and production abroad, is also one of the objectives and one of the reasons for multinationalisation.[26] However, we are studying firms in a market economy, whose objective —or constraint—is to maintain profitability. It is almost a tautology to state that strategic decisions, such as multinationalisation, are taken with the motive of increasing profitability. The search for causes, which we prefer to call factors, must be directed at the structural determinants relating to the nature of firms (size, operations, etc.), the home economy (concentration, foreign control, crisis, etc.) and the host economies. This is what we have done in Parts I and II, and this is our justification for presenting the high profitability of multinational companies here as a consequence of multinationalisation itself.

NOTES

1　In the sense of the trilogy of the industrial economy, based on the work of Mason and Scherer (mentioned for example by Chevalier, 1977, p. 16), we are studying results in this part, whereas in Parts I and II we studied structures and behaviour.

2　See Bodinat, De Leershyder, Ghertman, Klein, Marois, 1978, pp. 305 ff. on this subject.

3　Savary, 1980, pp. 368 ff.

4　M. Hannoun, 1978, p. 453.

5　Savary, op. cit., pp. 465 ff.

6　Savary, ibid., p. 471.

7　A. Jacquemin, 1979, p. 209.

8　Jacquemin, ibid., pp. 209 and 210. J. Y. Chevallier and J. Y. Nizet, 1980, showed that between 1971 and 1977 the large firms more often 'constantly showed a profit' (p. 202).

9　Jacquemin, ibid., pp. 192 ff.

10　B. Marois, 1979-1, cf. pp. 38 and 58.

11　INSEE, 1980.

12　INSEE, ibid., Table 26, p. 55. for the ratio, gross profit after tax/equity, companies belonging to French private groups did however have a higher profitability than independent companies.

13　Savary, op. cit., pp. 367-72.

14　F. Mader and J. Rocher, 1980.

15 D. Encaoua, B. Franck, A. Jacquemin, 1981.
16 Jacquemin, op. cit., p. 195, also quotes two studies where exports sometimes have positive effects and sometimes have negative effects on profitability.
17 In fact, P. J. Buckley, J. H. Dunning and R. D. Pearce, 1981, showed that for all the world's 200 biggest industrial groups, 'The degree of multinational production cannot statistically be considered to help explain profitability, when the impact of other explanatory variables, such as size, industrial sector and nationality have already been taken into account.' However, these statistical tests were not carried out by country of origin.
18 CNPF, 1979-1, cf. pp. 191 and 257.
19 J. Cohen, 1979. See also on this subject B. Soulage, 1981, p. 296.
20 M. C. Kaplan, 1979. The author also shows that certain foreign operations show a deficit and are net consumers of the financial resources of the group, particularly when they correspond to a start-up phase.
21 See S. Chouchaoui, 1979.
22 See A. Reynes, 1979.
23 See J. Cohen, 1979, and our refutation in Savary, op. cit., pp. 496–500.
24 These trends confirm the proposal made in Chapter 3, p. 70 that foreign production in the developed countries is above all a sign of competitiveness, while production in the NICs and LDCs is more a sign of the search for competitiveness. We do in fact see here that production in these NICs and LDCs increases the short-term profitability more than production in the developed countries. We confirm the fact that production in these developed countries also corresponds to a search for competitiveness, described here as an improvement in medium- or long-term profitability (or short-term profitability thanks to related exports, where these exist).
25 Marois, op. cit., pp. 49 and 76 ff.
26 If we refer to the general structure of the industrial economy, this emphasises the interaction between structures, behaviour and results: high profitability (results) is a consequence of production abroad (behaviour) and at the same time an objective which may determine this behaviour. One may add that high profitability linked with multinationalisation (result) increases growth in France, and hence the position of the firm on its market (structures), which then tends to accentuate multinationalisation.

6 Production Abroad and Exports

Does production abroad promote French exports or, on the contrary, does it substitute for them? Apart from cases where on-the-spot production is a technical necessity (for example, to obtain raw materials, building, public works and general contracting (assembly of heavy equipment)), there are two ways of gaining access to foreign markets: exporting products manufactured in France, and direct production abroad. In certain cases direct production can be a substitute for exports. The question of substitution is, however, very complex: we do not know to what extent exports could have substituted for direct production abroad, as the latter may be the only possible way of gaining access to the market in some cases, for example when exports are prohibited or made difficult by customs duties, or when on-the-spot assembly is imposed by the authorities. Finally, without being a form of access which is imposed, on-the-spot production may be preferable in the long term, if it provides greater cost savings and better competitiveness, or if it provides protection from possible commercial restrictions. Since to answer this we would need to look at a number of particular characteristics, specific to each individual company and to each foreign economy, we shall leave this delicate question on one side.

On the other hand, we shall look at the relations which we can actually check, that is we shall answer the following question: to what extent is production abroad by French companies accompanied by French exports to the foreign production subsidiaries?[1] We shall base our examination on the organisation structures for production abroad outlined in Chapter 3, where each type of organisation or strategy involves a particular relation, and the sectoral specialisations in adopting these strategies enable us to identify the trends for each sector.

We shall then test these results with regard to the development of French exports between 1974 and 1977: certain sectoral developments, or those relating to certain types of country, can be explained by the locational spread of production by the companies in these sectors or areas.

THE ROLE OF THE ORGANISATION STRUCTURES FOR
FOREIGN PRODUCTION

Strategies of Foreign Production and Consequences on French Exports

The organisation structures for foreign production have been analysed
in Chapter 3, where we considered that they showed up the strategies
of multinationalisation. For each company in the sample, we set out
the French exports to foreign production subsidiaries, the destination
of foreign production and in particular any reimportation into France:
we could try to assess, for each company, whether or not the locational spread of its production leads to any exports and reimports and
what the balance of this induced trade is.[2] It is not possible to obtain
precise figures for each company, or for each sector, as our information is either incomplete (few firms replied to our questionnaire), or
covered by statistical secrecy (this questionnaire was confidential).

So, assuming that the characteristics highlighted for 1974 on the
basis of our sample are significant, we have to carry out some global
tendential analyses, indicating how the main strategies and specialisations in their adoption by companies in a particular sector, or for production in a particular area, must induce flows of trade.

1. Table 6.1 sets out the consequences on foreign trade of each strategy
for production abroad. The supply strategy always has an adverse
effect, since foreign production is imported into France. The production strategy is used in a great many different situations, depending
on the geographical area where this production is carried out and the
area to which this foreign production is exported.

In both cases where foreign production is exported to Third World
countries, that is to countries other than France (cases marked III and
IV in Table 6.1), foreign production may have a positive effect on the
French trade balance, if French exports are processed by these foreign
production subsidiaries.

When foreign production is carried out in a developed country and
is re-exported in part to France ('international specialisation', case I),
the effect on foreign trade is undetermined, as there may be both
French exports of semi-finished products to these foreign subsidiaries
and French imports from these subsidiaries.

On the other hand, in the cases of 'pure production strategy', which
we know are the most common (case II), that is production carried
out in a Third World country and exported to France, the net effect on
France's foreign trade is still negative: even if all the parts are exported
from France to be assembled abroad, the value of reimports is always
higher (the difference includes at least the transport costs and foreign

Table 6.1 Strategies of multinational production and consequences on foreign trade*

	Foreign production carried out in:	
	Developed countries	NICs or LDCs
Supply strategy	*Negative effect* French imports	*Negative effect* French imports
Production strategy (foreign production exported)		
Production exported to the developed countries	I international spec. *Undetermined effect* (related to international organisation)	II 'pure production strategy' (common) *Negative effect* (French imports greater than exports)
Production exported to the NICs–LDCs	IV 'int. spec. to gain access to an economic area' *Possible positive effect* (if related French exports)	III 'production strategy for the NIC–LDC market' *Possible positive effect* from related French exports
Market strategy (foreign production intended for the local market)		
Autonomous production (or integrated: low imports of French products)	Common strategy *no effect* (no related exports)	Strategy Rare not common strategy *no effect* (no related exports)
Assembly production (with high imports of French products)	Rare strategy *Positive effect* (related French exports)	Common strategy *Positive effect* (related French exports)

Note: See Table 3.8 for the definitions of the different strategies and Tables 3.6 and 3.7 for the groups and sectors specialised in each strategy.

*For each type of production abroad, or strategy, the effect of this production on the foreign trade of France is noted in italics.

wage costs, and often the manufacture of semi-finished products carried out or subcontracted abroad).

In the market strategy there are no reimports, but various effects on exports are possible, depending on the extent of French exports of semi-finished products for processing by the foreign subsidiaries. We have made a distinction for autonomous production, where the effect on foreign trade is nil or small. In assembly production, on the other hand, the effect on foreign trade is positive.

2. Each strategy therefore has specific effects on French foreign trade. As we have seen, there are geographical specialisations in the adoption of these strategies: each of them is used mainly in one particular area of the world economy. Because of these specialisations, specific consequences on foreign trade can be related to the locational spread of French companies to each area of the world (read Table 6.1 vertically).

In the case of the developed countries of Europe and North America, foreign production rarely adopts the supply strategy, the production strategy and the market strategy with assembly production. On the other hand, the most common cases, involving the biggest subsidiaries, correspond to the market strategy with autonomous production, that is with no related exports. On the whole, without making any distinction between particular sectors or firms, the multinationalisation of French companies in the developed countries has very little effect on French exports and little effect on imports, only applicable to cases of international specialisation of production (case I in Table 6.1): Poclain, Crouzet, Renault and Citroën in Belgium . . .

On the other hand, when foreign production takes place in the NICs and LDCs, it has two opposite effects on French foreign trade:

— a negative effect for the common cases of supply strategy and pure production strategy;
— a positive effect for the common cases of market strategy with assembly production, that is related exports.

If one excludes the energy sector, one can consider that for French industry the positive effect will prevail, as the pure production strategy, although on the increase, is still not very common. One could try to make a distinction of the LDCs in Africa and in particular in Asia, where the pure production strategy is more common and where the overall effect on the locational spread of French industrial companies does perhaps have a less favourable effect on foreign trade.

If, as we do later on, we concern ourselves only with the consequences on French exports, production in the NICs and LDCs is found, on the whole, to have a very marked positive effect, as the production strategies often include French exports of semi-finished products.

Sectoral Specialisation in the Use of Strategies and Consequences of the Locational Spread of Production on Exports

Sectoral specialisations in the adoption of each strategy have been highlighted:[3] companies belonging to particular sectors often adopt particular production strategies abroad. Because of these specialisations, we can show how, on the whole, the multinationalisation of the companies in each sector has different consequences on foreign trade.

For the oil sector (1A) and the mining sub-sector (sector 2), the supply strategy is the most common: hence the effect on foreign trade is adverse.

For the textiles sector (7A) cases of market strategy exist, but the pure production strategy in the NICs and LDCs is more important: the multinationalisation of companies in this sector therefore has a negative effect on foreign trade, as reimports from foreign subsidiaries largely exceed the exports sent to them.

For all the intermediate products sectors (2: construction materials, glass; 3: iron and steel, metallurgy; 4: chemicals; 5: paper, rubber, plastics), parachemicals, pharmaceuticals (sector 6), non-textile consumer products (sector 7B), the agricultural and food industries (14C), we know that production strategies are not very common, and market strategies with assembly production not very important by volume (cf. clinker-crushing, metal and paper processing, in Africa, pharmaceutical operations with imported active constituents, Bic, Rossignol, etc.) Market strategies with autonomous production are, on the other hand, very common: they involve the biggest subsidiaries and are often located in the developed countries: on the whole, then, the multinationalisation of these sectors has very little positive effect on French exports.

For all the capital goods sectors (8: mechanical engineering; 9: electrical and electronic engineering; 10: transportation equipment) there are two types of specialisation in the adoption of production strategies abroad with two conflicting consequences on foreign trade:

— the importance of the pure production strategy, in the NICs and LDCs, has an adverse effect on foreign trade because of the big reimports;
— the importance of the market strategy with assembly production has a positive effect on foreign trade, because of the related exports of parts, components and CKD kits for cars . . .

For the latter sectors, if one is only concerned with the effects on exports, the locational spread of production by companies generally has a very marked effect on exports (as the pure production strategy leads to exports, and reimports are not taken into account).

THE DEVELOPMENT OF FRENCH EXPORTS BETWEEN
1974 AND 1977 AND THE MULTINATIONALISATION
OF COMPANIES

By studying the multinational companies in our sample, we have identified the main trends: depending on the sectors and location of foreign production, the multinationalisation of companies has different consequences on French exports. By extrapolating these results for all companies we can explain some of the developments of French exports over the period 1974-7, a time of both economic crisis and the further multinationalisation of the economy.

Between 1974 and 1977, French exports increased considerably, but so did imports, and the trade balance remained in deficit. The development of foreign trade was very uneven as regards the contribution made by different operations to exports as a whole, and as regards the position with respect to different foreign countries.

Table 6.2 shows that industry made a considerable export effort, but one which was unequally distributed between the sectors.[4]

Table 6.2 Development of sectoral export rates between 1974 and 1977

| | Export rates* | |
	In 1974	In 1977
Intermediate products	24.5%	25.7%
Consumer goods including	17.7%	17.9%
non-chemical consumer goods	17.7%	17.1%
Capital goods	21.9%	39.7%
Total industry (in strict sense)	21.9%	28.7%

*FOB exports excluding VAT/distributed production of product (excluding VAT).
Source: INSEE National accounts.

The growth was small for all the intermediate products industries (+ 1.2 per cent) and consumer goods (+ 0.2 per cent)—for which the trade balances are moreover deteriorating, with the balance for consumer goods, for example, slipping into deficit for the first time. There are also disparities within these very large sectors. For the intermediate products industry, growth is high in the chemical sector and sector 5 (particularly high in the rubber subsector), average in sector 3 and almost nil in sector 2 (mining, construction materials, glass). Within the consumer goods industries, the rate is growing rapidly in sector 6 (parachemicals, pharmaceuticals), and is negative in the other sector 7 because of the subsectors leather and shoes and printing and publishing in particular.

On the other hand, the growth in the rates was very high for the three capital goods sectors: transportation equipment (rate rising from 34.6 per cent to 41.6 per cent), mechanical engineering (rate rising from 33.6 per cent to 41.5 per cent) and electrical engineering (28.1 per cent to 34.1 per cent).

The Table in Annexe 6 (p. 210) shows the development of exports, imports and trade balances for France with the main geographical areas of the world.[5] One can see that exports to Europe and Japan have increased more slowly since their share of the total has fallen by 4.8 per cent and 0.3 per cent respectively.

Although exports to the United States have increased slightly more than average, the most rapid growth has been:

— to the oil-producing countries: their share of total exports has increased by 1.5 per cent and is linked here with the rapid growth of imports from these countries, which they do not offset;
— to the countries of eastern Europe: their share has increased by 0.9 per cent;
— to all the other less developed countries: their share has increased by + 2.8 per cent, mainly for Africa (+ 1.7 per cent) and the free trade area (0.9 per cent).

Note also that between 1974 and 1977 there was a large trade deficit with Brazil and Spain.

These different developments of foreign trade can be explained in part by the characteristics of French multinationalisation as analysed by us on the basis of our sample for 1974 and for the period 1974-7. We propose the following interpretations:

1. *Multinational production by capital goods companies has permitted the growth of exports in these sectors.*
The companies in these sectors very often adopt a 'market strategy' with 'assembly production' for their production subsidiaries abroad. A typical example of this strategy is automobile construction and its exports of 'kits'. This partly explains the rapid growth of exports for these sectors, especially since a large number of new subsidiaries were set up between 1974 and 1977, according to our sample. The companies in these three sectors also have foreign subsidiaries whose production is reimported into France: hence the adverse effects on the trade balances of these sectors. However, these cases of 'production strategy' are relatively limited, and the predominant trend is towards a positive effect on foreign trade.

The recent development of operations to transfer technology without any legal control over the foreign plants is not incompatible with this trend, to the extent that exports are often associated with these new forms of operations abroad.

2. *This can explain the rapid growth in exports to the NICs and LDCs.*
Here we refer to countries where market strategies with assembly production, carried out by the companies in these sectors, are the most common, together with pure production strategies (which as we have seen often induce French exports). From this point of view, the rapid

growth of exports to these countries is largely due to sectors 8, 9 and 10, which the statistics confirm.

These two effects of the multinationalisation of French companies in the capital goods sectors seem to be a *specifically French characteristic*, related to both the geographical specialisation of plants in less developed countries, and a type of multinationalisation which is not yet very marked among French groups: they have rarely reached the stage of world-wide organisation, with international specialisation of operations and complex flows between French and foreign plants (corresponding for example in our typology in Table 3.7 to the 'international specialisation of operations', the upper level of production strategy). On the other hand, for example, American companies in the same sectors have frequently reached this stage, are more often multinational in the developed countries and in Europe, and their multinationalisation has less of an effect on American exports.

3. *The multinational production of intermediate products companies limits the growth of exports in these sectors.*

Indeed, we have seen that the strategy most often adopted by companies in these sectors is a strategy to gain access to the local market, with autonomous production, especially for the biggest subsidiaries located in the developed countries: this is the case for BSN, Lafarge, Schneider, Imétal, Vallourec, SGPM, Rhône-Poulenc and Michelin. We have found that the export rates for these sectors have increased very little: one would think that the weight of these big multinational groups with this type of production abroad would explain this development in part. In a report to the Economic and Social Council, P. Bataille pointed out, 'In the glass sector, the tendency for companies to develop their production capacity abroad more rapidly than their domestic capacity increases the tendency for the cover ratio to deteriorate.'[6] This is shown by the fact that SGPM's export rate rose from 17 per cent in 1974 to 18.6 per cent in 1978, which was an average increase. However, the growth of the group's French production has been slow, rising from 13 472 million francs to 15 380 million francs (+ 14 per cent) while production increased considerably abroad: from 7409 to 16 449 million francs (+ 122 per cent). Hence the effect of SGPM on the absolute amount of French exports was not proportionate to the group's growth. The fact that the BSN group does not clearly publish the amount of its exports is also significant. Our estimates based on figures from *Le Nouvel Economiste* show that its low exports increased more slowly than total operations, rising from 5.25 per cent of the group's French production in 1974 to 5 per cent in 1977. On the other hand, the exports of Rhône-Poulenc increased more rapidly (+ 57 per cent) than its production abroad (+ 47 per cent) between

1974 and 1977, while the export rate for national production rose from 28.3 per cent in 1974 to 41 per cent in 1977.

4. *This partly explains the deterioration of trade balances with developed countries.*
To the extent that the companies in these sectors are mainly multinationals, adopting the strategies indicated. . .

5. *The multinationalisation of textiles/clothing companies can explain the drop in the trade balance for this sector.*
Since the 'production strategy' predominates in this sector, this partly explains why the cover ratio of imports by exports for all consumer goods fell from 139 in 1974 to 129 in 1977, and also why the trade balance in the textiles/clothing branch fell from + 3605 million francs in 1974 to + 235 million francs in 1977. Simple imports of competing products, not manufactured by the subsidiaries of French companies, do however play an important part in this.

6. *The multinationalisation of companies in Asia can explain the poor trade balance with countries in this area.*
The operations of firms in the textiles/clothing sector and other sectors (Thomson, Essilor) in Asia can explain the small positive trade balance with this area (2132 million francs in 1977).

7. *The multinationalisation of French companies in Brazil and Spain can explain the trade deficits with these two countries.*
We have seen that in Spain and Brazil pure production strategies are common (Lainière de Roubaix in Brazil, Jaz, Renault and Citroën in Spain). At the same time, market strategies with assembly production are clearly becoming less and less important here as the local authorities are restricting imports by foreign subsidiaries setting up on their territory: there is an increasing integration of local production.[7]

THE MULTINATIONALISATION OF FRENCH COMPANIES:
A POSITIVE EFFECT ON FOREIGN TRADE WHICH
WILL GRADUALLY DECREASE

In conclusion, even though our statistical data, which are either only qualitative or are covered by secrecy (confidential survey), do not permit figures to be given for the above trends, we can see that the actual organisation structures for production abroad partly explain the development of sector exports and imports.

There is no single answer, as it would seem that in certain cases multinationalisation leads to exports and improves the foreign trade position, while in other cases, it has a zero or even negative effect on foreign trade. Having stated this, we can make two more general remarks.

First, we again find a division between sectors where foreign production corresponds above all to a search for competitiveness (sectors 7A, 8, 9 and 10) and sectors where multinationalisation is more a sign of competitiveness (sectors 2, 3, 4, 5, 6, 7B and 14C) (see Chapter 3). The latter do to some extent constitute the strong points of French industry, are mainly multinational in the developed countries, but with little effect on French exports. The former, which constitute the weak points of industry, are mainly multinational in the NICs and LDCs, mostly with a positive effect on exports. To some extent, the positive consequences of the locational spread of production on foreign trade are the opposite of the competitive position of industries at world level, which is a paradoxical result.

Second, looking more to the future, it is possible to anticipate that the multinationalisation of French companies will have a less and less marked favourable effect on foreign trade, particularly for companies in the three capital goods sectors (8, 9 and 10), for whom foreign production is often accompanied, even today, by large French exports. There are two trends behind this current development:

— as these companies reach a higher level of multinational development, with world-wide organisation, international specialisation of the operations of different subsidiaries and increasing production in the developed countries, transfers between foreign and French plants will become more and more complex, they will tend to balance one another out and the positive effect on French foreign trade will diminish (for Renault, we can mention the efforts to set up in the United States and the plan to produce engines in Portugal for reimportation into France[8]);

— the NICs and LDCs will make increasing demands for the restriction of imports by foreign subsidiaries established on their territory: for the multinational firms, the obligation to increase the integration of foreign production in these countries reduces French export opportunities and often requires compensatory reimports to France. This also applies to plants in the Eastern bloc, and to cases of transfer of technology to independent plants. The example of the car sector is significant for these developments. The same demands for the integration of foreign production[9] are being made for these increasingly common cases, analysed in Chapter 4, although they may be accompanied by French exports.

The present geographical relocation of the multinational operations of these companies is therefore often coupled with a reduction in the positive effect of their foreign operations on French foreign trade.

This question of the consequences of multinationalisation on the trade balance of the economy is very topical. Present economic policy is largely directed at ways of improving this trade balance. In addition, and as a result, the French government is backing French investment abroad where it improves the foreign trade position, in particular by permitting exports. The recent trends which we have identified are apparent in some of the present concerns of the multinationals themselves. In 1979, at a seminar on foreign investment, the CNPF demanded that the government abandon its criterion for backing direct 'export-promoting' investment abroad in favour of the criterion of 'investment as a vehicle of redeployment', taking into account 'the long-term effects on employment and the balance of payments.'[10] And in January 1981, in its report to the Economic and Social Council on 'French investment abroad and foreign investment in France', J. Ehrsam, chairman and managing director of Singer S. A., repeated a similar proposal, which was in fact noted in the resolution voted by the Council.[11] These demands formulated by company representatives confirm the trends we have already highlighted: because of the new phase reached by the multinational development of many large groups (world organisation etc.), and because of the increasing demands of the NICs and LDCs for local integration of the production of subsidiaries, the multinationalisation of French companies will increasingly be a way of improving their competitiveness, but its positive effects on foreign trade will increasingly diminish.[12]

NOTES

1   In an econometric study on 1446 Belgian exporting companies, H. Glesjer, A. Jacquemin and J. Petit, 1980, showed that the existence of foreign subsidiaries promoted exports. In France, a sub-study group at the Commissariat Général au Plan has carried out a study based in part on two French analyses by CEREM and the University of Pau and principally on studies concerning foreign economies. This assessment concludes that on the whole French investment abroad has a positive effect on France's trade balance. See: Commissariat Général au Plan, 1978.

2   Tables 3.6 and 3.7 give qualitative data which need to be quantified to measure what type of production abroad is the most important (in the frequent cases where the same French company adopts different strategies for spreading the location of production).

3   See Tables 3.6 and 3.7

4   See Savary, 1980, p. 634.

5   For a full analysis, we would need to compare the geographical destinations against the type of goods. This would for example show that the deficit with regard to developed countries is largely due to capital goods, and that these same goods are responsible for most of the surplus with the Eastern bloc, the Middle East, Africa and the free trade area.

6   P. Bataille, 1978, p. 758.

7   See C. V. Vaitsos and Ph. Saussay, 1980, for a study of the establishment of European multinationals in Greece, Portugal and Spain and their effects on foreign trade of these countries and the European economies.

8   One can assume that many very big American groups have reached this stage,

which would explain their low export rates (see *Fortune* magazine, 22 September 1980, for the ranking of the top fifty American exporters, and Table I.4 for the overall export rate of the United States).

9   See the excellent study of the car sector in CNPF, 1979-1, pp. 15-37.
10 Introductory report of committee 1. Proposal taken up by F. Giscard d'Estaing, chairman of the BFCE, and emphasised in summing up the seminar by G. Perebeau, see CNPF, 1979-3, pp. 133 and 145.
11 J. Ehrsam, 1981, p. 118, and Resolution of the Council, p. 13.
12 An analysis of all the files examined by the Committee on foreign investment (Treasury) between 1972 and 1978 drew a distinction between three types of French investment abroad:

(1) Investment resulting directly in exports intended to promote either the marketing of French exports or the local manufacture of certain parts for these exports;
(2) Investment resulting indirectly in exports because:
    (a) it relates to certain ranges of products which will continue to be manufactured in France;
    (b) its existence gives the local buyer confidence and promotes other French sales;
    (c) French exports are used for one or two years in the.actual composition of the investment to be made;
(3) Investment for which no link with exports is in any way apparent.

In spite of the difficulties inherent in this type of classification, the study shows that over this period, 30 per cent of total investment corresponded to the first type, 30 per cent to the second and 40 per cent to the third. Between 1972 and 1978 cases with an indirect impact (second type) increased considerably. The link between foreign production and exports is therefore becoming less and less marked (see M. C. Kaplan, 1979, volume 1, Annexe Table 9).

7 Multinationalisation and Employment

What are the specific effects of the multinationalisation of French companies on employment in France?

This is a particularly controversial question at a time when, simultaneously, the French economy is becoming much more multinational and industrial employment is falling. 1974 was a turning point: while industrial employment had increased to reach 5 245 600 jobs at the end of 1974, it has fallen each year since then: 235 600 jobs were lost in three years. This drop has been general in all sectors, except for car construction, and very high in some of them which were hard hit by the crisis, such as textiles (−85 000 jobs in three years[1]). These trends have continued since 1977 and there have also been job cutbacks in the car sector in France in 1980 and 1981.[2]

There are two possible but conflicting answers to this question:

— the multinationals, by spreading the location of their production, are causing job losses in France, either through the transfer of production, the non-growth of production, or through cutbacks as a result of competition by foreign reimported products. This is the argument, for example, of the trade union organisations.

— the multinationals, which are more competitive because of their activity abroad, are the only companies creating jobs in France, if only because of related exports, work on foreign sites, induced operations in the research laboratories and all the jobs produced in the long term by the improvement in competitiveness, financial results, and technical and commercial know-how. This is the argument of the companies and the employers' organisations.[3]

Unfortunately these two assertions are not based on detailed analyses and no study has to our knowledge examined the real impact of production abroad on employment in France.[4] This is due primarily to the lack of official statistical data and surveys relating to the operations of French multinationals. However, the very difficulties involved in making such a study can also explain its absence. We have already pointed out how difficult it was to say whether, in general, French exports could have substituted for production operation abroad to gain access to a market. This is the essential point at issue.

In fact, a study of the consequences of multinationalisation on employment in France could try to draw a distinction between:

— cases where this locational spread has a positive effect on employment in France:
  (a) when it promotes French exports of semi-finished products for processing, or finished products;
  (b) when it improves the competitiveness of companies.
— cases where the locational spread has a negative effect on employment in France;
  (a) when it substitutes for potential exports;
  (b) when it corresponds to a real transfer of French production abroad, immediately or as a result of competition, or when in the long term it limits the growth of French production.

But we come up against the problems of substituting exports for foreign production. In addition, a study of this type is made all the more complex as there are two essential phenomena, other than multinationalisation and exports, also involved in changing employment patterns in France. The economic crisis in France has led to a reduction in activity and hence job losses. It has also accentuated the trend towards the resultant productivity investments and employment cutbacks. Companies, particularly the biggest of them, are adopting a particular method of growth, that of the take-over (or disposal) of existing companies, or external growth. These two phenomena make it very difficult to interpret employment trends in France for a given company or group of companies. On the basis of the consolidated data published by companies, changes in the extent of consolidation can alter employment figures, without there being any change in the operations under the economic control of the group. This further distorts the picture. In particular we lack the precise figures which will give us a better idea of the impact of multinationalisation on employment in France. We shall try here to present original factual data:

— from a survey on employment in France and abroad carried out among the companies in our sample we shall analyse the development between 1974 and 1977 of employment figures for seventy-seven French multinational companies;
— from our surveys and results relating to the organisation structures for foreign production, already set out in Chapter 3, we propose a set of interpretations: we shall try to relate the specific consequences on employment in France to each strategy for activity abroad.

THE FACTS: THE DEVELOPMENT OF EMPLOYMENT
IN FRANCE AND ABROAD FOR SEVENTY-SEVEN
MULTINATIONAL COMPANIES[5]

Increase in the Rate of Employment Abroad

Table 7.1(a) shows how for sixty-seven industrial companies employment in France increased by + 9.4 per cent between 1974 and 1977, while employment abroad increased by + 26.4 per cent: the rate of employment abroad rose from 22.5 to 25.2 per cent in three years. The economic crisis was therefore accompanied by an increase in the multinationalisation of French industrial companies, as we have already noted (Chapter 4). For companies in building and public works the trend is even more marked, as these companies, which in 1974 were less multinational, have expanded considerably abroad, while for the majority of them the number of their employees in France has fallen. Table 7.1(b) shows the situation in the building and public works sector.

We shall illustrate further the importance of the external growth operations carried out in France by groups such as Peugeot, Renault and Thomson. As regards the overall result which we are commenting on here, these operations obscure the fact that very many companies have suffered very big cutbacks in jobs in France. These large cutbacks have, as we shall see, also affected the big European subsidiaries of groups such as BSN, Penarroya and Vallourec. The employment cutbacks of these three groups abroad obscure the many other jobs created abroad, and if they are excluded employment abroad then increases considerably more, as does the rate of multinationalisation (from 20.6 per cent to 24 per cent).

If we pick out twenty-four large groups[6] which in 1974 each employed a total of over 10 000 people, Table 7.1(a) shows that these groups became more multinational between 1974 and 1977, but to a lesser extent than the other groups. In fact, their rate of employment abroad only increased by + 2.3 per cent as against + 4.7 per cent. This is primarily a result of the job cutbacks of certain big European subsidiaries of BSN, Vallourec and Penarroya, as well as the real dynamism of the multinationalisation of medium-sized groups such as Rossignol, Essilor, Delalande, Fichet-Bauche, Rousselot, Ciments Français, Nordon, Amrep and Jaeger, a dynamism which represents a departure from the stable or falling rates of multinationalisation for big groups such as Renault, Poclain, L'Oréal and Hachette (which is also a result of the rapid external growth of some of these groups in France). However, even though their share is falling slightly, the biggest groups still account for a massive proportion of total employment abroad, 94 per cent in 1974 and 93.1 per cent in 1977.

Table 7.1(a) Trend of employment in France and abroad for
sixty-seven French multinational companies, overall
results (total employees in 1974 and 1977 for
67 industrial companies)

		Employees France	Employees abroad		Total employees
			Total	%	
Total companies	1974	975 892	284 190	22.5	1 260 082
	1977	1 067 548	359 462	25.2	1 427 010
	change	+91 676			
		+9.4%	+26.4%	+2.7	
Total companies	1974	913 735	237 047	20.6	1 150 782
excluding BSN,	1977	1 007 983	319 001	24	1 326 984
Penarroya and	change	+10.3%	+34.6%	+3.4	
Vallourec					
24 large	1974	851 255	267 152	23.9	1 118 407
groups*	1977	944 458	334 735	26.2	1 279 193
	change			+2.3	
38 smaller	1974	124 637	17 038	12	141 675
groups†	1977	123 090	24 735	16.7	147 825
	change			+4.7	

*Groups of over 10 000 employees in 1974, including Merlin Gerin and fraction of Schneider group only.
†Including Jaz, groups of less than 10 000 employees in 1974 (France + abroad).

Table 7.1(b) Employees France/abroad of companies in the building and
public works sector

		Employees France	Employees abroad (subsidiaries + sites) %		Total employees
Total	1974	87 664	19 779	18.4	107 443
10 companies*	1977	87 820	46 298	34.5	134 118
	change	+156	+26 511	+16.1	
Total	1974	61 900	15 732	28.3	77 632
8 companies	1977	56 158	31 499	35.9	87 657
(excluding SPIE	change	−5 742	+15 767	+7.6	
and SGE)†					

*A. Cochery, Coignet, SPIE Batignolles, Saunier Duval, Bouygues, Routière Colas, SAE, SGE, Dragages et TP, Fougerolle.
†For these two companies growth in France is due in part to the electro-nuclear programme.

For the Majority of Sectors and Firms: Reduction of Employment in France and Increase Abroad

An examination of the employment trends for seventy-seven companies grouped by main sectors of activity (Table 7.2) shows that for nine sectors out of thirteen employment fell in France between 1974 and 1977, which confirms the trends for the economy as a whole.

Because of the small number of companies considered, the development of some big groups obscures the general trends. For instance, the growth of employment in France in sector 5 is due to Michelin which created 18 200 jobs in France: if this group is taken out, employment for other firms falls in France (for the sector, the total drop

Table 7.2 The trend of employment in France and abroad for French multinational companies: typology according to sectors (based on the data of 77 companies in industry and building and public works)

		Employment in France 1977/1974	
		Reduction	Increase
Employment abroad 1977/1974	Reduction	I 2 building mat. glass (41.3% → 41.6%) 6 parachemicals/pharmaceuticals (44.2% → 43.7%) 14 agr./food industry (17.5% → 18.4%)	II
	Increase	III 3 iron & steel, metallurgy (15.5% → 19.4%) 4 chemicals (30.7% → 33.8%) 7A textiles (15.9% → 39.4%) 8 mechanical engineering (17.2% → 25.4%) 9 electrical, electronic engineering (9.5% → 11.3%) 11 building and P. Works, excluding SPIE and SGE (28.3% → 35.9%)	IV 10 transport. equipment (19.6% → 20.6%) 5 paper, rubber, plastics (39.7% → 45.3%) 7B consumer goods (51.1% → 56.9%)

Note: We have noted in parentheses the trend of the employment rate abroad between 1974 and 1977. The exclusion of BSN, for which there were big job cutbacks by the foreign subsidiaries, which distorts the trend, would put sectors 2 and 14 in box III, that is the box for the sectors where the number of employees abroad is increasing.

The exclusion of Michelin, with Sommer the only company in the sector to increase its French employees, would put sector 5 in box III.

in employment was 16 700 jobs, according to INSEE). Similarly, the data for sector 7B only relate to two companies, Bic and Rossignol, which have undergone rapid internal and external growth in France, and are not therefore representative of a general trend in this sector. On the other hand, the growth in the number of employees in sector 10 ties up with the overall economic trend and is a result of the internal and in particular external growth of Renault and Peugeot (in fact Chausson, Motobécane and Jaeger cut back their French employees).

A comparison of job cutbacks in France between 1974 and 1977, for our sample and for all French companies, is given in Table 7.3.

Table 7.3 Employment in France between 1974 and 1977 for 67 multinational companies and for all companies by sectors

		Changes in employment in France between 1974 and 1977 as a percentage/employment in 1974	
		All French companies	67 multinational companies
2	Construction materials, glass	−6.3	−9
3	Iron and steel, metallurgy	−3.7	−4
4	Basic chemicals–fibres	−3.7	−10.6
5	Paper, cardboard, rubber, plastic	−4.4	+5.8
6	Parachemicals, pharmaceuticals	−0.8	−5
7A	Textiles, clothing	−12	−13.5
8	Mechanical engineering	−5.3	−11.5
9	Electrical and electronic engineering	−1.6	−1.2
10A	Land transportation equipment	+3.9	+43.2

Source: for the 67 companies, survey by Savary, 1980; for all companies, INSEE collection, series No. 76, July 1979.

The multinationals are therefore in general cutting back jobs in France more than French companies as a whole—because the multinational groups are more involved in world-wide competition as part of a move to adapt, restructure and invest to be competitive. But does not the locational spread of production increase job cutbacks in France? A characteristic example is the Rhône-Poulenc group, which between 1974 and 1977 cut back jobs in France by 11.2 per cent compared with 3.7 per cent for the sector as a whole.[7] The trend is all the more marked as the internal growth of Michelin and the internal and external growth of Renault and Peugeot account on their own for the favourable trend for employment in France found for the sample.

These job cutbacks in France are accompanied by the growth of employment controlled by firms abroad, embracing a total of eight sectors, for five of which employment is falling in France. This growth in employment abroad is a general phenomenon, which is obscured here for two sectors (sectors 2 and 14) by the job cutbacks of the big European subsidiaries of BSN, both in glass and in fresh products. The exclusion of BSN shows that the construction materials sub-sector (five companies) has increased employment abroad by 1209 jobs. The same applies for sector 14 where the increasing activity of GMP in Africa is hidden by the job cutbacks of BSN in Europe. Hence the increase in the sectoral rates of employment abroad compared with total employment: between 1974 and 1977 these rates increased for almost all sectors (shown in parentheses in Table 7.2).

These phenomena do without doubt show the main trends, although the sectoral compositions give very great weight to the big companies. The real picture varies considerably from this (Table 7.4). Most of the companies are in box III: there was a reduction in employment in France and an increase abroad between 1974 and 1977. For Rhône-Poulenc, Usinor and Rochette Cenpa, growth abroad was only small but the drop in France was very large. This trend is therefore very marked as it appears both at sector and at company level. It is especially marked as it is obscured by the frequent take-overs of existing companies in France. These external growth operations limit the effects of the development of employment in France which would be apparent 'with constant structures'—a capital point in our analysis. To take one example, the staff in France of the Lafarge group was reduced by 674 people between 1974 and 1977. But in 1976 Lafarge took over Rigips-France (plasterboard) and Promonta (plaster tiles), and in 1977 it absorbed Ciments du Sud-Ouest (335 people). With equal structures, the reduction in employment in France would therefore have been much greater. It is basically the figures at whole branch level which show the most remarkable developments as these figures are not influenced by the concentration of companies, at least not in the short term.

Box I includes cases of reductions in employment abroad already mentioned, mostly due to job cutbacks in industrial subsidiaries in Europe, suffering from the same difficulties as French companies. This is the case for the BSN glass and fresh products factories, those of L'Oréal in Europe and Crouzet (but here production jobs are increasing). Finally for Hutchinson, where the cutbacks in France were much greater, the rate of employment abroad is still rising. An example of these difficulties in European subsidiaries is given by Cérabati. In 1978, this company had to make 410 people redundant in France and jobs had already been cut back from 2634 in 1974 to 1993 in 1977. The difficulties due to the market situation also affected the Belgian subsidiary, which showed a deficit in 1977 and whose turnover was stagnating, and the Luxembourg subsidiary, which showed a deficit in 1977 and 1978, and which had to be turned over partly to produce glazed

Table 7.4 Trend of employment in France and abroad for 67 French
multinational companies: typology of situations

			Employment in France, 1974–7	
			Reduction	Increase
Employment abroad 1974–7	Reduction	I	Poclain BSN (% ↓) Cérabati (% ↓) Hutchinson (% ↑) L'Oréal (% ↓)	II P. M. Labinal (EG) Penarroya
	Small increase	III	Rhône-Poulenc Usinor Rochette-Cenpa	IV Vallourec (EG % ↓) Olida Labaz (EG % ↓)
	Large increase		Lafarge – Ciments français – C. Vicat – Salins du Midi – Quartz Silice – Carnaud – I. F. Pompey – Schneider* – Arjomari Prioux — Cellulose — Charfa – Delalande – Crouzet – Jaz – Amrep – Nordon – Frankel – HES – CGE – Saft – Moulinex – Télé- mécanique – Chausson – Motobécane – Acier, outillage – Peugeot – Lainière Roubaix – Vitos – Jaeger†	Fichet–Bauche (% ↑) Michelin (% ↑) EG Rousselot (% ↑) Moët (% ↑) Imétal (% ↑) Sommer (EG % ↓) Bic (EG % ↑) Rossignol (% ↑) Engrenages (EG % ↓) Essilor (% ↑) Seb (% ↑, EG) GMP Thomson (% ↓, EG) CGR (% ↑) Merlin Gerin (% ↑) Cycles Peugeot, Peugeot group (% ↑, EG) Renault group (% ↓, EG)

Note: (% ↑) or (% ↓) indicates a rising or falling rate of employment abroad; EG: external growth.
  *Iron and steel, metallurgy sectors only.
  †All companies in the building and public works sector would be here, except for SPIE and SGE.
Source: survey J. Savary, 1980.

earthenware flooring (with modernisation: in these two subsidiaries job cutbacks were also made—source: 1978 report). The case of Penarroya is also clear: its subsidiaries in Spain, Greece and Italy which produce lead and zinc (metals) lost 750 jobs in three years. They are suffering from 'the falling consumption of lead in Spain, as in the rest of the world', the 'world zinc crisis', the big increases in costs due to inflation in Spain, 'excessively high' costs in Italy, and insufficient diversification (source: company reports).

Finally, the total employment in eighteen companies had increased both in France and abroad, which means employment rates abroad which are either rising or falling. A distinction can be made between two groups of companies depending on the way in which jobs are created in France:

— For certain firms the growth of employment in France is essentially due to the growth of the existing plants or the setting up of new factories. Jobs are then created in the economy. This either means that the firm is dynamic or its position on the market is growing rapidly, or both. In almost all these cases it should however be noted that employment abroad is increasing faster than in France. The typical case is Michelin which created 8200 jobs in France and 16 600 abroad. And these really are new jobs. This category includes, sometimes for part of their employees, Skis Rossignol, CGR, the Thomson group, part of the Renault and Peugeot groups, Rousselot, Fichet-Bauche, Essilor, Imétal, GMP, with the last three simply maintaining employment levels in France.

— For other firms, the growth of employment in France is primarily due to take-overs of companies, hence operations which do not create employment in the economy and which hide job cutbacks in existing plants. This category includes Bic, Olida, Engrenages et Réducteurs, Labaz, Vallourec and Sommer-Allibert, Seb, Thomson and the Peugeot and Renault groups, with rapid parallel growth in the case of the last five groups.

Employment in the Labaz group in France has risen from 2300 jobs to 2543 jobs. This group has however made 'great efforts to improve productivity', disposed of two small diversified subsidiaries and in particular taken control of a company producing pharmaceuticals (Février Decoisy Champion in 1976) and a sterilisation equipment company (Thenot S.A. in 1977). With identical structures, employment in France has then certainly fallen, especially since the medical equipment division has set up a subsidiary in Malta, producing simple equipment which is reimported into France, and which has easily been able to substitute for part of the former production of Dubesnard-Hospital in France. We could also mention the take-overs in 1976 by Bic of Dim-Rosy and Colroy, SFMO in 1977 by Seb, LMT and Générale de téléphones Ericsson in 1977 by Thomson (11 451 jobs), Engrenages Dugrand in 1977 by Engrenages et Réducteurs, Triconfort and Claritex in 1976, and Rudloff in 1975 by Sommer-Allibert (+ 250 jobs approximately with a change in France of + 825 jobs), Citroën by Peugeot (in 1977 the Citroën car company employed 55 600 people while the number of employees in the Peugeot group in France has increased by 71 400).

Three Essential Conclusions

1. Employment rates abroad for French multinationals increased between 1974 and 1977, either because employment abroad increased faster than employment in France, or because it increased while employment in France fell. The only cases where employment rates abroad fell were due to:

— rapid external growth in France (Thomson);
— rapid external and internal growth in France (Renault, Labaz, Sommer);
— big job cutbacks by European subsidiaries (Vallourec, BSN, Penarroya, Cérabati and L'Oréal).

2. From the point of view of the number of jobs in France, in absolute terms, these:

— are falling in France for the majority of firms (39 out of 67) and the majority of sectors, where they are not simply remaining stable (Imétal, Essilor and GMP). Even big groups such as Rhône-Poulenc, CGE, Lafarge, Schneider, Télémécanique and Jaeger are cutting back on jobs in France (in spite of certain external growth operations);
— when they are increasing, they are not generally increasing as fast as the jobs of groups abroad, except in the three situations mentioned in point 1;
— when they are increasing, this is often because of companies being taken over, without any net creation of jobs.

3. There are, then, three phenomena which are essential in explaining employment trends in France and abroad:

— the economic crisis and the resultant rationalisation operations are causing job cutbacks in France and in European subsidiaries;
— French groups often develop in France by external growth, which then hides the general trend towards reductions in employment levels;
— all the multinational companies are becoming more multinational, hence there is an increase in numbers of employees controlled abroad.

MULTINATIONALISATION STRATEGIES AND EMPLOYMENT IN FRANCE

The question is then: does the very development of activity abroad result in job cutbacks in France? We can try to answer this question by looking at the types of organisation of production abroad, or strategies. The answers will not however be simple ones. In particular we need to ask, for each case of foreign production, whether the market could have been reached by French exports.

If a definite answer can be given to this difficult question, it would then be possible to calculate the positive effect on employment in France of a given amount of exports induced by foreign production— or the negative effect resulting from imports or a reduction in exports as a result of the locational spread of production. A table of inter-industry transfers in job-equivalents would enable the direct and indirect effects of foreign production on employment in France to be calculated.[8] We already know that it is very difficult to come to any conclusion on this possibility of substitution.

It can be assumed that all cases of 'pure production strategy' have an adverse effect on employment in France: either as a result of shutting down manufacturing in France to spread the location, the non-development of this production, or competition from imported foreign products. However, there are as yet few cases of this for French multi-nationals, though it is common in sectors 8, 9, 10 and in particular 7A, textiles/clothing. Certainly in the latter sector, the job cutbacks in France can be most clearly attributed to the multinationalisation of French companies.

For all cases of market strategy, the effect of production abroad on employment in France is difficult to interpret. The market strategy with autonomous production has few positive effects (increased profits, greater competitive capacity, technological and market know-how) or negative effects (reduction in financial resources, moving centres of interest). However, if one assumes that these foreign markets could have been supplied with French exports, then the locational spread of production substitutes for potential exports, and hence jobs in France. This is common for companies in sectors 2, 3, 4, 5, 6 and 7B and for their big subsidiaries located in the developed countries; we have already mentioned that the low growth of exports in these sectors, and to these countries, could be a result of the multinationalisa-tion of companies. We find here (Table 7.1) that the reduction of jobs in France in these sectors is no less than it is in sectors where the strategies are different and which are more often located abroad in the NICs and LDCs (sectors 8, 9 and 10). Does this not indicate that when these companies spread the location of production this reduces exports and hence jobs in France?

The market strategy with assembly production does on the other hand, have a positive effect on employment in France, especially if one considers that it would be impossible to export the finished pro-duct directly. The constraints of transport costs, customs barriers and the desire of the host countries to restrict imports in favour of local industrialisation frequently confirm this hypothesis. In this respect, two sectors whose foreign subsidiaries very often adopt this type of strategy have had few (−1.6 per cent for sector 9) or no (+ 3.9 per cent for sector 10) job cutbacks in France. However, for sector 8, mechanical engineering, the job cutbacks have been among the biggest (−5.3 per cent), although the multinational companies also often spread the location of their production and export semi-finished products for assembly. Is this initial interpretation correct or not?

Conversely, for assembly production, part of the production is carried out abroad, or at least the assembly operation, and often the production of certain parts, directly or by local subcontractors. If we assume that this production could have been carried out in France, and the foreign market supplied by exports of finished products, then this type of multinationalisation means job losses in France. This is especially true when the production stages relocated are very labour-intensive.

We do, then, arrive at certain interpretations. It is nevertheless difficult to deduce any distinct and certain consequences on employment in France from sectoral specialisations in the adoption of different multinational strategies.

A study of multinational strategies is not enough to answer the question asked. It has, however, highlighted the international division of labour which is almost always the reason behind production in the NICs and LDCs. By its very nature this IDL means that capital-intensive production, which does not create many jobs, is reserved for the developed countries and France, while in the NICs and LDCs it leads to the setting up of plants producing products or stages of production which are very labour-intensive. Production in the NICs and LDCs does, then, almost always imply more labour-intensive production than that reserved for France. In this sense the IDL by its very structure tends to distribute operations internationally to the disadvantage of employment in France.

CRISIS, COMPETITION AND MULTINATIONALISATION EXPLAIN JOB CUTBACKS IN FRANCE

Hence, in the majority of sectors and the majority of companies, employment in France is falling and employment abroad is increasing. This confirms the national statistics: between 1974 and 1977 industry lost 235 600 jobs. Over the same period, the sixty-seven multinational companies studied here saw a faster decrease in jobs, in many sectors, than that for all companies together, while the number of employees abroad increased by 75 272 jobs. If one could observe all French companies, one would note an even greater positive trend in the number of employees abroad. France would then be in a similar position to that of West Germany (Table 7.5).

Job cutbacks in France have, however, come later (after 1974) than in West Germany (before 1974) and were still relatively small between 1974 and 1977 (−235 600 jobs compared with −943 000 in West

Table 7.5 Employment in West Germany and abroad

Employees in industry	1971	1975
Number of workers in West Germany	8 407 000	7 464 000
Number of workers in the foreign subsidiaries of German companies	905 000	1 480 000

Source: F. Frobel, J. Heinrichs and O. Kreye, 1978.

Germany). Not all the jobs created abroad could have been created in France. But there is a dual movement in the reduction of employees in France and the increase in employees abroad which is very marked.

It is, however, essential to point out one other result. This is the highlighting of job cutbacks in the European subsidiaries of Vallourec, BSN and Penarroya, which confirms that the economic crisis brings with it these cutbacks in all the developed countries, just as in France. Competitive industries are created by cutting back jobs in French plants, in conjunction with efforts to rationalise and improve productivity. In this sense the statement by H. Couffin[9] to the effect that the same groups investing in the United States are those investing in France is true. Often investment in France does not result in the creation of employment; on the contrary.[10] Finally, it is the widespread competition and the economic crisis accentuating it which also cause cutbacks in employment in France.

When multinational production is carried out in Third World countries, this also tends structurally to reduce employment in France, as the production and stages of production which are relocated are the very ones which are the most labour-intensive.

The economic crisis does then indirectly cause job cutbacks in France in that it encourages firms to become multinational, and it is also apparent in the demands of the Third World for integrated production by subsidiaries of multinational companies. This limits related exports and the corresponding jobs.

In recent times, the trend of employment in France has therefore been a result of the combination of three inter-related processes: widespread competition, the world economic crisis from its two different aspects within the developed countries and the Third World, and the multinationalisation of companies with its corresponding international division of operations.

NOTES

1 Source: INSEE collections, Series C No. 76, July 1979.
2 While the number of employees of Fiat in Italy and Volkswagen in West Germany had already fallen between 1973 and 1977. See R. B. Cohen, 1980.

3　See, for example, the 'Journée de l'investissement français à l'étranger' where this subject was of primary importance: CNPF, 1979-1, and CNPF, 1979-3. See also J. Ehrsam, 1981, p. 113. For a presentation of the two arguments, see Savary, 1980, pp. 656 ff. For a summary of the information available, mainly in the United States, see ILO, 1973, pp. 27 ff., and B. Liebhaberg, 1980, which extends the analysis to industrial relations.

4　See Y. Berthelot, 1980, and Berthelot and Tardy, 1978, who analyse the effect of trade with the Third World (exports and imports) on industrial employment in France: the reports relate only to a single area of the world economy and the effect of the locational spread of production is not examined. However, the whole problem is an interesting one, as is the method of calculating the effects of trade on employment, as we shall see that the effect of production abroad on employment in France can be studied in terms of substituting for potential exports. See also a critical assessment of the work relating to the effects of foreign trade on employment by Ph. Hugon, 1980. Finally, see the recent article by F. Gèze, 1981.

5　For some results by company and a more detailed analysis, see Savary, 1980, pp. 643 ff. In B. Soulage, 1981, pp. 413 ff., there is also an analysis of the development of employment in seventeen big French industrial groups, supplemented by an interesting study of their 'social policies'.

6　These are Chausson, Peugeot, Renault, Lainière de Roubaix, Hachette, Poclain, CGE, Moulinex, Thomson, Télémécanique, Merlin Gerin, Hutchinson, Michelin, Cellulose du Pin, L'Oréal, Schneider S.A. (iron and steel and metallurgy sector), Vallourec, Imétal, Rhône-Poulenc, BSN, Lafarge, Carnaud, Usinor and Bic.

7　For Rhône-Poulenc the movement has continued, as it is anticipated that in 1982 2600 employees will be sufficient in R. P. Textile to achieve a turnover of 2000 million francs, while in 1977 13 200 were needed for 3000 million francs: the productivity gain is from 1 to 4 (*Le Nouvel Economiste*, No. 271, 2 February 1981).

8　See A. Tiano, *Le Monde*, 16 October 1979, and the articles quoted by Berthelot, 1980, and P. Hugon, 1980.

9　H. Couffin, 'Il faut investir aux Etats-Unis', *Le Monde*, 15 May 1979.

10　See for example on the subject of innovations which reduce employment within the big textile companies the article by F. Clairmonte, 1981.

8 Development and Performance of Multinationals

French companies always consider the consequences of their production abroad on French companies to be positive in the short or long term.[1] From the point of view of the nation, on the other hand, the consequences on exports and employment may be nil or even negative. This type of conflict between the objects of companies and the collective interest is a common economic reality and its raises problems with regard to economic policy: for example, the debate on the choice of criteria for backing investment abroad.

The multinationalisation of French companies also has very different consequences depending on the geographical area of its location: in the developed countries the positive consequences on exports and employment are less marked, and the consequences on profitability are longer term. In the less developed countries, the positive effects of multinationalisation are more marked and more immediate. A change in location does, then, on the whole mean a change in the consequences.

In view of the current development of the multinationalisation of French companies, what will the consequences of this multinationalisation be in the future? A marked change in the trend is predicted because of the joint effect of the following developments:

— increase in the multinationalisation of companies which are already multinational;
— relocation of foreign operations on the developed countries, or some of the big NICs such as Brazil;
— new forms of operation in the NICs and LDCs, by means of transfer of technology without any legal control over the production units;
— increasing demands of the NICs and LDCs, relating to the local integration of the production of foreign subsidiaries, hence restriction of their imports;
— for certain companies, frequent use of the 'pure production strategy' with the extent of this trend being uncertain.

As regards profitability, these developments, in particular relocation to the developed countries, and the new forms of operations in the other countries will mean a reduction in the short-term gains. Only the development of the 'pure production strategy' will, for certain firms and certain sectors, mean an immediate improvement in competitiveness. Multinational production will increasingly form part of a long-term development strategy to spread production and sales world-wide, at least for the biggest French groups. There will be a growing distinction between them and companies with little or no multinational development, through their organisation and the position which it will help them to achieve in world competition. This distinction will also be more and more marked with regard to competitiveness and profitability.

As regards exports, present developments will mean that the locational spread of production will in future have either positive or limited effects, or be accompanied by parallel increases in imports (see on this subject Chapter 6, p. 118).

Finally, the effects on employment, because of the very reduction in the positive effects on exports, will also be less and less important. The spread of multinational companies in the developed countries will in fact be for market strategies with autonomous production with no effect on employment, or strategies of international specialisation with high reciprocal transfers and with the positive and negative effects on employment offsetting one another. In the other countries, the NICs and the LDCs, the growing integration of foreign production will also limit the direct positive effects on employment.

A major trend is therefore becoming apparent. In the future the multinationalisation of French companies will correspond more and more to a search by groups for competitiveness within their branch at world level. But the international organisation of production which they will implement directly will be located primarily in the developed countries, because in the NICs and LDCs operations will relate to transfers of technology, subcontracting or subsidiaries with integrated production. This organisation will have limited positive or even negative effects on foreign trade and employment in France.

One other consequence of French investment abroad is essential from the point of view of the nation: the financial consequences as regards effects on the balance of payments. Are the outgoing flows of funds more than compensated for by the flows being repatriated? Studying the 'foreign exchange balance' of certain French multinational groups, M. C. Kaplan showed that, although the position differed considerably from one company to another, for the majority of them establishment abroad had had a positive impact on the French balance of payments. This effect should become more pronounced as the many recently created foreign subsidiaries come to maturity, for in the future they will finance themselves to a greater degree and show a profit. It could, on the other hand, be reduced when new plants are set up.[2] Without it being possible here to develop an analysis made difficult by the confidential nature of the little information available, we can stress that the consequences of French investment abroad on the balance of payments are not always positive.

After analysing the consequences of the multinationalisation of French companies, we have to give a summary of this multinationalisation, as it results from the three parts of our study: what is the overall multinationalisation process?

NOTES

1 An extreme position, but one which emphasises these conflicting points of view, is expressed by C. de Benedetti, Vice-Chairman of Olivetti, at a dinner to discuss the 'Journées de l'investissement à l'étranger', organised by the CNPF: 'The role of an industrialist is to create work where it is economically and socially useful to do so', CNPF, 1979-3, p. 21.
2 M. C. Kaplan, 1979.

9 The Multinationalisation of French Companies: an Interactive Process

Exports, production abroad: it is, of course, the companies who make the decisions. However, the structure of the French and the world economy and the economic crisis are also involved in these decisions. They are not therefore 'free' choices by the companies, but are part of *an overall process* of an interactive nature, which at the end of this study we can sum up as follows:

1. Two main structural characteristics of the French economy are involved. The concentration of production facilities encourages companies to look abroad for growth when this is restricted by the oligopolistic market structure and the dominant position of firms on these markets. This explains why French multinational firms are almost always in this position of domination on the domestic market. It also shows the parallel nature of the movement to concentrate French production facilities, which has been very intense over the last sixty years, and the expansion of firms by means of exporting and international production. On the other hand, the subsidiaries of foreign groups in France in general export very little and produce little or nothing abroad, so that foreign penetration of the French economy then limits export levels and the 'downstream' multinationalisation of this economy.

2. The structural characteristic of the world economy, that is the disparities in development, are also essential to an understanding of the multinationalisation of French companies. The large size of the markets in the developed countries explains why companies set up in these countries in order to increase their outlets and improve their shares of the market and their overall growth: this is an essential choice for French firms, for whom 59 per cent of their foreign investments were located in developed Europe and North America in 1974. The lower production costs, the narrowness of the markets and the lack of industrial competition in the NICs and LDCs explain why companies set up in these countries, not only to find outlets but in order to reduce their production costs. In both cases, multinationalisation, which is based on the structures of the world economy, interacts with them. The locational spread to the NICs and LDCs, because of

the low development of these countries, contributes to maintaining this disparity in development through the action of the international division of operations implemented by the multinational companies. The locational spread to the developed countries, in an attempt to increase the shares of the market controlled, takes competition right to the heart of these economies, reduces the number of companies in the branch and increases economic concentration: competition becomes world-wide, is carried out between bigger and bigger groups, but is not for all this any less intensive.

3. The consequences of multinationalisation on companies, that is increased competitiveness, profitability and sometimes exports, can all be considered as indirect causes of multinationalisation. These consequences vary in intensity and nature depending on the area of establishment and the strategy adopted: in this sense they are also linked to disparities in the world economy. Finally, as multinationalisation increases the growth and competitiveness of companies, it accentuates the movement towards concentration of French industry, and the very trends towards multinationalisation.

4. The world economic crisis finally has a conflicting effect on multinationalisation: while the reduction in the growth of the developed economies leads to a search for operations in the Third World, the new demands of the NICs and the LDCs lead French companies to intensify their multinationalisation of course, but by adopting new forms of operation in the Third World countries which limit the risks and also the opportunities for gain, and relocating the establishment of operations under direct control (subsidiaries) to the developed countries.

In our study of French companies we have brought to light an overall process of multinationalisation which must be verified for all the Western developed economies: the concentration of production facilities, the interpenetration of the economies due to reciprocal international investments, the disparities in the world economy and the economic crisis form the basis for the multinationalisation for all these economies.

Our study has only related to the multinationalisation of French industrial companies. We have omitted the international expansion of the banking groups, which is also very important,[1] and which in particular is one of the explanatory factors for the expansion of industrial firms outside France, and the establishment of foreign groups in France.[2] In view of the existence and weight of the big financial groups, which are themselves very international, it would have been useful to analyse their influence on the internationalisation of industrial companies. O. Pastré has already done this for the American economy[3] and M. Sagou has just done it for the French economy in a remarkable study on the financial group Paribas.[4] These groups can be regarded as 'decision centres where the different functions are coordinated on a national and world level in order to exploit individual decentralised capital to the maximum.'[5] Our study has therefore to some extent been only a preliminary observation, of the industrial firms, and has not analysed the role of the banking and financial groups in controlling the multinationalisation of the developed economies.

NOTES

1 See for example B. Marois, 1979-2, Ch. Barrère, 1974, Part 3, Chapter VI, C. Sauviat, 1981.
2 See on this second point O. Pastré, 1979, Chapter II, and J. Savary, 1980, pp. 394 ff.; W. Andreff and O. Pastré, 1979; and more generally the conference organised in 1979 by Cerem on the 'Multinational Banks', CEREM, 1979.
3 O. Pastré, 1979.
4 M. Sagou, 1981. See also O. Pastré, 1979, and F. Morin, 1975, for a study of the Paribas and Suez groups.
5 M. Sagou, 1981, p. 174.

PART IV

CONCLUSION

10 Place and Future of the Multinationals in the French Economy

After a period of growth which has accelerated with decolonisation, the formation of the Common Market and the policy of the Vth and VIth Plans which favoured big groups, the French economy, like the other European economies, has shown itself to be an open economy: its export level expressed as a percentage of the GNP is for example higher than that of the United States or Japan.

This integration into an international environment is mainly the doing of French industry: '25 per cent of its GNP is exported, imports represent 17 per cent of the GNP and 30 per cent of industrial production is carried out by foreign firms established in France.'[1] We have also shown that French industry controls production operations abroad which are the equivalent of more than 11 per cent of French production. The extent of this opening up to international trade and investment is also much higher in certain industrial sectors. It is primarily the big French industrial groups which have been set up gradually since the 1950s which are behind this opening up. For them today exports and/or production abroad represent a large proportion of their operations, and a strategic line in their growth.

However, the multinationalisation of the French economy is still lower than that of the United Kingdom, the United States and West Germany (on an industrial level), and its export level is lower than that of West Germany, Italy and the United Kingdom.[2] The French economy has been a late entrant to world competition.

Today, as with the other industrialised countries, French trade and direct investment is mainly carried out within the other developed economies. It is important to stress three specific characteristics of the multinationalisation of French companies, as they partly explain the relative under-multinationalisation of the economy. These are:

— the concentration of production facilities and production operations abroad, much higher than for the United States and West Germany, which reveals a great dichotomy between large groups and small and medium-sized companies and a certain weakness of the industrial fabric;
— considerable and often long-standing investments in North Africa

and Black French-speaking Africa, revealing the continuing political and economic influence over the former colonies;

— very large and long-standing investments in southern Europe, especially in Spain, and in Portugal, Greece, Iran and Turkey (and more recently in the Middle East).

These last two trends would seem to reveal less involvement in the industrial countries and distant countries (America and Asia) compared with West Germany.

FOREIGN EXPANSION: AN ESSENTIAL ASSET FOR THE COMPETITIVENESS OF FIRMS

Even though the international expansion of firms can rightly be considered a necessary response to international competition, this study has stressed that expansion also plays a part in improving profitability. Statistically, the multinational companies do have a higher and more stable profitability than companies which are not multinational. Though other factors are involved, we have shown how exports and foreign production have positive direct and indirect effects on the growth and financial results of French companies such as increase in market shares, scale economies, technological know-how, market awareness, access to raw materials and reduction of costs.

Growth abroad improves the competitiveness of French firms. It accelerates the growth of the big groups, and hence the concentration of production facilities: differences in the capacity to effect international growth accentuating the gulf between the small and medium-sized companies and the big groups.[3] Although some small and medium-sized companies are big exporters, or even produce outside France, the competitiveness of industry rests more and more with a few big very international groups. We should, however, stress that competitiveness and growth abroad are only possible for these groups when they have a strong position on the French domestic market.

THE TRADE-OFFS OF INTERNATIONAL OPENING UP

Foreign penetration in France, like French expansion abroad, has certain trade-offs.

1. First, because of the general multinationalisation of industrialised countries, investments are made in France by large foreign groups. This is an inescapable aspect of the opening up of the French economy, and a conflicting aspect, as it has adverse consequences too.

This investment creates dependence on foreign decision centres. A. Cotta noted in 1978 that 'an imbalance was being established to our disadvantage. French companies control a very small percentage of the industrial production of their partners, while these partners now have a very big say in our industrial choices.'[4] L. Stoléru, thirteen years ago, pointed out the risk of the gradual disappearance of French companies in certain sectors which were coming totally under foreign control.[5] One can add that the levels of foreign penetration are, in certain sectors, effectively so high that they make it difficult today for big competitive French groups to be formed. This can then only be achieved by taking over subsidiaries of foreign groups.[6] One can then say that foreign penetration of the French economy partly explains the under-multinationalisation already mentioned, especially since more and more works[7] have stressed a second constraint tied up with foreign penetration: the often adverse effect on French foreign trade.

2. Although the exports and production abroad of French groups show up the strong points of industry, conversely, foreign investment in France, when it is high, shows up the points of least resistance of French industry and the strong points of foreign industries. One can then deduce the industrial specialisations of France from a comparison of foreign investments in France and French investments abroad.[8] We find that industry is specialised in basic activities (intermediate products) and cars, and de-specialised in the activities of mechanical and electrical engineering, parachemicals and pharmaceuticals and the agricultural and food industries. The dual movement to internationalise French production facilities hence accentuates the weaknesses of French industrial specialisations, also revealed by looking at trade with the industrialised countries. This poor specialisation in trade has already been stressed by many authors, such as C. Stoffaës[9] or J. Mistral,[10] and the report on the accounts of the nation for 1980.[11]

This dual movement of specialisation/de-specialisation is inherent in any opening up of the economy to abroad. One will note that, for France, the acceleration of this process over the last twenty years has taken the form of an increased dependence on abroad in the main key sectors of industrial development. Within the world ranking of economies which has become established through these specialisations and this interdependence, we find France in a middle position, markedly below that of its main competitors, the United States, Japan or West Germany.

3. French investment abroad, although improving the competitiveness of firms and hence industry, is not in itself without adverse consequences.

As we have shown, foreign production in many cases has a positive effect on exports, but it may have no effect or even a negative effect on the French trade balance.

As regards employment, we have also noted how the locational spread of production can be a direct cause of reductions in employment in France, and why multinational firms are more involved in world competition and hence in an employment-reducing movement to adapt, restructure and modernise. So, between 1974 and 1977 there was a much greater reduction in employment in France for the sixty-seven multinational companies studied than for all companies together.

Finally the development trend noted between 1974 and 1980 shows that the changing international situation will encourage firms to invest more and more in other industrialised countries. The locational spread of production will then have less and less marked beneficial effects on exports and employment, which will then be limited to a long-term improvement in competitiveness.

The international opening up of the French economy, although accompanied by the modernisation and growth of industry, has at the same time resulted in weaknesses and new risks: global interdependence with regard to abroad, dependence with regard to imports and foreign groups investing in France, and de-specialisation in many key sectors.

At the end of 1981, what are the prospects facing the French multinationals?

AN INCREASINGLY RISKY WORLD

We have analysed the many forms taken by the widespread world crisis: reduction of growth in the industrialised countries and consequent intensification of competition between their industrial groups, rise in the economic and political demands of the Third World and reduction in opportunities for investment in these countries, and increasing competition from the industries of the newly industrialising countries.

The relocation to the rich countries, started by the French multinationals, and at the same time the new forms which their presence takes in the peripheral countries do, as we have seen, constitute a response to this new situation. The more and more frequent sectoral relocations also reveal the concern of the multinational groups to adapt to a world of more intense competition.[12] From the point of view of the multinational firms, the crisis is a permanent feature because of these different aspects. The forms in which it will manifest itself will however remain very unpredictable. Even though international investors are tending more and more to choose those countries considered to be safe, the events in Iran have shown to what point their predictions could be wrong. Might not the same happen tomorrow in Brazil, the country on which all the multinational firms are concentrating today? Under these conditions, and at a time when the crisis in the industrialised countries is encouraging companies to set up in the Third World, there seems to be a choice for the multinational groups between refusing to invest in the newly industrialising countries, and agreeing to invest, which will then be accompanied by increasingly higher risks.

The development of the international monetary situation is also another major concern of the multinationals. Even though they are still better armed than purely national firms to adapt to this type of problem, the total unpredictability of monetary parities prevalent today increases the risks and contributes to creating a very different context to that which prevailed in the 1960s.

The strategy of the international groups is therefore entering a 'period of high risks'[13] in all fields. 'With regard to the future' it is more and more difficult for multinational firms to achieve 'control over the probable, and management of the unpredictable.'[14]

THE UNCERTAINTIES OF THE SITUATION IN FRANCE

The massive electoral victory of the Socialist Party and its allies in the spring of 1981 has given the new Government the means of bringing about the profound economic and social reforms announced. These reforms will change the framework within which the French multinationals will operate. At the time of writing, however, there are still many unknown quantities and this will probably continue for several months. Two main questions are raised, relating to the extension of the public sector and the new economic policy.

1. First, what will be the extent and precise nature of the nationalisation? The new Government has committed itself to nationalising eleven big industrial groups, mostly leaders in their sector of activity. These include three groups under foreign control or influence: ITT-France, Roussel-Uclaf (Hoechst, West Germany), Honeywell (Honeywell, United States) and eight French groups: SGPM, PUK, Rhône-Poulenc, Dassault, CGE, Thomson Brandt, Usinor-Sacilor[15] and Matra (military department). But will all of these eleven groups be nationalised and when? In addition, all the private banks and insurance companies are in line for nationalisation. But what will happen to the companies which, because of the banks' holdings in them, would come indirectly under State control? The degree of the extension of the public sector might be doubled as F. Morin has shown.[16]

How will the nationalisations be carried out:

— will the existing structures of the groups be maintained?
— or on the other hand, will they be reorganised?
— what will happen to the foreign subsidiaries?
— what powers will be granted to the workers, users and local and regional authorities?

Leading questions as, even limited to the eleven groups concerned, the nationalisations will have a considerable impact on French industry. F. Morin has shown[17] that in terms of paid employees, the eleven groups concerned account for 10.5 per cent of the people employed in industry. With these nationalisations, the employees in the public sector would climb from 5.6 to 16 per cent of industrial employees.[18]

We have ourselves estimated that these eleven groups in line for nationalisation account for approximately 17 per cent of production operations abroad controlled by all French firms and 15 per cent of French exports.[19] This is not surprising as these eleven groups are almost all leaders in production abroad (cf. Table 1.5) and exports (cf. Table 1.6). However, some big French multinational groups seem to be excluded from the nationalisations: CFP, Michelin, Marine Wendel (with Carnaud), Compagnie du Nord-Imétal, BSN, Lafarge, Air Liquide, Denain-Nord-Est-Longwy (with Vallourec), L'Oréal (Nestlé), Empain-Schneider[20] and Peugeot. All these groups are concerned, on the other hand, by the second question.

2. The second great unknown quantity concerns the direction that the new public sector will take and the future conditions of existence for the foreign multinationals in France and the French multinationals. What new burdens will be imposed on these companies? What powers will the workers have? What control and what credit policy will the public banking sectors impose? What control will be exerted on the operations of foreign groups in France? Will the international expansion of firms still be encouraged? In more general terms, to what extent will the operating rules of the market economy at home and the movement of specialisation and international opening up abroad be called into question?

There are bound to be profound changes in structures, even if the new political leaders agree that the change 'will take into account the crisis situation, the fact that the economy of France is open to abroad, and the necessary economic and financial equilibria.'[21] However, external constraints may be complied with in a variety of ways. There will be three choices available here:

(a) First option. To improve the quality of industrial specialisations and reconquer some of the domestic market, without calling into question the principle of the integration of the French economy into the world economy. The maintenance of an industry integrated into world trade is vital, as stressed for example by M. Rocard, 'If we do not have an offensive political and economic strategy, we shall be swallowed up by protectionism. As it has no oil and hardly any uranium, France is obliged to export to ensure its independence.'[22]

The work in which A. Boublil, now the technical adviser of F. Mitterrand, defined 'industrial socialism',[23] or the industrial policy permitted by an extension of the public sector, now constitutes the fullest forward-looking analysis of future socialist choices. The description of the strategy desirable for each group in line for nationalisation still includes export and foreign production operations as they are considered to be elements of competitiveness which must be maintained and improved.[24] However, this does not exclude the possibility of extensive structural reforms since, for the author, the big public industrial group which would result from reorganising the operations of the groups in line for nationalisation would constitute essential industrial poles. They would form the basis for a 'policy of increasing supply' and of control over the key sectors and would hence make it possible to cast off constraints from abroad, making growth possible without a trade deficit. A suggested process would be vertical integration in intermediate products and capital goods, which would reduce the part played by the foreign multinationals.

(b) Second option. To create a big break-away from the world market, by adopting a defensive position, looking for a considerable reduction in imports[25] and more autonomous development. This slowdown in the adaptation of the economy to world-wide competition would involve a protectionist policy, that is strict foreign exchange control, a reduction in foreign investment in France and, for example, the gradual replacement of the foreign subsidiaries of nationalised groups through bilateral agreements,[26] that is a degree of 'disengagement by French-based multinational firms'.[27] This option is often accompanied by the desire to extend nationalisations.

The joint programme of the Leftist Government in 1972 provided for possible majority holdings being taken in the Schneider and Compagnie Française des Pétroles groups and water treatment and distribution companies. In 1977 the Communist Party proposed the total nationalisation of the Denain-Nord-Est-Longwy, Empain-Schneider, Chiers Chatillon, CFP Total, Peugeot and Citroën groups and a 'subsequent progressive increase in nationalisations'.[28]

(c) Third option. To adopt a mixed policy, half-way between the first two, making a distinction between those sectors exposed to world competition and those which are protected from it.[29]

Today, as the dominant political force in the Government coalition, the Socialist party is taking up the first of the three options which, although including far-reaching reforms, the reconquest of the domestic market and possibly limited protectionist measures, does not seem to call into question the integration of the French economy into the international trade and investment network. So, to mention only one significant development in the latter part of June 1981, some French multinational groups, including groups which are private, in line for nationalisation, or public, were authorised by the new government to take control of foreign firms or factories: PUK in Great Britain and BSN, Lafarge, Rhône-Poulenc, and in particular Elf-Aquitaine (take-over bid for Texasgulf) in the United States. In his speech to announce his programme on 8 July 1981, P. Mauroy confirmed this move and stated that the nationalisations announced would be carried out, but would be limited in scope, and would not call into question the very logic of groups. However, everything is far from settled.

The high level of internationalisation of French industry, on which our study has shed further light, explains why the choices of industrial policy, which are essential to any definition of a new development policy, necessarily have an 'international dimension'.

The choices to be made within this new policy affect all French companies (and some foreign companies) and all French people. There is a contradiction between the need for a national debate on this policy and the fact that the foreign groups and French multinational firms, whose weight in the economy we have seen, are waiting for this issue to be settled before they make any investments.

NOTES

1 G. Vitry, 1980.
2 See our Tables I.4 and I.5; Tardy, 1979; and Frobel, 1978, for the rate of multinationalisation of the German economy, equal in 1975 to 20 per cent.
3 J. P. Gilly and F. Morin, 1981, pp. 85 ff.
4 A. Cotta, 1978, p. 176.
5 L. Stoléru, 1969.
6 The take-over of CII–Honeywell Bull, carried out by SGPM in 1980, is an example in the data-processing sector. The planned nationalisation of Roussel-Uclaf seems to result from the same finding in the pharmaceuticals sector.
7 See J. Savary, 1980, and in particular J. Savary, 1981–2; STISI, 1980; Laubier and Richemond, 1980; J. L. Lienart, 1980.
8 See J. Savary, 1981–2.
9 C. Stoffaës, 1980, pp. 132 and 224.
10 J. Mistral, 1980.
11 Report on the accounts of the Nation 1980, INSEE Collections, Series C, No. 94, June 1981.
12 Cf. J. Savary, 1981–1.
13 As J. Mistral stresses in the introduction of the special issue of the *Revue d'economie industrielle* devoted to the new international division of labour (No. 4–1980).
14 These are the terms of an OECD experts report, prepared by J. Lesourne, OECD 1979.
15 The State and the nationalised banks already have majority control of Usinor and Sacilor.
16 F. Morin, A. and C. Alcouffe, M. Moreaux, X. Freixas, 1977.
17 F. Morin, 'Nationaliser?', *Le Monde*, 13 June 1981.
18 And to 21.6 per cent if we add four groups, as F. Morin proposes: Peugeot; Creusot–Loire, in which Paribas, the financial group in line for nationalisation, already has a minority interest (cf. A. Alcouffe and F. Morin, 'L'affaire Schneider', *Economie et Humanisme*, No. 258, March 1981); Générale des Eaux, in which nationalised insurance companies, CGE in line for nationalisation,

and the Caisse des Depôts already have a minority interest; Lyonnaise des Eaux, in which the financial group Suez, in line for nationalisation, already has a minority interest.

19 These percentages rise to 21.6 per cent and 24 per cent respectively if we add the four groups already mentioned above. (Our estimates of production operations abroad, based on the turnover of the production subsidiaries, relate to the situation as at 1 January 1975. Exports relate to 1979; we have taken the consolidated export figures for the groups—source, *Le Nouvel Economiste*, June 1980.)

20 This group, as we have seen, is already under the minority control of Paribas, the financial group in line for nationalisation.

21 Text of draft agreement of the Communist/Socialist government, 24 June 1981.

22 Speech at the Nantes Congress, August 1977. In the extreme, the consensus permitted by the Social Democrats coming into power would be a way of adapting the economic structures more quickly, as C. Stoffaës seemed to want in 1979 in the preface to the second edition of his book *La Grande Menace Industrielle*. (See C. Stoffaës, 1980, p. 13.)

23 A. Boublil, 1977.

24 Cf. A. Boublil, 1977, p. 182 for PUK, p. 179 for Rhône-Poulenc. SGPM is the only group for which a degree of relocation of investments in France is wanted, p. 198.

25 Cf. Ph. Herzog 'Rompre pour changer', *Le Monde*, 16 December 1977.

26 Cf. E. Izard 'Nationaliser: et les filiales à l'étranger?', *Economie et Politique*, No. 5, September 1977.

27 Cf. Socialist Party Conference 'Socialisme et multinationales', 1976, p. 118.

28 On these points see A. Le Pors, 1977, pp. 199 ff.

29 Cf. A. Cotta, 1978, p. 225, where this option is criticised and described by the author as a non-choice.

SUPPLEMENT

The French Multinationals since May 1981

On 17 June 1981, at the shareholders' general meeting, the chairman and managing director of Lafarge, O. Leclerf, expressed fears which at the time were shared by many company directors. In his view, the survival of his group in the face of international competition depended on the preservation in France of entrepreneurial freedom with its four component parts: 'freedom of prices, freedom to invest in France and abroad, freedom of financing facilities, and freedom of industrial organisation.' Did the Socialist plans really threaten this entrepreneurial freedom? After two years with the left in political power in France, have the changes that have been made justified these fears a posteriori?

We shall show that extensive economic and social reforms have in fact been carried out, but that ultimately they have essentially preserved these 'freedoms', in particular the freedom of international development. Of course the new rights granted to workers (Auroux laws) have imposed constraints on companies, but this has not for example prevented Lafarge from continuing its reorganisation, and cutting back the number of its employees.[1] Then again, the fiscal, welfare and wage costs borne by companies have increased, mainly during the first year. Firms have also had to suffer price controls and even a four-month price freeze, high interest rates, and a restrictive economic policy since the Delors plan of March 1983, but these therapeutic measures, often used by previous governments, do seem less severe than those administered in the United States and Great Britain, especially since French companies have benefited from a policy to boost the economy in France in 1981-2, in contrast to the deflationary policies being conducted in other economies. The international expansion of French groups, for its part, has been encouraged, as shown by the take-over by Lafarge in July 1981 of General Portland, the third biggest American producer of cement.

We shall now describe various aspects of the new French economic policy, paying particular attention to the modifications to industrial structures (nationalisations) and decisions relating to the international opening up of the economy. Since the beginning of the new legislature, the President of the Republic and the Government have announced their policy of maintaining this opening up. Even though the nationalisations were very quickly implemented, and although they have resulted in extensive industrial reorganisation, this policy has meant the pursuit of a dual movement of internationalisation, encouraged by the authorities: foreign groups have made extensive investments in France and French groups have continued with their international growth. In the spring of 1983, the return of French economic policy to a degree of orthodoxy, concentrating on defending the franc within the European monetary institutions and aiming for equilibrium, particularly in the balance of payments, as it were confirms that this policy is based on the respect of external constraints and the rejection of protectionism. The growth of French exporting and multinational firms is, then, an essential objective of economic development.

THE IMPACT OF NATIONALISATION

For the first Mauroy Government and its Secretary of State for the extension of the public sector, J. le Garrec, the rapid implementation of the nationalisation programme was a priority, as this gave the State the means of implementing its new policy.[2] At the beginning of 1982, these nationalisations had almost been completed, and covered most of the banking system and eleven big industrial groups.

The law of 11 February 1982 extending the public sector nationalised almost all the private banking sector: Paribas, Crédit du Nord, Suez, CIC, Crédit Commercial de France, Worms bank and Rothschilds. The only banks not nationalised were the small independent regional banks (with deposits of less than a billion francs), the mutual banks, the medium-sized merchant banks, and all the foreign banks in France. In 1980, the latter, 122 in number, represented 6.4 per cent of total French bank deposits, 14.95 per cent of the balance sheet totals, and much more as regards foreign currency operations. They now constitute the only private banks of an international dimension, and their role will certainly become more important. The British group Barclays, the biggest private bank in France, is going to set up a merchant bank there. The exclusion of the foreign banks in France from the nationalisations is a notable phenomenon, as is the maintenance for the nationalised banks, of the management criteria for private banks. Now some 75 per cent of French banking operations are under direct State control.

As regards industry, the existing public sector, consisting primarily of Charbonnages de France, Electricité de France, Gaz de France, Entreprise Minière et Chimique, Renault, Elf Aquitaine, SNIAS, SNECMA, CEA and BRGM, has been increased by eleven big industrial groups. This has, however, been carried out in four stages, and by different methods. When an amendment finance bill was passed in October 1981, the State converted into a capital holding the interests which the nationalised banks had held since 1978 in Usinor and Sacilor.

The two main heavy-iron and steel groups in France, employing a total of 60 000 people and with a turnover of over 32 billion francs hence joined the public sector, to which they really already belonged. In addition, the State was content to take a majority interest, but keeping the existing management teams, in two companies manufacturing civil and military equipment, which will remain private companies— Matra (11 000 employees, turnover 36 000 million francs) and Dassault (16 000 employees, turnover of 10 700 million francs, in which the State already had a 33 per cent holding). At the same time, through the nationalisation law, five big industrial groups, mostly leaders in their sectors and very multinational, were nationalised outright, and their management boards and directors changed. These were Saint Gobain Pont à Mousson (SGPM), Péchiney Ugine Kuhlmann (PUK), Rhône-Poulenc, Cie Générale d'Electricité (CGE) and Thomson (consolidated total employees in 1981: 460 000 people in France and 181 000 people abroad, plus consolidated turnover of 200 billion francs, including over ninety-four abroad). Finally, following long and difficult negotiations with the three foreign groups involved in the nationalisation programme, Hoechst, Honeywell and ITT, it was decided that Roussel–Uclaf, the leading pharmaceuticals company in France (17 000 employees world-wide, turnover 6 billion francs), would remain under the control and management of Hoechst, with the French State being content to take a minority interest of 34 per cent of its capital.[3] So only two foreign groups in France were affected. The American Honeywell group signed an agreement with the French Government in April 1982, in accordance with which it lost control of its big subsidiary CII–H.B. (20 267 employees, including 15 000 in France). Its holding was reduced from 47 per cent to 20 per cent, that is below the blocking minority, and the number of its directors was reduced from four to two. The American group thereby lost control of management, though it retained its important technological, industrial and commercial links. CII–H.B. may become the core of a national data processing industry. The ITT subsidiaries in France that were taken over in July 1982 were CGCT the main subsidiary (9200 employees and turnover of 2300 million francs) and its subsidiaries Pouget, La Signalisation and LCT. After much hesitation, it was decided in June 1983 that CGCT would not be merged with another public manufacturer of telephone exchanges, but would cooperate with the Thomson group.

Through the holdings of the nationalised banks, many industrial companies have found themselves virtually under State control. The most important of these holdings have not been handed back to the private sector.[4] However, where the State owned holdings in strategic sectors, or sectors being reorganised, it has sometimes used this control to consolidate the public sector. There are a few significant examples of this. The water distribution sector is dominated in France by two private groups, which in 1981 came under the minority control of public companies: Lyonnaise des Eaux (22 per cent of the capital held by Suez) and Générale des Eaux (holdings owned by CGE and the Caisse des Depôts). These groups were not, however, nationalised.[5] Another big holding, the Schneider group (150 companies, 130 000 people, with a turnover of 40 billion francs), is involved in strategic sectors such as the nuclear industry. This group was controlled by Paribas through a 35 per cent holding acquired in March 1981. This holding has been reduced to 13 per cent, and Empain Schneider, like its big subsidiary Creusot–Loire, have remained private groups. However, in April 1982, the State acquired 34 per cent of the capital of Framatome, thus ensuring a right to control this very profitable subsidiary working for the nuclear industry. In addition, two loss-making subsidiaries of the Schneider group were modified, Métallurgie de Normandie, which was taken over by Usinor–Sacilor, and Chantiers de France Dunkerque, which was combined with two naval shipyards as part of a sectoral reorganisation plan. Another case worthy of mention is the insurance sector. The insurance holdings of Suez (Victoire Group) and Paribas (le Secours group) have been retained. However, in June 1983, Suez signed an agreement with the private group Compagnie Industrielle, handing over to it control of the Victory group insurance operations (Assurance Abeille et Paix).[6] Finally, the Imétal group, with its subsidiaries Penarroya (lead), Mokta (uranium) and SLN (nickel) held by the former Rothschild bank, then by Suez in 1982, finally came under the control in May 1983 of a public company COGEMA, with the public holding company Erap in turn taking control of the big loss-making subsidiary SLN. This seems to be an attempt by the authorities to support a loss-making basic activity. Similarly, in June 1983, the Creusot–Loire group, which had suffered heavy losses, requested that the State take over all its iron and steel operations.

Did not the local shareholders of the foreign subsidiaries of the new French nationalised groups, on the basic principle of extra-territoriality, object to these companies passing over to the power of public firms in a Socialist country? Broadly-speaking, was not this public control of foreign companies going to hinder their development and, for example, prove an obstacle to their sales of equipment to the American Administration? In 1981, these risks were discussed in French and international financial circles. We can now see that almost all of the foreign subsidiaries of French nationalised groups have been preserved and have continued to grow. Only one subsidiary of a group under public control was nationalised, and this was Mines de Laurion, a subsidiary of Imétal, which was nationalised for reasons of control over mineral resources by the Greek Government. Of course in October 1981, the Paribas affair hit the headlines.[7] The foreign shareholders of the Swiss subsidiary of this financial group, Paribas Suisse, had made a take-over bid, which succeeded thanks to the action of some of the directors of Paribas, such as its chairman and managing director, P. Moussa. This operation, made possible by the many international financial alliances secured by this bank, finally ended in an agreement between Paribas and its former Swiss subsidiary. In addition, collaboration has been increased with foreign groups, such as S. G. Warburg in Great Britain, and A. G. Becker, the fourth biggest American investment bank. Paribas, which already held 20 per cent of the capital of this bank, bought up an additional 25 per cent and thus took over total control of a company whose chairman had announced in June 1981 that any collaboration with a nationalised foreign group was impossible. The following paragraphs will confirm that nationalisation has not been an obstacle to the international development of the groups.[8]

'Nationalisation will not be Statism. We shall preserve the autonomy of the nationalised companies.' In his speech to announce his programme to the National Assembly on 18 July 1981, the Prime Minister, P. Mauroy, thus publicly expressed the principle of the management autonomy of the nationalised companies.[9] At the same time, the public groups were asked to respect the criteria for private management, 'Your first objective will be economic efficiency, by continually improving competitiveness. The normal criteria for the management of industrial companies will apply in full to your group: all of the different operations must produce a sufficient trading profit to ensure the development of the company, and the return on the capital invested must be normal.'[10] In other words, economic objectives must be given priority over social objectives.[11]

However, the new public companies, controlled by their own guardian ministries,[12] were conceived from the outset as a means to serve the economic development of France. They must therefore respect the programmes set out in the national budget and development plan, and the main economic objectives of the State: investment, technological development, employment and foreign trade. This is to be achieved by a flexible and contractual system, the planning contracts. These are multi-annual contracts (four years) between the firm and the State, which are subject to revision and lay down strategic options, employment trends, financing requirements and forecast financial commitments of the authorities to the group. These contracts must therefore permit harmonisation of group strategies and the objectives of government policy, while clarifying relations, particularly financial relations, between the State and the nationalised companies. By February 1983, CII–H.B., SGPM, EMC, Rhône-Poulenc, Usinor, Sacilor, Renault and CGE had signed their first planning contracts, followed by PUK and CDF Chimie in June, and by Thomson on 1 July. These contracts, which form part of a considerable financing effort by the State,[13] must be harmonised with the law preparing for the IXth Plan, and with the industrial development bill, in the course of being drafted. Without it being possible to give details of these contracts here, we can say that they incorporate all the industrial logic of the search for competitiveness: technological investments and investments to improve productivity with State aid, focusing on the profitable or support sectors. In 1982, PUK has already disposed of its loss-making operations in special steels (Ugine Aciers) and chemicals (PCUK), and it is now developing its aluminium production in countries where electricity is cheap, in particular in Quebec where it has a big project. In its planning contract it undertakes to maintain aluminium production in France, concentrating it on two sites, rationalising its installations and reducing its employees. For so doing, it obtains State aid and a preferential price per kWh supplied by EFD (11 centimes instead of the previous 17 centimes, but in return PUK is financing an EDF nuclear power station). At the same time, it is choosing to invest in new materials such as carbon fibres.

The bill on the democratisation of the public sector, debated in May 1983, introduces new constraints on management, but these will ultimately be more limited than anticipated. In all public companies with over 200 employees,[14] workers will have one-third of the seats on the management boards, with their delegates being elected by direct universal suffrage from the lists sponsored by the trade union organisations or by at least 10 per cent of the workers' representatives. In addition, the works or office councils, in which all the workers meet at regular intervals and with which the managerial staff will be associated, will have powers to organise labour and look for technological innovations and improvement in competitiveness. This goes somewhat further than the Auroux laws, which apply to all French companies, in increasing worker participation in public companies. It is, however, too early to make any assessment of this reform.

Autonomy in the management of nationalised companies assumes that they are free to dispose of or acquire industrial assets, but this would mean a reduction or extension of the public sector, which is a political decision for which the legislator is responsible. The Government is thus drafting a bill designed to give the public sector room to breathe (the 'loi de respiration du secteur public'), governing transfers of ownership between the public sector and the private sector, which will authorise operations below a certain size threshold without any parliamentary control. Over the past two years the public groups have already made considerable adjustments to their boundaries.

We have described here the extent of the nationalisations carried out in 1982, and the new rules of operation for the extended public sector. These nationalisations have permitted extensive sectoral reoganisation.

INDUSTRIAL REORGANISATION

In 1982, the public sector of industry was considerably expanded. According to an estimate by default, covering only nine of the newly nationalised groups,[15] the weight of the public sector in industry has risen from 17.2 per cent of total sales before the nationalisations to 29.4 per cent after, from 11 to 22.2 per cent of the employees and from 43.5 to 51.9 per cent of investments. The public industrial sector is still predominant in the sectors in which it was already involved: coal, oil and electricity production and aeronautical engineering (where the percentage of employees it accounts for has risen from 56 to 79 per cent). There has been no change in the land transportation equipment sector.[16] It has acquired a significant position in other operations: iron and steel (rise from 0 to 51 per cent of employees), non-ferrous metals (15.6 to 64.3 per cent), glass (0 to 29.5 per cent), basic chemicals (9 to 52.8 per cent), parachemicals and pharmaceuticals (5.5 to 13.1 per cent), plastics (1.7 to 8.4 per cent), mechanical engineering (2.3 to 13 per cent), electrical and electronic engineering (0 to 26.8 per cent and in fact virtual control of certain subsectors such as telephones). The basic operations (intermediate products), chemicals in the wide sense, electrical equipment and electronic engineering, are the big areas into which the industrial public sector has expanded.

On the basis of these industrial nationalisations, and the companies controlled or influenced by the nationalised financial institutions, the State has stimulated extensive reorganisation: rationalisation of operations between public groups, with transfers of assets and concentration of production on certain strong points, amalgamating certain private companies with other private companies, or around public companies. Two or three big industrial groups have therefore been set up or reinforced in each of the sectors concerned. We give below a list of the principal operations.

— *iron and steel*: French production of special steels has been amalgamated into two public groups. In March 1981, Usinor took over the 'long products' (bars) subsidiary of Creusot–Loire. In January 1982, Sacilor took over PUK's subsidiary Ugine Aciers (stainless steel). In 1983, Usinor and Sacilor took over all the iron and steel operations of Creusot–Loire.

— *shipbuilding*: at the end of 1982, the five companies in this sector were amalgamated into two big groups, one public, the other private. Chantiers Navals de l'Ouest amalgamated with Alsthom (CGE) Chantiers de l'Atlantique of Saint Nazaire, and Dubigeon Normandie of Nantes. Chantiers du Nord et de la Mediterranée, under the industrial control of the Schneider group, includes Chantiers de France Dunkerque, Chantiers navals de la Ciotat, and CNIM of la Seyne.

— *non-ferrous ores*: COGEMA, an industrial subsidiary of the Atomic Energy Commission (CEA), took control of the Imétal group: Penarroya (lead), Compagnie de Mokta (uranium) and SLN (nickel).[17]

— *paper, cardboard*: in this crisis sector,[18] the State used to control La Chapelle d'Arblay through Paribas and IDI. It has not been able to find a national company to take over this group. In May 1983, the top French producer of newsprint was therefore handed over to the Dutch group Parenco which is responsible for leading a painful new start, with the loss of 1600 jobs.

— *chipboard panels*: the subsidiary of SGPM, Bois Déroulés Océan has merged with two private groups Rougier and Landex to form the leading French producer of chipboard panels. At the same time, three private groups, Leroy, Isorel and Baradel, have merged to create a second big group, Isoroy.

— *railway equipment*: two groups which dominated the sector have been amalgamated, one public with Alsthom (CGE) which took over Soferval in 1982, the other private with the Francorail group, led by the Schneider group, with Jeumont Schneider, Creusot–Loire which took over the railway operation of Carel Fouché in 1983, MTE, ANF and de Dietrich.

— *chemicals*: the whole French chemicals industry has been reorganised around the nationalised groups, with large amounts of public aid thrown in,[19] in two stages. In 1982, the assets of the chemicals subsidiary of PUK, PCUK (12 500 people, turnover of 17 200 million francs) were taken over by Elf Aquitaine (chlorine division, fluorine chemistry, hydrogen peroxide, foreign subsidiaries), Rhône-Poulenc (mineral chemistry, agrochemicals, pharmaceuticals), CDF Chimie (organic chemistry, plastics, inks) and ICI Great Britain (colourants). In June 1983, after tough negotiations and the departure of the chairman of Elf Aquitaine, A. Chalandon, Elf took over CPF's share of their joint subsidiaries. ATO Chimie and Chloe Chimie (former heavy chemicals of Rhône-Poulenc). Elf Aquitaine, with its new subsidiary Atochem, became the leader of French heavy chemicals (an operation which made a loss of 1600 million francs in 1982), alongside CDF Chimie.

— *fertilisers*: the entire French fertilisers industry has been reorganised, with the creation of two groups, one around CDF Chimie, whose subsidiary APC has taken GESA over from Rhône-Poulenc, the other around COFAZ (Paribas group), which has taken over Sopag (Gardinier group).[20]

— *machine tools*: in addition to the signature of multi-annual contracts between the State and several companies, two big industrial groups have been formed. The first, controlled by IDI and the big customer groups mostly nationalised, is called Machines Françaises

Lourdes. The second, Intelautomatisme, producing medium-sized machinery, is controlled by Huré, of the Suez group.

— *electronics branches*: this is one of the priority branches in the new industrial policy. Following the Farnoux Report, the French Government wants to develop its research and training effort and promote fourteen national projects. It is planning to release a financing package of 140 billion francs over five years. This wish has meant industrial choices like that of making Thomson the group leader for consumer electronics, CII-H.B. head of data processing, and CIT–Alcatel (CGE) an important office equipment group. In November 1983, CGE bought 10 per cent of Olivetti's capital from Bull and SGPM, and signed a technical and commercial agreement with this Italian group for office equipment.

— *electronic components*: the two groups built up around Matra and Thomson will be maintained; the third, Intertechnique, will be amalgamated with one of the first two.

— *data processing*: CII–H.B., partly freed of its dependence on Honeywell, has taken over SEMS, the data processing subsidiary of Thomson (Mitra and Solar ranges),[21] and Transac, data processing/peripherals subsidiary of CGE. This group has become the pivot of the French medium-sized and mini-computer industry.[22]

— *telephones*: the big telephone exchange industry in France is totally controlled by public companies: CIT–Alcatel (CGE), Thomson and CGCT, taken over in 1982 from ITT. After much hestitation, this last company will remain independent, but will coordinate its operations with those of Thomson. Finally, in September 1983, as part of an extensive agreement, CGE took over Thomson's telephone operations, thus forming a single 'French Telephones company'.

— *building and public works*: SGPM is increasing its operations in this sector by taking control of Générale des Eaux, and hence its subsidiaries Fougerolle and Campenon Bernard, and by taking over 26 per cent of the capital of the big subsidiary of the CGE group, SGE-SAINRAPT et BRICE (first stage towards bringing all the building branch under the wing of the CGE group).

— *other operations*: following the filing of the balance sheet of the Boussac St. Frères group in June 1981 (20 000 employees), the Government has worked out a solution for taking over the administration with the provisional support of IDI, with the survival of the group being made possible by public assistance. In aeronautics, a structural amalgamation has been brought about between the public companies SNIAS and SFENA and the private group Crouzet, with SNIAS and Crouzet taking joint control of SFENA.

On 8 September 1983, it was learned that a big agreement had been signed by CGE and Thomson to divide operations. CGE will transfer to Thomson its military, consumer electronics, and components operations. For its part, Thomson will transfer to CGE its wire and cable production subsidiaries, and the control of the whole of its communications division, in particular its telephone equipment operations. This will increase the concentration of producers of consumer electronics, components, cables, military equipment and in particular telephone exchanges. This recent operation shows that this movement will continue, with the public and private groups under State control still having competing operations in many sectors which can be reorganised in this way.

This reorganisation, initiated by the State and the public groups, has led certain large private companies to group together in the shipbuilding, machine tools, and chipboard panel sectors, for example. However, the movement to centralise capital financially, which has been developing within French industry since the 1960s, has also continued because of its own dynamism. In industry the operations carried out have remained modest compared with those we have just described.[23] We can mention the merger of the conglomerate Pricel (turnover of 1800 million francs) with Chargeurs Réunis (5 billion francs), the take-overs of the food division of Unipol by Lesieur, SIASMPA by Pernod, Lenzbourg and Vitrac by Bongrain, Editions C. Lattes by Hachette, SECRE by Jeumont-Schneider, the Revillon group by Cora, Doris by Amrep, Compagnie des Lampes by Philips, Solido by Marjorette, Preval by Besnier, Vitoux by Prouvost, Testut Aequitas by the Tapie group, and so on.

In the building and public works sector, on the other hand, big concentrations have been carried out in two years, involving some very multinational large groups. SCREG (turnover 10 billion francs) took control of Colas and Sacer (turnover 10 500 million francs), to become the top French public works group. GTM (8 billion francs) has merged with Entrepose (3 billion francs). SPIE (Schneider group, 9500 million francs) has taken over Trindel (1430 million francs). Campenon (5 billion francs) has taken over Entreprises Heulin. Finally, in February 1982, the Bouygues group (9300 million francs) failed in its attempt to take control of the Drouot group, the leading French private insurance group. In addition, in the services sector, Novotel merged with J. Borel to create the Accor group (turnover of 8 billion francs), Cie Internationale des Wagons Lits took control of PLM, Europe No. 1 of Affichages Giraudy, Codec Una of Viniprix, Crédit du Nord total control of Jacques Ribourel, and so on.

Between May 1981 and May 1983, the first two years of Socialist Government in France have therefore meant a very great acceleration of the concentration of the French production machinery. This development has without doubt exceeded the scope of the development which took place between 1965 and 1970,[24] and marked a turning point in 1980-1, which was characterised by a consolidation of industrial operations and take-overs of an essentially financial nature.[25] In 1982 and 1983, extensive reoganisation took place in industry, under the aegis of the State. These amalgamations of companies were carried out in order to form big competitive groups within sectors or branches of production and formed part of the *industrial project*. Even though this is not an absolute rule which is always confirmed—nationalised groups have continued to carry out diversification operations as well as financial operations[26]—the overall trend shows the voluntarist and industrial tendency of the new policy implemented through the nationalised groups.

THE POLICY OF OPENING UP INTERNATIONALLY

'Will not the reconquest of the domestic market be allied with a degree of protectionism?' To this question, asked in April 1981, the presidential candidate, F. Mitterrand, replied, 'No. No more than the conquest of foreign markets is allied with dumping. There are rules on the subject, those of the Common Market, and those of GATT. We shall respect them and we shall ask for them to be applied when they are evaded.'[27] This reply, on a particular point of commercial policy, illustrates that it has been the constant wish of the French authorities, for all international political, military, commercial, technological and direct investment relations, to maintain France's international commitments, to pursue the opening up of the economy abroad, without the economic and social reforms implemented within her frontiers calling this international integration into question.

The general economic policy followed by the Mauroy Government is, then, characterised by an increasing respect for 'external constraints'. The development of trade and direct international investment, keeping France in the European Monetary Agreement and accepting foreign exchange constraints are all proof of this. Of course, the policy to boost consumption, social transfers and reforms carried out during the first year still has as its primary objective the fight against unemployment—at the expense of the equilibrium of the budget, the social organisations and foreign trade, and to the detriment of the fight against inflation. The weakness of the franc against the dollar, the yen and the European currencies, sanctioned by three monetary adjustments within the European Monetary Agreement (4 October 1981, 12 June 1982 and 21 March 1983), the increasing deficits and the very much bigger increase in prices than for France's main partners, have led the Government to modify its policy: freezing prices and wages during the summer of 1982, measures to re-establish the equilibrium of the trade balance, and stringent measures accompanying the third devaluation in March 1983, with a shortfall of 65 billion francs for domestic demand, or 2 per cent of the national product. Since this date, priority has been given to regaining the equilibrium of the balance of payments, the fight against inflation and the defence of the franc. In order to continue with the development originally experienced, withdrawal from the European Monetary Agreement with the floating of the franc and a temporary return to protectionism might have been considered. On the contrary, in 1983, the authorities chose to give priority to the external economic and monetary constraints rather than to this development.

As regards foreign trade, the policy followed has been one of expansion, even though, as in other countries, the accent has been placed on controlling the domestic market and bringing the trade balance into equilibrium. For P. Mauroy 'the reconquest of the domestic market does not for all that mean a relaxation of our export effort or France drawing back on to itself through protectionist measures.' The measures aimed at reconquering the domestic market consisted of aid to certain sectors where foreign trade was causing big losses (textiles, wood, furniture, leather, toys), encouragement to reach agreements between national producers and distributors, and guidance given to the public sector companies.[28] Industrial-type measures seem to be limited, compared with the protectionist steps being taken throughout the world, particularly in the United States.[29] The only authoritarian decision to restrict imports related to video tape recorders, by setting up in October 1982 dissuasive customs clearance in Poitiers.[30] This slowed down the flow of purchases, and accelerated the establishment of production plants in France (Philips in 1982, then Grundig, Akai and Thomson through an agreement with JVC). One can add that the strict foreign-exchange control set up in 1981 upset both importers and exporters. At the same time, there was a degree of continuity in the support for exports. Even though M. Jobert, Minister of foreign trade, has obtained the rank of Minister of State, the promotion of sales outside France has been carried out for eighteen months with measures which are very little different from those used during the previous seven-year term. In October 1982, faced with the worsening trade deficit, the Government adopted a series of measures: an increase in aid for energy saving and exports (certain fiscal exemptions, improvement in credit-insurance system), the reinforcement of customs controls and supervision of transfers of patents and licences with foreign countries. In addition, the French authorities have, as before, continued to promote sales by French companies, in particular of capital goods through bilateral negotiations.[31]

The opening up of international investment takes two forms: the investments of foreign groups in France and those of French groups abroad. The Government has promoted the pursuit of this dual movement.[32] The many authorised operations which we describe in the following paragraphs are evidence of this. As regards the principles and procedures officially adopted, the desire to gain the confidence of international financial circles and to improve the balance of payments situation explains why the French authorities have been very active in attracting and publicly reassuring foreign investors, and have been content to authorise French groups to carry out their operations outside France.[33] As early as 11 September 1981, P. Mauroy made an appeal to foreign investors in Dunkirk, 'Our desire to develop our exports and the performance of our companies abroad implies that we accept, in return, that foreign companies can develop their operations in France.' On 8 and 9 February 1982, at a conference organised by the *International Herald Tribune*, P. Mauroy and eight ministers repeated this appeal and explained French economic policy to 300 directors of multinational firms. J. P. Chevenement and M. Rocard did the same on a visit to the United States, and P. Mauroy when inaugurating SICOB in September. The installation of foreign multinationals in France is desirable because of their contribution to the development of the country, 'Their contribution to the fight against unemployment, restoring the trade balance, providing training in new technologies and boosting industrial investment' (J. P. Chevenement, Minister of Industry, on 25 October 1982 in Besançon, at the inauguration of the Bergs Electronics factory of Du Pont de Nemours). At the same time, in replying to O. Lecerf, the Prime Minister stated in October 1981, 'Yes, France needs French-run multinational companies. In a world economy and with troubled but open international trade, the Government will help them play their cards.' He also asserted in his policy speech on 8 July 1981, 'The nationalised companies must be able to invest beyond our frontiers or sign cooperation agreements with foreign partners.' This trend was confirmed in the letter of appointment from the Minister P. Dreyfus to the general managers of the nationalised groups, 'You will be responsible for maintaining and developing the international dimension of the operations of your group, an essential condition for competitiveness and technical progress. In this field, the normal management criteria will apply to your group' (March 1982). However, as part of the reinforcement of foreign exchange control introduced in May 1981, the maximum amount of direct investments abroad dispensed without prior authorisation was reduced from 5 million francs to 1 million francs. Since this date these investments must also, unless specifically exempted, be financed to the tune of three-quarters by foreign currency borrowings on the international financial markets, that is without any francs leaving the country.[34] As regards direct investments, the constraint to maintain the equilibrium of the balance of payments does change the fundamental free-trade objectives.

THE GROWTH OF FOREIGN GROUPS IN FRANCE

Foreign investments in France continued actively in 1981, 1982 and 1983.[35] In fact, the characteristics of the French economy, in particular the size of the market and the existence of wage costs lower than those of Germany, continued to act as an attraction. This was accentuated by three phenomena tied up with the new policy. The increasing weakness of the franc with respect to the dollar, the deutschemark and the yen reduces the costs of investments and increases the costs of direct exports.

In addition, the more protectionist policy increases the risks of these direct exports and encourages companies to set up locally, as in the case of Japanese video tape-recorder producers. Finally, the prospects for economic growth in France contrast, at least they did up until 1982, with the general stagnation of the Western economies. The American *Fortune* magazine proclaimed in 1982, 'Business's not so bad year with Mitterrand.' As we have seen, the Government is encouraging this investment, and has only objected to two or three operations.[36]

So the number of jobs created in conjunction with the new production investments decided upon by foreign groups in France, which reached 12 000 people per annum in 1978, 1979 and 1980, have been maintained: 11 667 jobs planned in 1981 and 12 086 in 1982 (source: DATAR).

An estimate of the operations carried out over the first two years of the Socialist Government, from May 1981 to May 1983 is given in Table S.1.[37] Two main results are found. First, the take-overs of French companies have been very important (57 000 jobs involved), compared with the plants set up (approximately 6000 jobs). This reflects a trend for direct international investment increasingly to take the form of take-overs of companies, and, as a result, to have little effect on the net jobs created. Second, the years 1982–3 correspond to a period of consolidation of foreign penetration in the French economy and even of reduction in the rate of foreign control in industry, especially in the electrical and electronic engineering sector. This comes solely from the intervention of the authorities, with the nationalisation of CII–H.B. and CGCT, and French control being taken of Chantiers Navals de la Ciotat. The trend to pursue new foreign investments in France is confirmed by these figures.[38] If this is maintained, it will in the next few years mean an increase in the weight of foreign groups in France.

In two years, several big French companies, equipped with competitive

Table S.1 Foreign investments in France between May 1981 and May 1983
(survey of main operations)

	Number of operations	Employees under foreign control
New plants set up*	41	5 846
(including 50/50 subsidiaries)	(7)	(530)
Investments and extensions of existing subsidiaries	33	645†
1. Total plants set up and extensions	74	6 491
2. Take-overs of French companies	45	56 859‡
reductions in activities	17	−3 083
closures	16	−5 906
transfers to French shareholders	19	−39 728§
3. Total disinvestments	51	−48 543
4. Change in holder of foreign control (transfers between foreign groups)	15	(8 108)
Net change in employees under foreign control		+14 623

*Excluding Mitel (announced as 1000 jobs, then delayed).
†Taking into account a reduction of 650 jobs at Ford Bordeaux.
‡Including 4000 for Trois Suisses, 8000 for Quillery, 18 000 for Colas and Sacer.
§Including 27 656 connected with the nationalisations (CGCT and CII-H.B.) and the action of the authorities (Ch. navals Ciotat).
Source: press review.

production facilities and holding large market shares, have become subsidiaries of foreign groups: Table S.2 shows the biggest of these take-overs.[39] Hence, Logabax, the top French producer of data processors/peripherals was taken over in June 1981 by Olivetti. Then Boussois, with 50 per cent of French flat-glass production capacity, was sold to PPG Industries (USA). This was followed by Benson, 'number two' in the world in computer graphics, taken over by Schlumberger, Médicornéa by Nestlé, Fenwick by Linde. Companies depending directly on the State have also been transferred to foreign competitors. La Compagnie des Lampes, a subsidiary of Thomson, has come under the control of Philips, the colourants division of PCUK under the control of ICI and La Chapelle d'Arblay under the control of Parenco. These three operations clearly confirm the French policy of opening up to abroad.

The plants set up, on the other hand, mostly involved small companies, and high-technology operations. By associating with French groups, the Hercules and Toray groups have set up carbon-fibre plants,

Table S.2 The establishment of foreign groups in French industry between
May 1981 and May 1983 (operations involving over 500 jobs)

Date	Foreign group	Operation	Employees in France
I Plants set up or extended (projects)			
7/81	Mitel (Canada)	telephone switching plant set up (Vosges), project altered in '83 to 500 jobs, and delayed in April '83	1 000
3/82	Sony (Japan)	Video cassette plant set up in Dax	530
9/81	Hewlett Packard (USA)	Extension at Grenoble, plant set up in Lyon (data processing)	900
10/81	Nestlé (Switzerland)	Ice cream factory in St. Etienne	500
11/81		Take-over of Médicornéa at Tise (lenses)	+236
3/82	Unilever (Netherlands)	Milk products factory in St. Etienne + detergents factory	936
9/81	Ford (USA)	Investments Bordeaux factory	−650
II Take-overs of French companies			
10/81 4/82	British Petroleum (GB)	50% take-over of Naphtachimie (petro-chemicals) refinery closed in Dunkirk	2 500 −400
2/82	Sabot investments (Netherlands)	acquisition 40% of Quillery (Building–public works)	8 000
12/81	PPG Industries (USA)	take-over of Boussois SA (flat glass)	4 000
6/81	Olivetti (Italy)	take-over of Logabax (data processing)	1 700
11/81	RD Shell (Netherlands)	take-over of Application des Gaz (gas man. distr.)	1 389
7/81	Chicago Bridge (USA)	take-over of Constr. Met. de Provence (boilermaking)	1 180
3/82	Grammer (West Germany)	take-over of Sable (lorry seats)	545
6/82	Philips (Netherlands)	take-over of Cie des Lampes (lighting equipment)	4 000
7/82	ICI (GB)	take-over colourants division PCUK	1 700
9/82	Schlumberger (USA)	take-over of Benson (computer graphics)	900
4/83	Petrofina and Soc. Gen de Belgique (Belgium)	SCREG (minority interest) take-over of Colas and Sacer (public works)	18 000 (in France)
5/83	Linde (West Germany)	take-over of Fenwick (forklift trucks)	1 750
5/83	TBG (Switzerland)	33.5% holding in Schaefer (textiles)	4 000
5/83	Fläkt (Sweden)	Control taken of Solyvent-Ventec (fans)	600
5/83	Parenco (Netherlands)	'industrial control' and acquisition of 34% of the capital Chapelle-d'Arblay	2 000
III Disinvestments (closing-down operations or transfer to national shareholders)			
12/81	Lightning Opti (West Germany/GB)	refusal to resurrect subsidiary Elair Prestil (zip fasteners) take-over by Petrotec-suisse (10/82)	1 870
5/81	Mohasco ind. (USA)	transfer of Ranger (furniture) to CFM	1 100
12/81	Wasag chimie (West Germany)	filing of balance sheet of Bella (dolls) take-over by Berchet (France) with 500 jobs	800

Table S.2 (*cont.*)

Date	Foreign group	Operation	Employees in France
12/81	Norton (USA)	closing-down operations of Eurocéral (gas diffusion barrier supports) 50/50 subsidiary with Lafarge	615
2/82	Brooke Bond Liebig (GB)	transfer of food subsidiaries to BSN	500
6/82	Honeywell (USA)	transfer to State of 27% of capital in CII–H.B., with Honeywell retaining 20% (data processing)	15 000
6/82	Int. Harvester (USA)	plan to cut back jobs in French plants	867
7/82	ITT (USA)	transfer to State of CGCT (telephone exchanges)	9 000
10/82	Intra. invt. (Lebanon)	loss of financial control of Chantiers Navals de la Ciotat (sectoral reorganisation plan)	3 656
11/82	Bauknecht (West Germany)	plant closed down	800
1/83	Sandwik (Sweden)	transfer of part of Eurotungstène to the mining company Anglade (tungsten carbide)	700
2/83	BBC (Switzerland)	transfer of Cie Electromécanique CEM to Alsthom Atlantique (electrical engineering)	7 700
5/83	Montefibre (Italy)	dissolution of Montefibre France (nylon and polyester)	570

Source: press review.

Applied Micro-circuit, Harris, Intel and CGA have set up integrated circuit factories and AVX has set up an electronic components plant. Finally, many consumer electronics plants have been set up, primarily by the Japanese groups, which are hence penetrating French industry significantly for the first time: video tapes with Intermagnetics, hi-fi systems with Akai and Pioneer, video cassettes with Sony, video tape recorders with Philips, Akai, Grundig and JVC.[40]

THE INTERNATIONAL EXPANSION OF THE FRENCH GROUPS

French firms have continued over 1981–3 to extend their commercial and productive establishments outside France. International expansion has remained an essential strategic policy for all groups, with the political change which has taken place in France not having altered any of the factors of multinationalisation. The continuing crisis has exacerbated the fight to share world markets, while the increasing concentration of production machinery and the stagnation of the national markets are stimulating internationalisation. The authorities have encouraged exporting and international growth by firms which are already deeply committed on foreign markets, and have not changed the main rules of operation for these companies in France, even for those which have been nationalised.

Since June and July 1981, four big French groups have implemented four big investment operations in the United States: Elf Aquitaine with a take-over bid of 14 billion francs for Texas Gulf, Lafarge with the take-over of General Portland, BSN with that of Dannon and Rhône-Poulenc with that of the agrochemicals division of Mobil. This wave of establishments illustrates the extent of the trends involved, the attraction of the American market and the part played by public companies. After describing all of these phenomena in more detail, we shall ask whether this international expansion will permit new relations with the Third World countries, and whether it constitutes an end to the economic crisis.

The Pursuit of Investment Abroad

In 1981, French industry was very broadly multinational. The top thirty-nine multinationals, which are all big companies, employed 571 000 people in their foreign subsidiaries, compared with 1 356 000 in their French plants (cf. Annexe 7). This phenomenon is also very marked within the firms in the building and public works sector, where it has been accentuated recently (cf. Annexe 8) and in the banks.

The flows of French investments abroad, as accounted for in the balance of payments, have increased considerably in 1981.[41]

Over the first two years of F. Mitterrand's seven-year term, the big French groups have implemented some very big investment operations abroad, as part of already very advanced multinational strategies. The thirteen biggest establishments (Table S.3) alone represent investments of a total cost of over 17 billion francs, and foreign operations a turn-over of over 54 billion francs (estimate). Even though certain take-over processes which were completed in 1982–3 had been instigated a long time before (in the cases of American Motors and Mack Truck), this was a very big wave of investment. Take-overs are predominant with only two out of thirteen operations relating to the setting up of plants (PUK in Quebec and Renault in Mexico). The United States and more generally North America are found to be the preferred area for these big external growth operations. Of course, other French companies carried out big investments abroad during this period: Rhône-Poulenc, Valéo, DMC, Bouygues in the United States, Michelin in Brazil, etc.[42]

After 1981, the United States continued to exert a big attraction for French firms. The biggest of their investments abroad over the last two years have, as we have seen, been in the United States. But this movement westwards has involved firms of all sizes, and from

Table S.3 French investments abroad between May 1981 and May 1983—
main operations (industry only)
(the public companies are italicised)

Date	Group	Operation	Cost of investment	Size of activity set up or taken over
6/81	BSN	Take-over Dannon division (fresh products) from Beatrice Foods in USA	84.25 m$ 480 mfr.	130 m$ T/O 730 mfr. T/O
7/82	*CGE*	Take-over of Kable Metall (cables) in West Germany by Cables de Lyon (and in '81 of Chester cable in USA)		5 000 jobs 2 000 mfr. T/O
6/81	*Elf Aquitaine*	Successful take-over bid made for Texas Gulf (chemicals, mining) in USA (real cost to Elf 2315 m$, or 13 500 mfr.)	4232 m$	1 100 m$ T/O 6 160 mfr. T/O
81/82/ 83	General Biscuit	Take-over of 3 cos. in USA: Barry, Salerno biscuits, Mother's Cake and Cookie biscuits	50 m$	2 170 jobs 90 000 tonnes prod. cap.
7/81	Lafarge	Successful take-over bid for General Portland (cement) in USA (10 plants, 7% of American production)	326 m$ 1 850 mfr.	312 m$ T/O 1 769 mfr. T/O
9/81	Lyonnaise des Eaux	Take-over of Aqua Chem (heat prod. and water treatment equipment in USA)		130 m$ T/O 760 mfr. T/O
1/83	Lyonnaise des Eaux	Take-over of 50% capital of General Waterworks (water dist.) in USA		64 m$ T/O
5/83	*PUK*	Sale of American subsidiary Hownet aluminium (aluminium)		3 300 jobs 200 000 tonnes
		Aluminium electrolysis plant project in Quebec (51% of cost borne by PUK)	1 000 m$	230 000 tonnes
1/82	*Renault*	Increase in its share in the capital of American Motors (cars) in USA (Control taken with 46.4% of capital and technical and comm. agreements, cf. production of the Alliance)	40 m$ (350 m$ in all since '79)	146 000 jobs
5/83	*Renault*	Increase of its holding from 20 to 45% in Mack Truck (heavy lorries, 19% of market) in USA (control taken)	100 m$	17 000 lorries 1 300 m$ T/O
82/83	*Renault*	New engine plant set up in Mexico (and increase in control exerted over VAM and Renault Mexico)	400 m$ (in 3 years)	

Table S.3 (*cont.*)

Date	Group	Operation	Cost of invest-ment	Size of activity set up or taken over
5/82	*Thomson*	Take-over of Dual (record players, cassette players) in West Germany		2 000 jobs 620 mfr. T/O
3/83	*Thomson*	Take-over of Telefunken (consumer electronics, 9% of German Market, 4 000 jobs) in West Germany	70 mDm.	1 400 mDm. 4 200 mfr. T/O

Note: T/O: turnover; m: million.
Source: review of press, company reports.

all sectors, as shown by Table S.4. In spite of the rising dollar and the severe American recession, the factors encouraging local production have remained the most important: large market size, increasingly protectionist policy of the Reagan Administration, stability and quality of labour, exceptional technological and managerial environment. Almost all French firms which have embarked on a process of international expansion were already present in the USA in 1983, or were planning significant establishments in the near future. Rhône-Poulenc, which makes only 5 per cent of its turnover in the United States, stated in June 1983 that it wanted to develop in the pharmaceuticals sector there; CGE for its part wanted to take over a private American telephone company. In May 1983, Prouvost added North America to its list of priority areas for expansion. Essilor, Leroy Sommer, Rallye and Casino mentioned the same objectives. Finally, as illustrated in Table S.4, take-overs of companies are found to be more common for industrial establishments, with the commercial subsidiaries mostly being created piecemeal.

Small French companies, when they are leaders in their market or have a technical or commercial advantage, do not hesitate to set up abroad. This dynamism was confirmed over the recent period. CIMA, the top French producer of rear-view mirrors with 522 employees, set up a commercial subsidiary in the USA in 1983. Outilleurs Champenois, with seventy-five employees, set up a production subsidiary in Tunisia.[43]

In the building and public works sector, where the groups have been very multinational for ten years (cf. Annexe 8), establishment outside France has continued, although the persistent crisis has made competition keener on the markets of the Third World. Big contracts have continued to be signed (cf. Bouygues in Algeria, SGE in Abu Dhabi) subsidiaries set up (cf. SPIE in Saudi Arabia), and firms taken over (cf. Bouygues in USA).

The commercial companies (distribution),[44] and the services companies (particular the hotel industry)[45] have set up outside France.

Table S.4 Direct investment decided on by French industrial firms in the USA between May 1981 and May 1983, according to types of companies and investments

Nature of establishment	Type of French company	Methods of investing in the USA			
		Plant set up	Company taken over	Joint Fr./Amer. subsid.	Licence or common agreement
Industrial establishments	Public companies		Elf Aquitaine—Renault—Cogema—Rhône-Poulenc—Inst. Mérieux (RP) Cables de Lyon (CGE) PUK (transfer) CEA (minor. interest) Rousselot (Ato Chimie)	Sanofi (Elf)	
	Big private companies	Rossignol (shutdown ski production)	BSN—General Biscuit—Lafarge—Lyonnaise des Eaux—Générale des Eaux—Air Liquide	Neyrpic (Creusot Loire)	DMC
		Prouvost	Joucomatic—Delalande (transfer) Ciments Français—Pernod Ricard Moët Hennessy	Synthelabo (L'Oréal) Vallourec Moulinex	
	Small private companies	Bolloré	Manitou BF—Sfernice—Roederer		Sarasin
Commercial establishments	Public companies	Alsthom (CGE)	CDF (minor. interest) CDF Chimie	Matra	CIT Alcatel (CGE) CDF Chimie
	Big private companies	Motobécane & SCOA—Dim—Potain—Machines Françaises Lourdes—Franco-rail	Essilor	Jeumont Schneider	Laboratoire Fabre
	Small private companies	6 furniture companies 12 small cos. of Graulhet Cima			Potel & Chabot—UPSA

Source: review of press and company reports.

The banks were already very multinational in 1981: in 1979 and 1980 they had for example been open to foreign countries—30 branches, 11 subsidiaries, 48 representative offices,[46] and in 1980 18 per cent of total banking operations were dealt with by the offices set up abroad.[47] In 1982 and 1983, the big French banks, all nationalised, increased their establishments abroad. Paribas took control of AG Becker, the fourth biggest American investment bank and Sung Hung Kai in Hong Kong (in association with Merrill Lynch). It consolidated its reciprocal holdings with the British merchant bank Warburg, set up a merchant bank in Ireland and opened several branches. Indo Suez set up subsidiaries in Finland, Sweden, Australia and West Germany. CCF set up branches in Great Britain and Hong Kong. The Worms bank set up a subsidiary in Singapore. Crédit Lyonnais set up a subsidiary in Mexico and took over the Dutch Slavenburg bank.

The Main Role of the Public Multinationals

This action has already appeared to be essential in the biggest industrial operations carried out over the last two years abroad (Table S.3) and in establishments in the United States (Table S.4). Of course, companies in the old industrial public sector, such as Renault, Elf and EMC, were among the first multinationals. However, one of the characteristics of the nationalisations in 1982 was that it concerned big industrial groups in the competitive sector, which were big exporters and very multinational. So, out of the top thirty-nine French multinationals (Annexe 7), eleven are today public multinationals, employing 285 000 workers in their foreign subsidiaries, that is half of the total work-force outside France of these thirty-nine multinationals. The State controls seven groups out of the top ten multinational groups, SGPM with 72 000 employees outside France, and Renault with 50 000 employees are in second and third place, slightly behind Michelin.

In addition, the public multinationals account for almost all of the very multinational banking sector which, as we have seen, is continuing its expansion abroad. The part played by the Government in the international growth of industry is hence reinforced, and the international development of the banks is closely tied up with that of the industrial and commercial firms: the establishment of the latter outside French boundaries has led the financial institutions to follow their customers and, conversely, the existence of an international banking network assists the multinational companies.

A brief outline of the main international development operations carried out over the last two years by the French public multinationals enables us to show how, in spite of the different strategies, expansion abroad has remained a constant factor in the policies now clearly incorporated into the planning contracts signed with the State.

Usinor and Sacilor are the least international of the public groups in the competitive sector: being primarily exporters (cf. 39 per cent of turnover in 1982 for Usinor), they have commercial subsidiaries abroad and some minority interests in mines or coking plants. Their development policy has consisted of reorganisation measures, in particular in special steels, production cutbacks decided upon in conjunction with the other European groups, and expensive investment programmes to modernise their installations.

Dassault is a big exporter: in 1981, 77 per cent of its turnover was accounted for by sales of aircraft outside France. It was therefore afraid that the new direction being taken by French foreign policy would affect exports of military equipment and hence sales. In the end nothing came of these fears.[48]

Matra is another big exporter, with the parent company making 73 per cent of its sales abroad in 1981. As it always had before, it has continued to cooperate with foreign groups to acquire technology and produce certain equipment in France: with the Japanese group Hattori (Seiko trade mark) in watch- and clock-making, then with the American group CGA in semi-conductor production equipment. The Government authorised this foreign investment in France, even though Thomson is producing the same type of machines with State financial aid. In addition, Matra has set up a company in the USA in which the group has a 30 per cent holding and the local distributor Tymshare, responsible for selling 560 000 remote data-processing and telecommunications terminals, 70 per cent.

CII–H.B. made 43.2 per cent of its consolidated turnover abroad in 1982, thanks to an important commercial network. It has just opened a branch in Singapore, and obtained authorisation to set up a production and marketing subsidiary for DPS7 systems in Brazil, with local partners.

EMC has commercial and industrial establishments abroad for its three main operations: potassium, chemicals and animal feedstuffs. In 1983 it reorganised its big chemical companies in Belgium (over 2700 employees). In 1982 and 1983, the groups carried out two big investment projects, one in France, in the Mines de Potasse d'Alsace, the other in Canada, with an interest in the exploitation of a potassium deposit in New Brunswick.

CDF chimie, the chemical subsidiary of Charbonnages de France, has commercial subsidiaries abroad, one set up in the USA in 1982, two medium-sized industrial subsidiaries, and interests in industrial companies in Venezuela, Mexico, Portugal and Qatar. It is carrying out project engineering contracts outside France. In 1982 it granted a licence for linear polyethylene to two Japanese groups and in 1983 to Kodak, which shows that development abroad has long been one of the main aspects of its strategy.

SGPM is a group which is very multinational for all its operations (glazing, insulation, cast-iron piping, paper, cardboard) in Europe, the USA, and Brazil: one employee in two works outside France. Having had to dispose of its interests in CII-H.B. and Olivetti, SGPM is now concentrating on its traditional operations. 1982 and 1983 were marked by difficulties in certain sectors such as insulation, and by modernisation investments which often meant job cutbacks, both in France and abroad: reorganisation of Vegla in West Germany, closure of a Skanglass glass factory in Denmark. Its interest in the big American subsidiary Certain Teed was increased in 1982. In July 1983 the group embarked on an extensive diversification programme in France and abroad, and acquired 20 per cent of the capital of Générale des Eaux (water distribution). It also reinforced its public works operations by taking over from CGE 25.7 per cent of the capital of Société Générale d'Entreprises–Saintrapt et Brice, a firm which has developed widely outside France.

PUK, after disposing of its chemical and special steels operations, is involved mainly in the very international aluminium branch. In 1981, the group took control of the British international ore and metal trading firm Brandeis Goldsmith, and in 1982 of the flexible tube operation of VDM in West Germany. It has invested a lot in Australia, one of the cheap energy countries where it wants to develop its aluminium production by constructing a plant in Tomago and increasing its interest in the Arukun bauxite deposit. In 1983, thanks to the signature of an attractive electricity supply contract, it decided to build a big aluminium electrolysis plant in Quebec (220 000 tonnes). Fifty-one per cent of this investment of 1 billion dollars, or 3.5 billion francs, will be borne by PUK, and the disposal of its American subsidiary Hownet Aluminium will serve to finance part of this big project.

Rhône-Poulenc employs 37 per cent of its staff outside France, in Great Britain, Switzerland, West Germany, Spain, the USA and Brazil. Its position in fine chemicals has been reinforced in France following recent reorganisations. The group has continued with its rationalisation investments in its loss-making textile fibres operations and with the development of its other operations, especially abroad. In the USA, it has started up a rare earth plant and taken over the agrochemicals division of Mobil.[49] In Japan it has set up three joint subsidiaries with Daï Nippon (silicon based products), Mitsui Petrochemical Cy (polyimide resin) and Toyobo (magnetic tapes). In Korea, a pharmaceuticals factory has been opened. In Australia, the group has taken over a silicon mastics manufacturer.

CGE has carried out an extensive reorganisation programme in France, in particular in electrical engineering (cf. take-over by Alsthom of Compagnie Electromécanique, a subsidiary of the Swiss group BBC) and in contracting operations (cf. take-over of Cochery by SGE, then transfer of 25.7 per cent of the capital of SGE, corresponding to a disengagement from public works operations). This group, which makes 35 per cent of its total turnover abroad, and is still moderately multinational, has continued its expansion outside France. This is shown by an analysis of a sector and a geographical area. In the cables sector, the subsidiary Cables de Lyon took over Chester Cable Corp. in the USA, and took control of a German group Kable Metall in 1982, and thanks to this external growth operation became the second biggest producer of cables in the world. In the United States several establishments were carried out: a commercial subsidiary TGV Inc. was set up, the portable batteries division of Gould was taken over, the capital of the subsidiary Friden Alcatel was increased, and a 25 per cent interest was taken in the capital of Lynch Communications Systems, who will make the CIT–Alcatel E 10 S electronic exchange.

Elf Aquitaine has considerably reinforced its position in the chemical industry in France, at the request of the Government, as part of the sectoral reorganisation plan. Its pharmaceuticals subsidiary has taken control of Charles Jourdan perfumes. The international expansion of the group[50] was marked by the take-over bid for Texas Gulf, which was the biggest French investment operation abroad for ten years, and the biggest take-over of an American company by a foreign company. It shows Elf's wish to set up a development base in North America which will give it permanent flows of revenue, to replace those of the Lacq gas field which is nearly exhausted. While in 1980 the Minister of Industry had forbidden Elf to take over the American oil group Ker MacGee, in June 1981 the Socialist Government authorised the group, run by A. Chalandon to make a take-over bid for Texas Gulf. This group, which has a turnover of 1.1 billion dollars in chemical operations, has big mineral reserves (phosphates, copper, zinc, oil) and a good profitability rate up until 1980. The take-over bid, costing the French group 2 315 million dollars, or 13.5 billion francs, was to be financed by the disposal of the Canadian Elf subsidiary (994 million Canadian dollars) and by borrowing 1.4 billion dollars on the financial markets. The oil group undertook not to take any currency out of France, but in fact, because of Texas Gulf's difficulties, Elf has already transferred over 1 billion francs out of France in 1982 alone, and these flows are bound to increase. This operation illustrates a financial investment strategy on the part of a big group which has extremely large liquid assets. The Government, by authorising this operation, has clearly shown its desire to open up abroad. But is this decision consistent with the desire announced to make big investments in French industry?

Renault carried out an extensive international expansion programme in 1982 and 1983. It confirmed two strategic choices which had already been outlined in previous years; firstly industrial establishment in North America, and secondly investment in the heavy goods vehicle sector. This double ambition of the public group contrasts with the very great prudence of its private competitor Peugeot.[51] In fact, of the many international operations carried out over the last two years (in Taiwan, South Africa, Tunisia and Colombia), three would seem to be very important. In January 1982, the group subscribed to 40 million dollars of convertible debentures in AMC, in which it had had a minority holding since 1979. With 46.4 per cent of the capital and technical agreements signed, Renault thus has virtual control over the fourth biggest American car manufacturer—employing 146 000 workers and with a turnover of 3 billion dollars—and has appointed its managing director. AMC distributes the R5 and R18 in the United States, assembles the Fuego and in September 1982 began the local production of the R9, christened the Alliance, with a target of 100 000 sales per annum. In 1983, Renault invested a further 50 million dollars for AMC to produce the American version of the R11. Renault now therefore has a massive and irreversible commitment in the USA, where it is taking big commercial, industrial and financial risks. The investments made in Mexico complete Renault's establishment in the North American continent. In this country, Renault took total control of two companies which were already assembling Renault and AMC cars in June 1983. In 1984 it is to commission a new engine plant, 80 per cent of which will be exported to the USA, which will reduce production costs for the Alliance and the other AMC models. The third strategic decision, in May 1983, was for Renault to double its stake in Mack Truck, a heavy lorry producer which accounts for 19 per cent of the American market. Renault, which already held 20 per cent of the capital, took over 25 per cent of the shares, giving it a majority of the votes on the board and responsibility for management. Mack, which already distributes Renault 9-15 tonne lorries, is to buy components in France and manufacture urban buses. In view of the take-over in 1981 of the heavy goods vehicles branch of Chrysler in Europe, Renault has become the second biggest producer in the world of utility vehicles—but with companies making losses and the market in a state of crisis, this is a second massive strategic gamble.

Thomson is a big diversified group, primarily an exporter, whose growth has largely relied on State aid and public orders for military equipment (cf. arms systems) and professional equipment (telephone exchanges, radar, radiology). Since May 1981 it has accelerated its sectoral relocation by trying to offload its loss-making operations. In May 1982, one of the first decisions of the new chairman and managing director was to sell La Compagnie des Lampes (4000 employees) to Philips. The civil data-processing division was transferred to CII–H.B. The group has tried to get out of the medical equipment branch, and it might do the same in the telephone branch. However, the strategic decisions taken over the last two years are characterised by the pursuit of two policies which it had been following for several years: the conclusion of technological and industrial agreements with foreign groups in France, and the expansion abroad of its consumer electronics activity. Thomson, which already distributed small Japanese televisions and video tape recorders under its own name, decided in December 1982 to market Hitachi compact disc players. In November 1981 it planned to sell JVC video tape recorders and video discs produced by AGE and Thorn EMI, under an agreement reserving the production of cameras for itself. This agreement was, however, blocked by the Government. Similarly, in September 1981, SEMS, the group's data-processing subsidiary, planned to produce a 16-bit microcomputer and a 32-bit minicomputer in France, under technical agreements with the American groups Fortune and SEL, for whom it was going to market other products too. This agreement was cancelled as the Government wanted SEMS to collaborate with CII–H.B. Another decision in April 1982 was for Thomson to give up marketing the professional video disc for which it did have a technical advantage, as the prospects did not guarantee a sufficient return. Finally in 1983, in view of the losses of the subsidiary CGR, Thomson planned an agreement to share production and marketing areas with the American group Technicare, in accordance with which CGR would stop all activities to produce advanced medical electronics (RMN) and on the markets of North America. The conclusion of this agreement, which has caused controversy in French political, trade union, industrial and medical circles, is still uncertain.[52] These operations show that the Thomson group, in those activities where it is faced with technological lags, often goes for solutions which are profitable in the short term, at the expense of production investment and research which could give it control in the longer term.

Another of the group's policies is to try and reach a reasonable size in traditional consumer electronics (radio, television, hi-fi). In May 1982, it took over the German record and cassette-player producer, Dual. Then, in November 1982, it concluded a project to take over 75 per cent of the capital of the German Grundig group, number one in consumer electronics, with 30 000 employees, a turnover of 9 billion francs and producing 1.8 million televisions and 830 000 video tape recorders per year. However, opposition from Philips, which refused to transfer the 25 per cent of Grundig's capital which it held, opposition from the German politicians and trade unions, partly because of Thomson's bad reputation as a company in West Germany, and finally the refusal announced in March 1983 by the German Cartels Office, forced the group to abandon this project. Thomson immediately took over Telefunken, the AEG subsidiary under receivership, which produces 700 000 televisions and 200 000 video tape recorders per year. It then signed an agreement in April 1983 with the Japanese group JVC to produce video tape recorders with imported components and Japanese technology in France (mechanical part) and in Germany (assembly).

Thomson is one of the nationalised groups most dependent on the State through the aid and public orders it receives. It is firmly entrenched in the electronics branch, a priority in the new industrial policy. However, although the Government has blocked certain decisions, it did ratify the sale of Compagnie des Lampes to Philips, the agreement with JVC and the abandonment of the professional video disc, and it would seem that it had difficulty in preventing the CGR-Technicare agreement. Does this not emphasise both a degree of hesitation in economic policy and the power of a group whose management team has been little changed? The failure of the Grundig takeover, and the agreement signed with JVC also mark the failure to find a European solution in the consumer electronics industry. Instead of a Thomson-Grundig-Philips agreement, adopting the V2000 standard for video tape recorders, we have a Thomson-Telefunken-JVC agreement with the VHS standard for video tape recorders, with the Thomson group signing in April 1983 an agreement which, although it was more advantageous and involved a real transfer of technology, was similar to the one the Government blocked in November 1981.

In conclusion, over the last two years, the nationalised groups have vigorously pursued international expansion, with methods similar to those of the private groups. No operations abroad have been banned by the Government, which has hence recognised the autonomy of the nationalised groups and the need for them to set up outside France. Certain operations such as the Elf operation in the USA or certain agreements of Thomson do, however, seem inconsistent with the trend of industrial policy, which poses a problem of articulation.

New Relations with the LDCs?

The Government wants to promote new economic relations between France and the Third World countries, which would in particular promote more autonomous growth by these nations. Is this shown by changes in the action taken by French multinationals abroad, for example by the public multinationals? Two short answers can be put forward.

Transfers of technology, without any direct control by the foreign company setting up production, have continued to develop, without this being a new trend. On the other hand, the French Government has publicly repeated the wish expressed a long time ago by the less developed countries, which has assisted in the signing of agreements. Dassault has obtained the manufacture under licence of 40 Mirage 2000 aircraft in India. And in May 1982, thanks to an outline agreement between the two governments, CIT–Alcatel won a big contract to supply 200 000 telephone lines and install a plant with a production capacity of 500 000 per annum, with complete transfer of the technology for telephone exchanges and the training of researchers, engineers and workers.[53]

In February 1982, Gaz de France signed an agreement with Sonatrach in Algeria in accordance with which Algeria would supply France with 9.15 billion cubic metres of gas per annum at a price which was some 20 per cent above the world price. This agreement, which 'is not a simple commercial agreement but a basic co-development agreement', corresponds to the 'desire of the leaders of the two countries to give themselves security and to make the best use of the income from natural resources, a fundamental aspect of North–South relations often highlighted by the Algerian Government, and to which the French Government intends to contribute' (Joint communiqué, February 1982). This decision has considerable significance for both economies. It was implicitly coupled with the award of fifteen Algerian industrial projects, worth 12 billion francs, to French companies, which is a positive trade-off for French industry.

The Multinationals out of the Crisis?

This question is raised in two recent works which have shown that over the years 1973-80 direct international investment from the industrial countries, in spite of slowing down slightly, has held up better than national investment within these economies, and has given rise to more and more reciprocal investment between these nations. Analysing the adaptation strategies of the world multinationals the authors show how they are standing up to the crisis better than the national companies.[54]

This trend has been confirmed here with regard to the development over the last two years and for the French economy: we have shown that foreign investment in France and French investment abroad have continued at a high level. Internationalisation is still one of the best ways for firms to fight competitors, with world markets being shared today both by exports and direct production abroad. This multinationalisation is then an essential factor in improving competitiveness and profitability. For example, in its annual report, the French group Valeo stressed that during 1982 its sales had fallen by 5 per cent in volume in France and increased abroad by 20 per cent.

Recent data have confirmed that these international investments very often take the form of companies being taken over, which in particular has no effect on creating employment. This leads us to stress that the rapid international growth of the multinationals does not necessarily mean a bigger increase in employment within these groups, either in their home economy or in their host economies. In fact, the French subsidiaries of foreign multinational groups did on average reduce their employees between 1974 and 1983 at the same rate as French companies as a whole.[55] For their part, the French multinationals do not seem to have been any more dynamic in employment in France. An examination of the thirty-nine top multinationals listed in Annexe 7 shows that between the end of 1974 and the end of 1981, the number of their employees increased much more outside France, by +39.7 per cent, but only by +11.9 per cent in France. We do, however, need to eliminate the big company take-over operations in France which inflate the number of employees without meaning that French plants are intrinsically dynamic.[56]

The considerable losses made by several big French groups in the 1980s, in particular the nationalised groups, are evidence of the difficulties encountered by these leaders of French industry, with big commitments to world competition. In general these results illustrate the fact that this multinationalisation movement does not constitute a general solution to the crisis of the world economy, as the multinationals are sharing a market which on the whole is stagnating.

Finally, certain recent developments of the French multinationals stress the risks of multinationalisation. The firms obtaining a big part of their turnover and profits in these foreign countries are becoming very vulnerable to the economic situation prevalent on these markets, and to monetary fluctuations. The Lafarge group, which invested heavily in the USA in 1981, was a victim of the severe American recession in 1982: its operations over the Atlantic, which in 1982 represented 38 per cent of its consolidated turnover, fell in terms of tonnage delivered by 25 per cent in Canada and 6 per cent in the USA, and they did not make any contribution to the result, only balancing their accounts (1982 company report). Another significant example is that of the Michelin group which made losses of 290 million francs in 1981 and 4 billion francs in 1982, the equivalent of 10 per cent of its turnover. This very multinational group, which recently made big investments in North America and Brazil, is thus suffering from a particularly marked world recession in the USA where the car market has collapsed. The deficit of the American subsidiaries has been accentuated in the group accounts thanks to the rise in the dollar compared with the franc. Over the period 1982–3, French multinationals have therefore had to bear considerable losses from their foreign establishments.[57]

The development of the French economy might seem paradoxical, particularly in the eyes of a foreign observer. In spite of the nationalisation of almost the whole banking system and eleven big industrial groups, the extension of public involvement in research and industry and the constitution under the aegis of the State of big industrial groups in several sectors, in spite of the wish it expressed to 'reconquer the domestic market', the French Government would like to maintain the international opening up of its economy and promote the expansion of foreign groups in France and French groups outside France, without fundamentally changing the rules of the game. The facts show that over the last two years the French production system has become more international. The French multinationals, including the old and new public multinationals which already had many involvements outside France, have continued to establish themselves throughout the world, particularly in the USA. At the same time, the foreign groups have continued to concentrate their investment in France, which clearly shows that in their eyes it is still a market economy and a free trade economy.

NOTES

1 Cf. reorganisation of refractory operations in France with loss of 448 jobs in 1982 (1982 company report, p. 12).
2 Cf. J. F. Lemettre, 1981. See also C. Stoffaës, 1983.
3 Roussell Uclaf was excluded from the scope of the public sector democratisation law, and did not sign a planning contract with the State in 1983.
4 The Government has not followed the advice of the Council of State, which in September 1981 recommended that it get rid of its non-banking interests in the two financial companies Suez and Paribas within the year.
5 During the summer of 1983, SGPM, the nationalised group, when taking over the holdings of CGE and the financial institutions, did, however, obtain 20 per cent of the capital of the Générale des Eaux group, while BNP and Stern bank, allied with SGPM, obtained 13 per cent. SGPM is therefore now able to exert financial and industrial control over Générale des Eaux.
6 But confirming its wish to set up an international shop group around SAGA.
7 Another publicised affair was when the former private shareholders of Saint-Gobain did not obtain a receiving order for the Swiss subsidiary of the group (cf. *Le Monde*, 23 September 1982).
8 Similarly, we can remark that the nationalisations did not result in a massive brain drain, which some people had predicted.
9 Which is confirmed in the Law of 11 February 1982 by the dispensation from having State controllers for CGE, Thomson, PUK, SGPM, and Rhône-Poulenc.
10 Letter of appointment from P. Dreyfus, Minister of Industry, to the general managers, February 1982.
11 On 23 February 1982, P. Mauroy told the chairman and managing directors of the nationalised groups, 'As regards social policy, you must give the example, without ever calling into question the competitiveness of your companies and even more so their financial equilibrium.'
12 The Ministry of Defence for Matra, Dassault, Snias, Snecma; Ministry of Industry for Renault, PUK, SGPM, Thomson, CGE, Rhône-Poulenc, CII-H.B., CGCT, CDF chimie, EMC, EDF, GDF, CDF, Elf Aquitaine, Usinor and Sacilor.

13 Twenty billion francs capital contribution in 1982 for all public companies, 20 billion in 1983 for the eleven companies under the Ministry of Industry, compared with 9 billion in 1982 (iron and steel 6.45 billion; CII-H.B. 1.55; PUK 2.4; Rhône-Poulenc 1.8).

14 Approximately 600 companies and 1.8 million employees. The bill became law on 26 July 1983 and it carried with it numerous exceptions.

15 Cf. STISI, 1982. The nine groups are: CGE, Thomson, Dassault, Matra, PUK, Rhône-Poulenc, SGPM, Usinor and Sacilor. We should add: CGCT, CII-H.B., Imétal, Cofaz (Paribas) Métallurgique de Normandie, Dubigeon Normandie, Cie Electronique CEM (acquired by Alsthom in 1982).

16 With 28.8 per cent of employees, however, if Alsthom were taken into account (railway equipment) this would increase this percentage.

17 ERAP, Elf Aquitaine holding company, has a majority interest in the capital of SLN.

18 With two companies threatened, La Cellulose d'Alozay and La Chapelle d'Arblay, this is a sector in which the State is present in La Cellulose du Pin (subsidiary of SGPM), Rochette Cenpa (15 per cent holding by Paribas) and Beghin Say (12 per cent holding by Suez).

19 One billion francs in 1983, added to each group's own contributions.

20 With a specific contribution of 650 million francs by the State in 1983.

21 Thomson retains CIMSA, military data processing.

22 The cost of the investments necessary to develop national production of big computers makes it probable that the present dependence on the USA will continue (essentially IBM).

23 Especially since we have omitted certain reorganisations of the public groups such as the take-over by Alsthom of Cie Electromécanique CEM (7700 employees) or the transfer by this group of its small engine activity to Leroy Somer.

24 Cf. J. P. Gilly and F. Morin, 1981, p. 33.

25 Cf. control taken of Hachette group by Matra, and Schneider group by Paribas.

26 The diversification policies of SGPM in urban services, with virtual control of the Générale des Eaux group over the summer of 1983 (in particular by taking over its interest in the Compagnie Générale d'Electricité group which is relocating its production), illustrate this diversification phenomenon. This water distribution activity is, however, much closer to the traditional activities of SGPM, cast-iron piping and insulation, than its diversification into data processing, abandoned in 1982 at the request of the Government.

27 *Le Nouvel Economiste*, 20 April 1981.

28 With, for example, the obligation to publish their foreign currency payments balances.

29 For steel, shoes, machine tools, for example. In 1982, a bill supported by the Democrats proposed that any car sold on the American market should include a minimum number of parts manufactured on the spot (cf. *Le Monde*, 5 August 1982).

30 And an annual licence of 471 francs payable by all video tape-recorder owners.

31 Cf. the contracts of Dassault and CIT Alcatel in India, or those corresponding to fifteen Algerian industrial projects reserved for French companies following an agreement on the price of gas signed in February 1982.

32 Contrary to what one might have thought hearing President Mitterrand declare 'If nationalisation were not carried out, far from being nationalised, these companies would soon be internationalised. I reject an international division of labour and production decided in distant countries, serving interests which do not accord with our own'—statement made at a press conference given 24 September 1981.

33 The Government has thus abstained from making any public comment on the European project to control multinationals (Verdeling project); cf. G. Caire, 1982.

34 Cf. Note bleue No. 21 of June 1981, Ministry of the Economy. Several big operations authorised in 1981 will comply with this rule: the take-over bid of 14 billion francs for Texas Gulf was to be financed in part by the disposal of Elf Aquitaine's interests in Canada, the acquisition for 315 million dollars of General Portland in USA was made by a subsidiary of Ciments Canada Lafarge.

35 The total gross flows of foreign direct investment into France rose from 19 630 million francs in 1980 to 20 170 million francs in 1981, and from 6565 million francs to 8440 million francs for industry (the balance of payments figures for 1982 at the time of writing were not available).

36 The association of PUK with Occidental Petroleum (already blocked under Giscard d'Estaing), the setting up of a fertiliser factory by the Dutch SKF group, the transfer of the advanced activities of Compagnie Générale de Radiologie (Thomson) to the American Technicare group.

37 The setting up and take-over operations are underestimated compared with those of disinvestments which get better coverage in the press because of the social consequences.

38 One phenomenon has become apparent in the preparation of these statistics: during the second year, reductions in activity and closures of subsidiaries of foreign groups have seemed to accelerate, as if the Government were accepting reorganisations which the previous Government had blocked (cf. case of Montefibre France), and as if the persistence of the crisis were accelerating this reorganisation. This adverse trend still has to be confirmed.

39 Of the many take-overs of medium or small companies we can mention Oberthur, Heller, Spepic, Fond. et at. du Rhône, Chaussure Kicker, Richaux, fonderie de Merlin Gerin, Fram, Mep, CIG, Nord Morue, Quercy, Paulhet, Baube, Calvet, René Garaud, Magister, Peintures H. Lappartient, Parfums Grès, Papeteries de Pont, Audemer, Watco, L. J. Oxford, Verreries des Trois Fontaines, SIPAP.

40 Other plants set up or extended include those of the groups Bahlsen, WH. Brady, Quaker Oat, Tandy, Citizen, Ocor, Union Carbide, Cummins Engines, Groko, Computer Vision, WR Grace and Co, Du Pont de Nemours, Merck, Macrodyne, Emag, Danly Machine Corp., Alfa Riceti, Van Pelt, General Foods and Baumann.

41 The total gross flows of French investment abroad amounted to 12 596 million francs in 1979, 18 021 million francs in 1980 and 38 264 million francs in 1981. 10 000 million francs of this high figure is accounted for by big operations in the USA and the take-over bid for Texas Gulf. Source: Ministry of the Economy, Note bleue No. 88, September 1982, French balance of payments in 1981–March 1983.

42 Excluding the operations in the USA, described in the following paragraph, we can mention the following operations:

Agricultural/food industries: Sodima, Pernod Ricard, Marie Brizard, Piper Heidsieck, Grands Moulins de Paris, Socopa.

Capital goods and intermediate products: Pompes Guinard, Outilleurs Champenois, Rousselot.

Consumer goods: Cycles Peugeot, Synthelabo, L'Oréal, Essilor, Sommer Allibert, Prouvost, SAIC, Seb.

43   UPSA laboratories, with a turnover of 245 million francs, are going to market a product in the USA in conjunction with Hoffman La Roche. Potel et Chabot, 240 employees, top French catering firm, is setting up in Germany in 1983 (franchise contract). Six small companies making furniture are opening a shop in New York. Bolloré SA, a paper manufacturer employing 700, set up an industrial subsidiary in the USA in 1982. Twelve small fancy leather goods companies, de Graulhet, set up a commercial subsidiary in the USA. Manitou BF, a small company with a turnover of 650 million francs, is taking over 50 per cent of the capital of an American firm to sell its forklift trucks.

44   Cf. Printemps in Singapore, Carrefour in Argentina, Darty in Spain and Euromarché in Saudi Arabia.

45   Cf. Mériden in the USA (seven hotels in 1981), India and Hong Kong, Novotel in the USA, club Méditerranée and Accor.

46   For a full analysis see P. B. Ruffini, 1983.

47   Report of the Bank Control Commission, 1980.

48   In 1981 the Government banned aircraft from being represented at the air show at le Bourget with their arms systems. However, the new ministers have continued to support arms sales to many foreign governments.

49   But it had to dispose of its 20 per cent holding in the capital of the pharmaceuticals company Morton-Norwich, following a legal dispute.

50   The pharmaceutical subsidiary Sanofi also set up a commercial subsidiary in the USA and signed two cooperation agreements in Japan. In France, Elf has associated with Union Carbide (USA) and Toray (Japan) to produce carbon fibres. For an analysis of Elf Aquitaine's strategy see P. Péan and J. P. Sérini, 1982.

51   Peugeot signed a financial and industrial agreement with Chrysler, but in February 1983 gave up producing a small car with this group in the USA. Peugeot, making a loss, is getting to grips with important reorganisation investments to be carried out in the Talbot plants in Spain and Great Britain (cf. also the closure of a Citroën plant in Belgium, the disposal of its financial interest in its commercial subsidiary in Argentina, the failure of the factory project in Romania). It also announced in July 1983 a plan to cut back 7371 jobs in its French Peugeot and Talbot plants.

52   The planning contract was signed without this question being settled.

53   One year later, in July 1983, CIT-Alcatel was again selected to construct a second telephone exchange plant in the south of the country. In January 1981, the PUK group had also obtained a big transfer of technology contract in India, with the group setting up a mine, an alumina plant and an aluminium plant and supplying all the knowhow, with the back up of French public credit. See J. Lamant, 1982 for a recent analysis of the new objectives of the NICs, and for the wish of the French authorities to develop these new types of agreements see De Bandt and Judet, 1983, and Berthelot, Pineye, Sid Ahmed, 1983.

54   Cf. W. Andreff, 1983, and Delapierre, Madeuf, Michalet, Ominami, 1983.

55   Cf. J. Savary, 1983, pp. 16 ff.

56   Cf. ibid., pp. 37 ff.

57   Elf hoped that Texas Gulf would make profits: this was not the case in 1982. Rossignol has for two years been the victim of poor winter snow falls in the USA where it has had to close down its factories. Moulinex is having great difficulty in its North American plant, which has had an adverse effect on its financial results. The consolidated profit of Carrefour did not increase very much in 1981 because of the poor results in Spain and Brazil. Prouvost has suffered from the losses of its Brazilian subsidiary. In 1982 Imétal, as well as SLN, bore a deficit from its American subsidiary Copperweld, Creusot-Loire

(Empain Schneider group) had to bear the loss in 1982 of 17 million dollars by its American subsidiary Phoenix Steel, which it finally ceased to support in August 1983.

ANNEXES

Annexe 1 List of the 413 French companies in the sample by sector of activity and size

(Within each sector the companies are classed by decreasing size, measured by the amount of their equity as at 31 December 1974.)

SECTOR 1—*PRIMARY INDUSTRY*

SNPA
Esso SAF
Antar PA
Générale des Eaux
Parisienne de Chauff. urbain
Plant. Terres Rouges
Electricité Strasbourg
Compagnie Cambodge
Primagaz
Hydrocarbures Saint-Denis
Gaz et Eaux
Caoutchoucs de Padang
Oxygène Acet. Ext. Orient
Urbain Air Comprimé
Eurafrep
Compagnie Eaux ozone
Eaux Banlieue Paris
Compagnie Agr. Ind. Commerce
Comores Bambao

SECTOR 2—*MINING, CONSTRUCTION MATERIALS, GLASS*

BSN GD
Lafarge
Salins du Midi
Ciments français
Carbonisation entre. céra.
Ciments Vicat
Lambert Frères et Cie
Origny Desvroise
Ciments d'Origny
Compagnie de Mokta
Cérabati

Dong Trieu
Tuileries Marseille Med.
Placoplâtre
Ardoisières d'Angers
Sabla
Ciments Port. Lorraine
Quartz et Silice
Verreries Puy-de-Dôme
Dannes Lavocat
Cristalleries Baccarat
Ardoisières d'Anjou
Ciments et Matériaux
Tuileries Gilardoni

SECTOR 3—*IRON AND STEEL, METALLURGY*

Usinor
Imétal
Vallourec
Min. Met. Penarroya
Marine Wendel
Laminoirs tr. cabl. Lens
Hauts Fourneaux Chiers
Schneider s.a.
Lyon Alemand Louyot
J.-J. Carnaud
Forges de Gueugnon
Ind. Fin. Pompey
Neuves Maisons Chatillon
s.a. Paris et Outreau
Profilés Tubes Est
La Mure
Ets Gantois
Fichet-Bauche
Vincey Bourget
Arbel

Laminoirs froid Thionville
Fab. fer Maubeuge
Tissmetal Lionel Dupont
Métallurgique de l'Escaut
Cartoucherie française
Métal Déployé
Fonderie de précision
Keller et Lelleux
Ressorts du Nord
Man. Met. Tournus
Forgeval
Constr. Métalliques et entr.
Forges de Clairvaux
Boulonnerie de Thiant
Forges at. de la foulerie
Expl. min. de l'Indochine
Chantiers maritimes Paimpol

SECTOR 4—*BASIC CHEMICALS*

Rhône-Poulenc
Rousselot
Chimique de la Grande-Paroisse
La Carbonique
SIAS
Parcor
Thann et Mulhouse
Gerland
Duffour et Igon
Pts mat. col. Mulhouse
Givaudan, Lavirotte et Cie
Agricola
Gilot
Baïkowski

SECTOR 5—*PAPER, RUBBER, PLASTICS*

Man. Michelin
Compagnie générale Michelin
Pricel
Sommer-Allibert
Kleber-Colombes
Cellulose du Pin
La Rochette-Cenpa
Dunlop s.a.
Hutchinson-Mapa
Arjomari Prioux
Novacel
Charfa
Papeteries de la Chapelle
Paulstra
Papeteries Clairefontaine

Générale des Papiers
Paul Dumas
Pâtes, papiers et textilose
Cotex Union

SECTOR 6—*PARACHEMICALS, PHARMACEUTICALS*

L'Oréal
Institut Mérieux
Labaz
Laboratoires Roger Bellon
Lorilleux-Lefranc
RETI
Delalande s.a.
Ind. for des allumettes
Explosifs et produits chimiques
Lumière
Parfums Caron
IPA
Laboratoires Sarbach
Durrschmidt
Nivéa
Ruggiéri
Buhler Fontaine
Prochim
Johnson et Cie

SECTOR 7—*CONSUMER GOODS*

Libraire Hachette
Saint Frères
Agache-Willot
Lainière de Roubaix
Bic
Prouvost s.a.
Revillon frères
Imprimerie éd. d. nouv. Strasbourg
Tanneries de France
Imprimerie G. Lang
Skis Rossignol
Filés de Fourmies
Le Blan et Cie
Man. française tapis et couvertures
Vitos
Badin et fils
CICOR
Sarlino
Plastic Omnium
Librairie A. Quillet
Orfèvrerie Christofle
Maroquinerie Le Tanneur
Financière Valisère

Ets Gaillard
La Soie
Gaveau Erard
Ruby
La Brosse et J. Dupont
Société Morvan
Imprimerie de Strasbourg

SECTOR 8—*MECHANICAL ENGINEERING*

Appl. méca. SKF
Poclain s.a.
Essilor international
Crouzet
Soudure Autogène Française
Ernault Somua
Manhurin
Bernard Moteurs
Constr. Met. de Provence
Moteurs Baudouin
Gévelot
Nordon et Cie
BSL
Engrenages et réducteurs
Tref. Ateliers Commercy
Ateliers Bergeaud
Ets Neu
Cie transmissions mécaniques
Surgénérienne const. mécaniques
Amrep
Frankel
SKM
Soc. G. Vernier
Rateau
Jaz s.a.
Speichim
Ateliers GSP
Expl. usines métallurgiques
Industrie de fab. et de transf.
Appareils évaporateurs Kestner
Nantaise de fonderie

SECTOR 9—*ELECTRICAL ENGINEERING*

Compagnie générale d'électricité
Thomson-Brandt
Alsthom
CIT–Alcatel
La Radiotechnique
Seb s.a.
Moulinex
Télémécanique électrique

Française des téléphones Ericsson
CGR
Merlin Gerin
Sagem
SAFT
De Dietrich et Cie
Piles Wonder
Silec
P. M. Labinal
Arthur-Martin
Claude s.a.
Française Auer
Cipel
Océanic
Radio Maritime
Saxby
Soc. Electricité Mors
Man. réu Saint-Chamond
Expl. électr. indus.
Métanic
Lemercier frères

SECTOR 10—*TRANSPORTATION EQUIPMENT*

Renault
Automobiles Peugeot
Citroën s.a.
Dassault
Ferodo
Berliet
Chantiers Atlantique
Chausson
Paris et du Rhône
Acier et outillage Peugeot
Chantiers de France Dunkerque
Jaeger
SEV Marchal
Wabco Westinghouse
Franco Belge Matériel ch. fer
Cycles Peugeot
Cefilac
Motobécane
Trailor
Prov. ateliers Terrin
Carel Fouche Languepin
Fab. instruments de mesure
Floquet Monopole
ABG Semca
Dubigeon Normandie
CIMT Lorraine
Fauvet Girel
Mavilor
Decauville

Ets Ind. Dr Soulé
La Polymécanique

SECTOR 11—*BUILDING AND PUBLIC WORKS*

Soc. Générale entreprises
Fougerolle
Bouygues
Saunier-Duval
Routière Colas
A. Herlicq et fils
SPIE Batignolles
Auxiliaire d'entreprises
Campenon-Bernard
Mines bitume asphalte
Maisons Phénix
Coignet
Swartz-Haumont
Suburbaine canalisations
Dragages et travaux publics
Entreprise A. Borie
Balency Briard
A. Cochery
Trindel
Nationale de Construction
Wanner Isofi isolation
Entreprise Heulin
Nord France entreprises
Travaux éclairage force
Routière du Midi

SECTOR 12—*COMMERCE*

Au Printemps
Nouvelles Galeries
Davum
Ets éco. Casino
Radar s.a.
Galeries Lafayette
CFAO
Cedis
Paris France
Fisuma
Ets. Nicolas
Ets Nozal
Goulet Turpin
Cofradel
Viniprix
Forces et lumière électriques
Darnay
Safic Alcan et Cie
Econom. Troyens et Docks
Alsacienne Supermarchés

Stokvis et fils
L'Allobroge
Docks Fouquet
Mielle
Ruche méridionale
Docks du Nord les Echos
Doc François
Antargaz
Aux Trois-Quartiers
Nord-Ouest Alimentation
Docks, alcools, carburants
Economie bretonne
Gde Brasserie de Lille
Pyr. entreprises industrielles
Motoconfort
Docks lyonnais
Aux Cordeliers de Lyon
Lancel
Berton et Sicard
Matériel construction Sud-Est
Docks pet Ambès
Docks Ardennais
Magasins du Globe
Comm. Ind. du Midi
Maisons H. Devred
Favre Frères
Grand Bazar de Toulouse

SECTOR 13—*SERVICES*

Compagnie La Henin
Compagnie du Nord
Compagnie générale Transatlantique
Messageries Maritimes
Agence Havas
Française transports maritimes
Industrielle maritime
UTA
Club Méditerranée
Entr. Mag. gen. Paris
SAGA
Pompes Funèbres Générales
PLM
Bis s.a.
Sofitel
STEF
Pathé Cinéma
CEGF
Hôtel Meurice
Nationale Navigation
Française transports entreprises
Locatel
Simotra
Stemi

Mattei automobile
Ch. fer et tr. automobile
Avenir Publicité
Navale Caennaise
Hotel Casino Deauville
Immeubles de Lyon
Générale location serv. textiles
Imm. comm. Banville
Bertin et Cie
Tr. en commun de Nice
Citram
Entreprises et part. autom.
Pigier et Cie
SGTE
Royal Monceau Hôtel
Docks industriels
Africaine armement
Touage et remorquage
Soc. Gérance et Navigation
Tramways de Rouen
Mag. gen. Lyon Guillotière
Cie Int. Wagons Citernes
Ch. fer Saint-Etienne
Grand Hôtel Bordeaux

SECTOR 14—*AGRICULTURAL AND FOOD INDUSTRIES*

Pernod-Ricard
Moët-Hennessy
Mumm et Cie
Olida et Caby
Dubonnet

Veuve Cliquot Ponsardin
Brass. Glac. Internationales
Saupiquet
Grands Moulins de Paris
Eaux minérales Vittel
Ch. Pommery Greno
Cusenier
Piper-Heidsieck
Sant-Raphaël
Sogepal
Caves producteurs réunis Roquefort
Grands Moulins de Strasbourg
Rochefortaise Produits alimentaires
Malteries franco-belges
Lait Mont-Blanc
Pointe à Pitre
Distilleries Réunies
Sofical
Grands Moulins de Pantin
Eaux minérales Bassin Vichy
Grands Moulins de Corbeil
Banania
Costimex
Brasseries du Pêcheur
Benedictine
Ricqles Zan
Cie Française Grands Vins
Géo
Ets Rigal
Fromagerie P. Renard
Sucrerie Raffinerie de Bresles
Adeshoffen
Sogevals
Française de sucreries au Chili

Annexe 2 Note on methodology[1]

1. COMPILING THE SAMPLE, SOURCES AND CHOICE OF VARIABLES

In view of the lack of official statistics and information published by companies,[2] we have had to compile a data base on operations in France and abroad for a sample of 413 quoted companies. The figures have been obtained from various published sources and, as regards operations abroad, by a direct survey carried out among the companies.[3]

The figures researched had to describe the conditions under which the companies operate in France and their operations abroad. It was on the latter point, for which few data are available, that some simple figures had to be selected to make sure that figures could be collected for all the companies. For this reason we have just given figures for the amount of exports and the turnover of foreign commercial subsidiaries by area. For production abroad the measurement criterion used was the turnover of foreign production subsidiaries by geographical area. This figure does not give a very accurate picture of real production operations because of the imports included: the value added or the number of employees of these subsidiaries would have been a better criterion, but it was not possible to obtain comprehensive figures. All the data collected for the 413 companies were statistically processed by computer, and this was supplemented by the partial and qualitative data.[4]

We were faced with a dilemma in compiling the sample. We could either take figures at group level in France, which had the advantage of describing the whole of their organisation and the level at which the big decisions were taken. This did however make it difficult to make any comparison between operation abroad and the economic and financial consequences of operation in France. The latter cover several companies, often in several sectors. The second possibility is to take figures for French subsidiaries so that comparisons are easier as operation in France is more uniform. The companies were in fact drawn by lot from all the companies quoted, giving us both parent companies, or group leaders, and their French subsidiaries.[5] We kept to this 'cross-section' of the French production machinery, each time describing all of the direct or indirect foreign subsidiaries, that is the whole group controlled by the company in question.[6] Our sample therefore describes both the groups and some of their French subsidiaries.[7]

Finally, we have to add that we have always described the production operation abroad controlled by French companies using the wide definion of economic control: majority control or minority control of the capital.[8]

2. REPRESENTATIVENESS

To give a suitable picture of the multinationalisation phenomenon, the sample must include a wide spread of companies as regards the main characteristics deemed to have an impact on this phenomenon. This is the case, as the 413 companies cover fourteen sectors of activity, and include companies of all sizes with differing levels of operation abroad: in 1974, 182 of them controlled production operations outside France.

However, to form a suitable basis for extrapolating results for the whole of the French economy, the sample must also be representative of all companies or sub-groups considered to be important. The sample does therefore include 243 companies quoted on the Paris stock exchange (variable income securities, official listing), accounting for 47 per cent of this type of company and it can hence be considered to have a representativeness of around 50 per cent.[9]

With respect to the top 455 French groups,[10] the sample covers 192 which represent 43 per cent of the equity, corresponding to some 21 per cent of the equity of all French companies. As regards exports, the 413 companies represent 39 per cent of the total exports of the 1363 export leaders for 1974 and some 30 per cent of all French exports, which is representative. With respect to all French companies, the sample is of course less representative, but if we exclude the commerce and services sectors, it is representative of at least 20 per cent of the equity of all French companies in industry, building and public works and the agricultural and food industries.

The representativeness of our sample overall or by sector is then satisfactory. Even though the big and medium-sized companies are overrepresented, the existence of small companies will enable an analysis to be made of multinationalisation in all categories of French companies.

3. CRITERIA OF MULTINATIONALISATION

The statistical method used consists in particular of studying the characteristics of the multinational companies compared with non-multinationals, for example to highlight their major specific characteristics. It is therefore necessary to have a set of multination-alisation criteria.

Before selecting these criteria, a study which we cannot describe in detail here was made to compare the consequences of the different criteria possible. The two criteria finally selected concentrated on the presence of production abroad, as do the theories and analysts. The latter often add two constraints. First, there is a size constraint: for R. Vernon[11] the multinational company must have a total turnover of over 100 million dollars in 1971, which corresponds to 500 million francs in 1974 in France. For B. Marois, the French multinational groups are the forty groups which in 1977 had a turnover of over 2000 million francs.[12] Finally there is a constraint as regards production in a minimum number of foreign countries, fixed for example by R. Vernon as at least three countries.

We have rejected the adoption of a size limit as we want to show that there are small and medium-sized multinational companies. Size will therefore be a characteristic of the companies subsequently reintro-duced into the analysis, which will for example enable a distinction to be made of the sub-group of large multinational companies.

As regards the constraint of the number of countries, which amounts to measuring the extent of production abroad, particularly in organisa-tional terms, from this point of view we have used two definitions of multinationalisation based on the following criteria:

— 1st multinationalisation criteria: the 'multinational' companies are all companies controlling production operation in a foreign country;
— 2nd multinationalisation criteria: we define within the multi-national companies the 'very multinational' companies as those controlling production operation in at least five foreign countries or which have a production operation abroad representing at least 10 per cent of their total operations.[13]

These two criteria were used throughout the study. They reveal a group of 182 multinational companies and a sub-group of 101 very multinational companies, fairly well distributed over all sectors.[14]

NOTES

1 For a full analysis see Annexe No. 27, describing the method of analysing the multinationalisation of French companies on the basis of a sample of 413 com-panies, in Savary, 1980.
2 Paragraph 1 of Annex No. 27 describes these limits.
3 See paragraph 7 of Annexe No. 27.
4 See paragraphs 4 and 5 of Annexe No. 27 for a full description of the 119 variables described exhaustively for the 413 companies.
5 See Annexe 1 (p.189): 'List of the 413 French companies in the sample'.

6 See paragraph 2 of Annexe No. 27 devoted to the composition of the sample.
7 To avoid counting twice when using certain aggregate statistics, exclude the companies whose parent company is also described in the sample. The results will then be qualified as 'excluding subsidiary companies'.
8 See Annexe No. 27, paragraph 3. Choice of a definition of the control of foreign companies.
9 See Annexe No. 29, Savary, 1980, for a detailed assessment.
10 That is excluding the sectors Insurance, Banks and Finance, and Real Estate in the ranking of *Le Nouvel Economist*, 8 December 1975.
11 R. Vernon, *Les Entreprises multinationales*, 1973.
12 B. Marois, 1979-1.
13 Our 'very multinational' companies are comparable with R. Vernon's 'multinational companies', but here we are not setting a size limit.
14 See Annexe No. 30 in Savary, 1980, describing this breakdown.

Annexe 3 Sectoral Nomenclatures

INSEE Nomenclatures		Nomenclature in 14 'main sectors'	
Level 14*	**Level 100†**	**No.**	**Name**
U01 + U03	1 to 8	1	primary ind. (agr., for., fishing, gas, oil, elec. distr.)
Intermediate goods U04	9, 12, 14, 15, 16	2	construction materials, glass, ores
	10, 11, 13, 20, 21	3	iron and steel, metallurgy
	17, 43	4	basic chemicals, art. thread, fibres
	50, 52, 53	5	paper, rubber, plastics
U06 Consumer goods	18, 19	6	parachemicals, pharmaceuticals
	44 to 49, 51, 54	7	consumer goods (non-chemical)
U05 Capital goods	22 to 26, 34	8	mechanical engineering
	27 to 30	9	electrical engineering
	31, 32, 33	10	transportation equipment
U07	55	11	building and public works
U08	57 to 64	12	commerce
U09 + U10	65 to 99, 56	13	services
	35 to 42	14	agricultural and food industries

*See for example pp. 14 and 15 of *Les comptes intermédiaires des entreprises en 1974*, INSEE collections, series E No. 51.

†See definitions in: *Nomenclatures d'activités et de produits 1973*, Ministry of Economy and Finance, 1975.

Annexe 4 The top eighty-eight foreign groups investing in France

Name	Country	Capital controlled in France 1978 (millions frs.)	Consolidated group sales 1978* ($US millions)	Operations of the group
1 Royal Dutch Shell NV	NE	3 104.2	44 054	Oil
2 Fiat Spa	IT	1 452.6	15 813	Cars
3 Hoechst AG	GER	1 198.6	12 068	Chemicals
4 International Business Machines (IBM)	US	1 184	21 076	Data processing
5 Exxon Corp.	US	1 166	60 334	Oil
6 Philips Gloeilampen-fabrieken NV	NE	1 128	15 121	Electronic equipment
7 Schlumberger Ltd.	US	998.3	2 619	Scient. & Meas. equipment
8 Nestlé SA	CH	851.7	11 001	Food products
9 Electrorail	BE	847.6		Electrical equipment
10 Unilever NV	NE	765.5	18 893	Food products
11 Maus Frères SA	CH	713.4		Holding/comm.
12 Chrysler Corp.	US	654	16 340	Cars
13 British Petroleum Co. Ltd.	GB	600.8	27 408	Oil
14 Mobil Oil Corp.	US	491	34 736	Oil
15 Cockerill SA	BE	396	3 145	Metallurgy, iron and steel
16 Sandoz SA	CH	391.7	2 420	Pharmaceuticals
17 Tenneco Inc.	US	378	8 762	Oil refining
18 International Telephone and Tel (ITT)	US	359.7	15 261	Electronic equipment
19 Tate and Lyle Ltd.	GB	359.6	2 152	Food products
20 Goss Bank	USSR	350		Bank
21 Goodyear Tyre and Rubber Co.	US	338.8	7 489	Rubber, tyres
22 Petrofina SA	BE	319.1	5 612	Oil
23 Ciba Geigy AG	CH	282.8	5 030	Chemicals, pharmaceuticals
24 Solvay et Cie SA	BE	274.6	3 027	Chemicals
25 Ford Motor Co.	US	270.4	42 784	Cars
26 Motorola Inc.	US	268.8	2 220	Electronic equipment
27 BASF AG	GER	265.4	10 732	Chemicals
28 UBAC Nederland NV	NE	250		Financial Holding company
29 Caterpillar Corp.	US	244	7 219	Industrial equipment

Name	Country	Capital controlled in France 1978 (millions frs.)	Consolidated group sales 1978* ($US millions)	Operations of the group
30 Hoffman La Roche et Co. AG	CH	240.1		Chemicals, pharmaceuticals
31 Lucas Industries Ltd.	GB	228.7	1 789	Car accessories
32 International Harvester Co.	US	224.4	6 664	Industrial & agr. equipment
33 Firestone Tire and Rubber Co.	US	223.3	4 878	Rubber, tyres
34 United Technologies	US	222.4	6 265	Aeronautics
35 Eastman Kodak Co.	US	215.8	7 013	Photographic equipment
36 Generali spa	IT	203.1		(insurance)
37 Mercury Securities Ltd.	GB	200.6		Finance
38 Bass Charrington Ltd.	GB	200.5		Drinks
39 Sté Financière européenne	LUX	200		Financial holding company
40 Algemene Bank Nederland	NE	196	†	Bank
41 Union Carbide Corp.	US	195.7	7 870	Chemicals
42 Merck and Co. Inc.	US	192.5	1 981	Pharmaceuticals
43 Grace and Co. (W.R.)	US	191.9	4 310	Chemicals
44 Electrolux A/B	SW	189.6	2 662	Electronic equipment
45 SKF A/B	SW	188.8	2 132	Steel processing
46 Intershop Holding AG	CH	180.4		Holding company, real estate
47 Seagrams Ltd.	CA	174.1	1 346	Drinks
48 Bendix Corp.	US	170.9	3 625	Cars
49 Fiduciaire et de Gérance SA (sté)	CH	163.4		
50 Intra Investment Co. SA	Lebanon	161.7		Financial holding company
51 Massey Ferguson Ltd.	CA	161.4	2 925	Agricultural equipment
52 Banca commerciale italiana spa	IT	160.8	‡	Bank
53 Semkler AG§	CH	160.3		Holding company
54 Hoescht Werke AG	GER	157.9		Metallurgy, materials
55 Akzo NV	NE	153.4	4 938	Chemicals
56 Grand Metropolitan Ltd	GB	149.4	3 654	Hotels, food products
57 C and A Nederland BV	NE	146.4		Commerce, clothing
58 Henkel KGA	GER	146.1	1 692	Chemicals
59 Control Data Corp.	US	144.6	1 846	Data processing
60 Brown Boveri et Cie BBC AG	CH	143.2	4 562	Electrical equipment
61 Clark Equipment Co.	US	140	1 503	Ind. & agric. equipment
62 Xerox Corp.	US	138.4	5 902	Scient. meas. & phot. equipment
63 Imperial Chemical Ind. Ltd.	GB	138	8 701	Chemicals
64 Rank Hovis McDougall Ltd	GB	137.5	2 283	Food products
65 General Motors Corp.	US	132.8	63 221	Cars

Name	Country	Capital controlled in France 1978 (millions frs.)	Consolidated group sales 1978* ($US millions)	Operations of the group
66 Electrowatt AG	CH	132.1		Elec. ind. holding company
67 Bosch Gmbh (Robert)	GER	128.4	4 798	Car accessories
68 Courtaulds Ltd.	GB	125.2	2 834	Textiles
69 Montedison spa	IT	121.1	6 815	Chemicals
70 Schweizerische aluminium AG	CH	120.4		Metallurgy (aluminium)
71 Monsanto Co.	US	119.6	5 019	Chemicals
72 Siemens AG	GER	118.6	13 865	Electronic equipment
73 Barclays Bank Int. Ltd.	GB	117.7	¶	Bank
74 Allis Chalmers Mfg Co.	US	116.5	1 762	Industrial equipment
75 Generale immobiliare spa	IT	116		Fin. building, real estate
76 Schindler holding AG	CH	112	625	Lifts
77 Ogem Holdings NV	NE	109.8		Com. equip. constr. ind.
78 Agfa Gevaert AG	GER	108.9	1 842	Photo lab. equipment
79 American Can Co.	US	107.9	3 981	Metal products
80 Mac Millan Bloedel Ltd.	CA	107	1 758	Paper, wood
81 Olivetti et Co. spa	IT	105	1 873	Office equipment
82 Royale Asturienne des Mines	BE	103.4		Mining and non-ferrous metals
83 Du Pont de Nemours	US	102.7	10 584	Chemicals
84 Dana Corp.	US	102.4	2 253	Cars
85 Veba Chemie AG	GER	101.5	3 931	Oil, chemicals
86 Kone Oy	Finland	100.3		Lifts, cranes
87 Daimler Benz AG	GER	100.1	12 091	Cars
88 Ready Mixed Concrete Ltd.	GB	100	1 214	Construction materials

*The consolidated group sales for 1979 are given either in the rankings drawn up by *Fortune* magazine, 7 May 1979 (the top 500 American industrial groups), 18 June 1979 (the second 500 American industrial groups), 13 August 1979 (the top 500 non-American companies), or *Business Week*, 23 July 1979, although the methods of calculation for these two sources are different: our aim here is to indicate the order of size of the groups.

†26th non-American bank, by balance sheet total (*Fortune* ranking).

‡45th non-American bank according to balance sheet total for 1978 (according to *Fortune*).

§This is a holding company partly controlled by Michelin France, and controlling Kléber-Colombes.

¶15th non-American bank by balance sheet total (*Fortune*).

Annexe 5 Geographical specialisations of production operations abroad for all French companies, by sector

(turnover of foreign production subsidiaries, establishments and sites, direct or indirect in 1974, by area as a percentage of the total)

	1A Oil	2 Mining constr. mat. glass	3 Iron & steel met.	4 Chem- icals	5 Paper Rubber Plastics	6 Para- chem. Pharma- ceutic.	7 Con- sumer goods	7A incl. textiles
Area 1 (Africa)	30.4	2.6	3.1	1.7	6.2	6	21.2	27.8
Area 2 (Asia, Latin America)	40.6	1	3.2	5.2	1.6	15.9	13.1	22.6
Area 3 (North America)	11.6	26.9	12	17.7	6.9	1.3	14	0.2
Area 4 (Developed Europe)	17	52.1	62.6	55.4	70.1	60	47.4	44.8
Area 5 (Brazil, Spain, Portugal)	0.3	17.4	19	19.9	16	16	4.2	4.5
TOTAL	100	100	100	100	100	100	100	100
Developed countries (areas 3 + 4)	28.7	79	74.6	73.1	76	61.3	61.4	45
Less developed countries (areas 1 + 2 + 5)	71.3	21	25.3	26.8	23.8	37.9	38.5	54.9
Total production (all areas) (in millions francs)	25 088	15 281	15 340	8 394	9 034	3 294	2 984	1 731

*Including foreign trading subsidiaries.

Sources: our sample of 413 French companies of all sizes, plus examination of the 200 biggest French groups and the biggest groups in each sector.

8 Mechanical engin.	9 Elec. electronic engin.	10 Transport. equip.	11 Building, public works	12A* Internat. trading cos.	12B National Commerce	13 Services	14A Food/agric. industries multinat. by nature	14B Food/agric. industries French base
4	2.8	5.1	49.1	81.4	0.4	57.3	78	44.6
3.4	16.3	22.7	8.1	1.7		6	22	0.4
16.3	7.1	2.1	5.5	3.9		2		3.6
32.1	34	24.6	22.2	11.5	42.2	29.5		40.3
44.1	39.7	45.5	15.1	1.5	57.4	5.1		11.1
100	100	100	100	100	100	100	100	100
48.5	41.1	26.7	27.7	15.4	42.2	31.5		43.9
51.5	58.8	73.3	72.3	84.6	57.8	68.4	100	56.1
1 317	3 217	9 679	5 583	8 205	1 685	2 162	1 081	1 760

Annexe 6 The foreign trade of France by geographical area in 1974 and 1977

(CIF–FOB trade in millions of current francs—customs statistics)

	1974				
	Imports	Percentage	Exports	Percentage	Trade Balance
Common Market*	120 998		117 281		−3 717
Other Western Europe	22 016		33 027		11 011
Total Europe	143 014	56.3	150 308	68.1	
North America	22 332	8.8	12 740	5.8	−9 592
Eastern Europe	6 380	2.5	7 727	3.5	1 347
Franc Area	8 811		9 576	4.3	945
Africa	18 353		19 206	8.7	853
Latin America	5 209		6 002	2.7	793
Oceania	2 411		992	0.4	−1 419
Asia	47 514		13 845	6.2	−33 669
—— including Middle East†	(36 011)	(14.2)	(3 634)	1.6	(−32 377)
—— including Japan	(4 553)		(2 232)	1.0	(−2 318)
—— including other Asian countries	(−6 950)		(7 979)	3.6	(1 029)
Total less developed countries (Franc area, Africa, Lat. Am., Oceania, Asia except Middle East and except Japan)	41 734	16.4	43 755	19.8	−2 021
General total	254 031	100	220 584	100	−33 447
including NICs (Brazil, Spain, Greece, Portugal, Turkey, Yugoslavia)	9 480	3.7	14 408	6.5	4 928 (Spain 1 428) (Brazil −135)

*Nine countries in 1977.
†Nine oil countries exporting to France: Iraq, Iran, Saudi Arabia, Kuwait, Bahrein, Qatar, Oman, Dubai, Abu Dhabi.
Source: calculations taken from CFCE, 1979.

1977				
Imports	Percentage	Exports	Percentage	Trade Balance
171 102		157 171	58.4	−13 931
31 945		40 361	4.9	8 416
203 047	58.6	197 532	63.3	
26 701	7.7	18 613	6.0	−8 088
10 908	3.1	13 685	4.4	2 777
12 019		16 259	5.2	4 240
20 079		32 316	10.4	12 237
8 260		8 132	2.6	−128
2 931		1 059	0.34	−1 872
62 363		24 471	7.84	−37 892
(45 014)	(13.0)	(9 527)	3.05	(−35 487)
(6 795)		(2 258)	0.7	(−4 537)
(10 554)		(12 686)	4.1	(2 132)
53 843	15.5	70 452	22.6	+16 609
346 364	100	312 072	100	−34 292
16 658	4.8	18 142	5.8	1 484 (Spain −1 534) (Brazil −1 578)

Annexe 7 The top thirty-eight French industrial multinationals as at 1 January 1982

(ranked by number of employees abroad, only industrial companies under national control; the public companies are italicised)

Rank	Group	Employees as at 1 January 1982			Rate of multi-nationalisation
		Abroad (A)	In France (B)	Total (C)	A/C %
1	Michelin	73 000	50 000	120 000	59.3
2	*SGPM*	72 332	63 227	135 559	53.3
3	*Renault*	49 810	166 034	215 844	22.5
4	Peugeot*	47 000	171 000	218 000	22.6
5	*CGE*	34 200	146 200	180 400	19.0
6	*Rhône-Poulenc*	33 150	56 198	89 348	37.1
7	Empain Schneider	22 470	84 530	107 000	21.0
8	*Elf Aquitaine* *	21 069	35 559	56 628	36.0
9	*Thomson*	21 000	128 000	149 000	16.3
10	*PUK*	20 311	66 531	86 842	23.4
11	CFP†	20 088	27 172	47 260	42.5
12	*Imétal* *	18 795	5 044	23 839	78.8
13	Lafarge	15 539	13 934	29 473	52.7
14	Bic*	15 500	11 000	26 500	58.5
15	Air Liquide*	15 000	10 000	25 000	60.0
16	BSN	10 786	30 965	41 751	25.8
17	DMC	8 474	10 649	19 123	44.3
18	Générale des Eaux*	8 000	44 060	52 060	15.4
19	Amrep	7 535	3 099	10 634	70.9
20	Prouvost	6 300	12 679	18 979	33.2
21	Valéo	5 200	22 000	27 200	19.1
22	*CII–H.B.* ‡	5 078	16 120	21 198	24.0
23	Vallourec*	4 500	20 435	24 935	18.0
24	Fives-Lille*	4 000	8 966	12 966	30.8
25	Télémécanique*	3 800	8 382	12 182	31.2
26	*EMC*	3 578	8 731	12 309	29.1
27	Lyonnaise des Eaux*	3 300	42 656	45 956	7.2
28	Carnaud	3 048	9 451	12 499	24.4
29	Pompey	2 368	7 736	10 104	23.4
30	Essilor	2 177	5 611	7 788	28.0
31	Legrand	2 031	9 204	11 235	18.1

Rank	Group	Employees as at 1 January 1982			Rate of multi-nationalisation
		Abroad (A)	In France (B)	Total (C)	A/C %
32	Sommer	1 851	6 851	8 702	21.2
33	Fichet Bauche	1 553	2 860	4 413	35.2
34	Lesieur	1 457	5 104	6 561	22.2
35	Bel*	1 606	5 695	7 301	22.0
36	Crouzet	1 282	7 540	8 822	14.5
37	Générale de Fonderie	1 140	10 214	11 354	10.0
38	Chausson	1 051	14 161	15 212	6.9

nd: not determined.

*Estimate.

†The State holds 40 per cent of CFP.

‡Under national majority control since April 1982 (employees abroad correspond to commercial operations).

Source: published data and survey (consolidated employees of groups). (L'Oréal, controlled by Nestlé, employs 11 388 people abroad, and Roussel Uclaf, controlled by Hoechst, employs 6 814.)

Annexe 8 The top twelve French multinationals in the building and public works sector as at 1 January 1982

(ranked by number of employees abroad)

Rank	Group	Employees as at 1/1/82			Rate of multi-nationalisation
		Abroad (A)	In France (B)	Total (C)	(A)/(C) %
1	Dumez	26 300	3 000	29 300	89.8
2	SCREG*	22 519	14 857	37 376	60.2
3	SGE (soc. gle d'entre-prises) (CGE group)	18 256	14 752	33 008	55.3
4	Fougerolle	17 673	8 880	26 533	66.6
5	SPIE (Empain-Schneider group)	17 580	14 750	32 330	54.4
6	Colas†	10 720	16 080	26 800	40
7	Campenon Bernard (Générale des Eaux group)	7 000	11 098	18 098	38.7
8	Bouygues	6 423	17 365	23 788	27
9	SAE Auxiliaire d'Entre-prises	3 435	14 830	18 265	18.8
10	Coignet	2 817	2 468	5 285	53.3
11	GTM Grands Travaux Marseille‡	2 000	7 967	9 967	20.1
12	SOBEA Socea Balancy (SGPM group)	2 812	5 814	8 626	32.6

*Minority interest held by Belgian shareholders.
†Taken over by SCREG in 1983.
‡Estimated.
Source: Company reports and survey, consolidated figures.

Bibliography

Adam, G., 'The Big International Firm and Socialist Countries: an interpretation', CNRS International conference No 549, Rennes, 1972; *La Croissance de la grande firme multinationale*, Paris, Ed. du CNRS, 1973.

ADEFI, 'Les Restructurations industrielles en France', Fifth national meeting, Chantilly, September 1979; Paris, Ed. Economica, 1980.

Alcouffe, A. and Morin, F., 'L'Affaire Schneider, ou la naissance d'un nouveau couple financier', *Economie et Humanisme*, No 258, March–April 1981.

Allard, P., Beaud, M., Bellon, B., Levy, A. M. and Lienart, S., *Dictionnaire de groupes industriels et financiers en France*, Paris, Ed. du Seuil, 1978.

Andreff, W., 'Pour une approche historique de l'internationalisation du capital', ACSES conference, Grenoble, June 1974.

Andreff, W., *Profits et structures du capitalisme mondial*, Paris, Calmann-Levy, 1976.

Andreff, W. and Pastre, O., 'Le genèse des banques multinationales et l'expansion du capital financier international', paper given to the conference 'Internationalisation des groupes financiers et des banques', CEREM, University of Paris X, November 1979; Paris, Ed. CNRS, 1981.

Anvers, M., 'L'implosion du social', *Le Monde Diplomatique*, December 1979.

Auquier, A., 'Sizes of Firms, Exporting Behaviour, and the Structure of French Industry', *Journal of Industrial Economics*, No. 2, December 1980.

Barrere, C., 'Equivalent général, monnaie et crise du système de crédit', thesis, University of Paris I, 1974.

Bataille, P., 'La Compétitivité des produits français à l'exportation', report to the Economic and Social Council, Official Journal, 19 July 1978.

Baudant, A., 'Une entreprise française face à l'exportation, Pont-à-Mousson: 1860–1940', *Revue Economique*, No 4, Paris, July 1980.

Beaud, M., Danjou, P. and David, J., *Une multinationale française: Pechiney Ugine Kuhlmann*, Paris, Ed. du Seuil, 1975.

Bellon, B., *Le Pouvoir financier et l'industrie en France*, Paris, Ed. du Seuil, 1980.

Bellon, B., 'Origines et conditions des restructurations en France', ADEFI conference: 'Les restructurations industrielles en France', Chantilly, September 1979; Paris, Ed. Economica, 1980.

Bennis, R. and Rhiati-Salih, A., 'Carnaud au Maroc et en Côte-d'Ivoire', research memorandum, University of Social Sciences, Toulouse, 1979.

Berthelot, Y. and Tardy, G., *Le défi économique du tiers monde*, Commissariat général au Plan, Documentation française, 1978.

Berthelot, Y., 'Emploi industriel et évolution de la division internationale du travail', *Tiers Monde*, No 81, January–March 1980.

Bertin, G. Y., 'Les Causes de la croissance des entreprises à l'étranger', *Revue Economique*, July 1972.

Bertin, G. Y., *L'Industrie française face aux multinationales*, Commissariat général au Plan, Documentation française, 1975.

Bodinat, H. and Marois, B., *Gestion financière internationale* (2 volumes), 2nd edition, Paris, Dunod, 1978.

Bodinat, H., De Leersnyder, J. M., Ghertman, M., Klein, J. and Marois, B., *Gestion internationale de l'entreprise*, Paris, Dalloz-Gestion, 1978.

Boublil, A., *Le Socialisme industriel*, Paris, PUF, Collection *Economie en liberté*, 1977.

Buckley, P. J., Dunning, J. H. and Pearce R. D., 'An Analysis of the Growth and Profitability of the World's Largest Firms, 1967 to 1977', International conference on 'The impact of the large firms on the performance of the European economy', European Institute for Advanced Studies in Management Brussels, 10-12 June 1981.

Bulcke, D. Van Den, Boddewin, J. J., Marten, B. and Klemmer, P., *Politiques d'investissements, réductions ou cessations d'activités de multinationales en Europe*, Paris, PUF, CEEIM, 1979.

Capian, A., 'Aspects internationaux de l'accumulation cyclique du capital (1870–1970)', doctoral thesis, University of Paris I, 1973.

Caves, R. E., 'International Corporations: the Industrial Economics of Foreign Investment', *Economica*, vol. 38, 1971.

CEPII, 'Les Economies industrialisées face à la concurrence du tiers monde, le cas de la filière textile', August 1978.

CEREM, 'Internationalisation des groupes financiers et des banques', Conference organised by CEREM at the University of Paris X, Paris 8, 10 November 1979; Paris, Ed. du CNRS, 1981.

CFCE (Centre français du commerce exterieur), Statistics on foreign trade from 1950 to 1977, 1979 edn., Paris, 1979.

Chevalier, J. M., *L'Economie industrielle en question*, Paris, Calmann-Levy, 1977.

Chevalier, J.M., *L'Echiquier industriel*, Paris, Hachette, 1980.

Chevallier, J. Y. and Nizet, J. Y., 'Résultats et comportements de 2800 sociétés privées 1971-1977', Etude de la Centrale des bilans, direction de la Prévision, Ministère de l'Economie; Journée d'étude des centrales de Bilan, Paris, 28 May 1980.

Chouchaoui, S., 'Bouygues en Côte d'Ivoire', research memorandum, University of Social Sciences, Toulouse, 1979.

Clairmonte, F., 'Comment les sociétés multinationales du textile renforcent leur emprise sur le marché mondial', *Le Monde diplomatique*, July 1981.

Claude, H., *Les Multinationales et l'impérialisme*, Paris, Ed. Sociales, 1978.

CNPF,* *Implantations à l'étranger, 70 témoignages d'entreprises*, Ed. ETP, October 1979-1.

CNPF, *Données comparatives et chiffres clés sur l'investissement français à l'étranger*, Ed. ETP, October 1979-2.

CNPF, *De l'exportation à la croissance internationale, propositions du CNPF pour une politique active d'investissement à l'étranger*, Report on the Journées de l'investissement français à l'étranger, 11-12 October 1979, Ed. ETP, 1979-3.

Cohen, J., 'Quelques remarques sur le redéploiement des grands groupes français', Fifth meeting of ADEFI, Chantilly, 20 September 1979; in *Les restructurations industrielles en France*, Paris, Ed. Economica, 1980.

Cohen, R. B., 'La restructuration internationale de l'industrie automobile', *Revue d'Economie Industrielle*, No 11, 1st quarter 1980.

Cohen, J. C. and Fondanaiche, C. P., 'Les Participations étrangères dans l'industrie française en 1971', *Economies et Statistiques*, No 52, January 1974.

Commissariat général au Plan, 'Crédit, change et inflation', Report of the applied monetary economy group (2 volumes), Paris, Documentation française, 1978.

Cotta, A., 'Pouvoir et stratégie de l'entreprise multinationale', International conference No 549 of CNRS, Rennes, September 1972; in *La croissance de la grande firme multinationale*, Paris, Ed. CRNS, 1973.

 * Conseil National du Patronat Français—National Council of French Employers

Cotta, A., *La France et l'impératif mondial*, Paris, Ed. du Seuil, 1978.

Couffin, H., *Les entreprises françaises sur le marché américain*, Paris, Ed. Economica, 1977.

Drugman, B. and Eisler, P., 'Capital financier et accumulation monopoliste, à propos du groupe SGPM', IREP Grenoble, June 1972.

Dubarry, J. P. and Cardot, Z., 'Les PMI et l'exportation', Chronical of SEDEIS-IV, 1981.

Dunning, J. H., 'The Determinants of International Production', International conference No 549 of CNRS, Rennes, September 1972; in *La croissance de la grande firme multinationale*, Paris, Ed. CNRS, 1973.

Dunning, J. H., 'The UK's International Direct Investment Position in the Mid-1970s', *Lloyds Bank Review*, No 132, April 1979.

Ehrsam, J., 'Les investissements français à l'étranger et les investissements étrangers en France', Report to the Economic and Social Council, January 1981.

Encaoua, D., Franck, B. and Jacquemin, A., 'Répartition fonctionnelle des revenus, pouvoir de monopole et groupes industriels', AFSE Conference, Paris, 17 June 1981.

Frank, D. and Mathis, J., 'Investissement direct américain et balances des paiements', *Statistiques et études financières*, No 355-6, 1979.

Franko, L. G., *The European Multinationals, a Renewed Challenge to American and British Big Business*, London, Harper and Row, 1976.

Frobel, F., Heinrichs, J. and Kreye, O., 'La Nouvelle Division internationale du travail et ses répercussions sur l'emploi', No. 1, 1978 of Gewerkschaftliche Monatshefte Cologne and *Problèmes économiques*, 11 October 1978.

Geze, F., 'Le Redéploiement international des grands groupes industriels français et ses conséquences sur l'emploi en France', *Revue d'économie industrielle*, No. 15, Paris, 1981.

Gilly, J. P. and Morin, F., 'Les Groupes industriels en France, concentration du système productif depuis 1945', Notes et études documentaires No 4605-6, Paris, Documentation française, 1981.

Glejser, H., Jacquemin, A. and Petit, J., 'Exports in an Imperfect Competition Framework: an analysis of 1446 exporters', *Quarterly Journal of Economics*, May 1980.

GRESI, 'La Division internationale du travail', Ministry of Industry, *Etudes de politique industrielle*, No 9 (2 volumes), Paris, Documentation française, 1976.

Groupe de recherche de géographie industrielle, *Les Investissements étrangers en France*, Grenoble, Presses universitaires de Grenoble, 1975.

Guibert, B. et al., 'La Mutation industrielle de la France', INSEE Collection, Series E, No 31-2, November 1975.

Guir, R., 'Logiques d'internationalisation et théorie de l'organisation industrielle, les investissements industriels français en Amérique du Nord', duplicated document, University of Quebec, Hull, June 1980.

Hannoun, M., 'Les Groupes industriels, structures et performances', *Journée d'études des centrales de bilans*, 6 June 1978.

Helleiner, G. K., 'Manufactured Exports From Less Developed Countries and Multinational Firms', *Economic Journal*, No 329, March 1973.

Hernandez, Cl., Peskine, B. and Saglio, H., 'La Pénétration étrangère dans l'industrie française', *Economie et Statistiques*, No 72, November 1975.

Hirsch, S., 'Multinational Corporations: how different are they?', International conference No 549 of CNRS, Rennes, September 1972; in *La croissance de la grande firme multinationale*, Paris, Ed. CNRS, 1973.

Horst, T., 'Firm and Industry Determinants of the Decision to Invest Abroad: an empirical study', *Review of Economics and Statistics*, No 54, August 1972.

Hugon, Ph., 'Chômage: le tiers monde est-il responsable? Mythes et limites des méthodes d'analyse', *Tiers Monde*, No. 81, January–March 1980.

Hymer, S., and Rowthorn, R., *International Big Business 1957–1967: A Study of Comparative Growth*, Cambridge, Cambridge University Press, 1971.

ILO, 'Les entreprises multinationales et la politique sociale', International Labour Office (Bureau international du travail), Geneva, 1973.

INSEE, 'Les Groupes de sociétés dans le système productif français. Année 1974', INSEE Collection, Series E, March 1980.

Jacquemin, A., *Economie industrielle européene* (2nd edition), Paris, Dunod, 1979.

Jeanblanc, P., 'L'industrie européenne des fibres synthétiques, la concurrence oligopolistique face à la crise', State doctoral thesis, University of Social Sciences, Toulouse, June 1981.

Kaplan, M. C., 'Analyse fine des investissements français à l'étranger'—'Fondation nationale des sciences politiques', study carried out for the Commissariat général du Plan (duplicated), December 1979.

Keller, P., 'Les Relations franco–suisses et les industries suisses en France en 1980', *Revue économique franco–suisse*, No. 4, Paris, 1980.

Kindleberger, C. P., *Six lectures on Direct Investment*, New Haven, Yale University Press, 1979.

Kraseman, T. and Barker, B. L., 'Employment and Payroll Costs of US Multinational Companies', *Survey of Current Business*, No. 10, October 1973.

Laubier, D. de and Richemond, A., 'Interpénétration des capitaux et concurrence industrielle mondiale', CEPII, March 1980. Provisional version at conference of ISMEA, 10–14 March 1980; *Economie Appliquée*, No. 2.3.1981.

Le Pors, A., *Les Béquilles du capital, transferts Etat-industrie: critère de nationalisation*, Paris, Ed. du Seuil, 1977.

Leibhaberg, B., *Relations industrielles et entreprises multinationales en Europe*, Paris, PUF, CEEIM, 1980.

Lienart, J. L., 'Dynamique des importations et croissance centrifuge', *Revue d'économie politique*, No. 4, Paris, 1980.

Mader, F. and Rocher, J., 'La Réussite sur le marché mondial', survey presented at seminar 'La réussite sur le marché mondial, six expériences d'entreprises', Crédit national, Paris, January 1980.

Magdoff, H., *L'Âge de l'impérialisme*, Ed. Maspero, 1970.

Marois, B., *Les finances des sociétés multinationales*, Paris, Ed. Economica, 1979-1.

Marois, B., *L'Internationalisation des banques*, Paris, Ed. Economica, 1979-2.

Masini, J., Ikonicoff, M., Jedlicki, C. and Lanzarotti, M., *Les Multinationales et le développement, trois entreprises et la Côte-d'Ivoire*, Paris, PUF, Collection CEEIM, 1979.

Maurino, J. D., 'Procès d'internationalisation et développement des luttes de classes', ACSES conferences, Grenoble, June 1974.

Metais, J., 'Le Processus de multinationalisation des grandes banques commerciales', *Revue Economique*, No. 3, May 1979.

Michalet, C. A., 'Pourquoi les entreprises deviennent-elles multinationales? Le cas français', International conference No. 549 of CNRS, Rennes, September 1972; in *La croissance de la grande firme multinationale*, Paris, Ed. CNRS, 1973.

Michalet, C. A., *Le Capitalisme mondial*, Paris, PUF, 1976.

Michalet, C. A., 'Typologie des FMN', *Cahier français*, No. 190, 1979.

Michalet, C. A. and Delapierre, M., *La Multinationalisation des entreprises françaises*, Ed. Gauthier-Villars, 1973.

Michalet, C. A. and Delapierre, M., *Les Implantations étrangères en France: stratégies et structures*, Paris, Ed. Calmann-Levy, 1976.

Ministry of Economy, 'Evolution des investissements français à l'extérieur et étrangers en France, de 1973 à 1979', Note bleue, July 1979.

Mistral, J., 'Filière et compétitivité: enjeux de politique industrielle', Annales des Mines, January 1980.

Monateri, J. Ch., 'L'Industrie pétrochimique: nouveaux acteurs et adaptations de l'ancienne structure oligopolistique', *Economie et Humanisme*, No. 256, November–December 1980.

Montavon, R., *L'Implantation de deux entreprises multinationales au Mexique BSN Gervais-Danone et Akzo*, PUF, Collection CEEIM, 1979.

Morin, F., *La Structure financière du capitalisme français*, Paris, Ed. Calmann-Levy, 1975.

Morin, F., Alcouffe, A., Alcouffe, C., Moreaux, M. and Freixas, X., *La Banque et les groupes industriels à l'heure des nationalisations*, Paris, Ed. Calmann-Levy, 1977.

OECD, 'Face aux futurs, pour une maîtrise du vraisemblable et une gestion de l'imprévisible', Report by OECD edited by J. Lesourne, 1979.

Pastre, O., *La stratégie internationale des groupes financiers américains*, Paris, Ed. Economica, 1979.

Payement, C., 'Les Petites et Moyennes Entreprises à l'exportation', Report to the Economic and Social Council, Official Journal, 15 February 1980.

Perrin, J., 'De nouveaux exportateurs de technologie: les pays semi-industrialisés', *Economie et Humanisme*, No. 256, November–December 1980.

Rainelli, M., *La Multinationalisation des firmes*, Paris, Ed. Economica, 1979.

Reynes, A., 'Armosig en Côte-d'Ivoire', research memorandum, University of Social Sciences, Toulouse, 1979.

Robbins, S. and Stobaugh, R. B., *Money in the Multinational Enterprise, a Study in Financial Policy*, New York, Basic Books, 1973.

Rolant, M., 'Evolution économique des Etats-Unis et ses incidences sur l'économie française', Study presented to the Economic and Social Council, 28 April 1981, Official Journal No. 10, avis et rapports du CES, Paris, June 1981.

Roussel, J., 'Le Redéploiement de l'industrie ouest-allemande à l'étranger', *Le Monde diplomatique*, December 1979.

Sagou, M., *Paribas, anatomie d'une puissance*, Paris, Presse de la Fondation nationale des sciences politiques, 1981.

Sauviat, C., 'Les Mutations du systeme bancaire et financier français sous la Ve République', doctoral thesis, University of Paris X, January 1981.

Savary, J., 'La Multinationalisation de l'économie française: spécialisation et dépendance', doctoral thesis, University of Social Sciences of Toulouse, June 1980.

Savary, J., 'Les Multinationales françaises à l'heure du recentrage', *Economie et Humanisme*, No. 257, January–February 1981-1.

Savary, J., 'La France dans la division internationale du travail: une approche par l'investissement direct international', special issue 'Spécialisation internationale et crise', *Revue Economique*, July 1981-2.

Soulage, B., 'Stratégies industrielles et sociales des groupes français', doctoral thesis, University of Social Sciences, Grenoble, IREP publications services, 1981.

STISI, 'Etude économique des entreprises et secteurs à forte pénétration étrangère', Ministry of Industry, 1976.

STISI, 'L'Implantation étrangère dans l'industrie', Ministry of Industry, Collection 'Traits fondamentaux du systeme industriel français', Documentation francaise; No. 3 as at 1 January 1975; No. 9 as at 1 January 1976; No. 14 as at 1 January 1977; No. 18 as at January 1978.

STISI, 'Les Exportateurs de l'industrie, entreprises, groupes, filiales de groupes étrangers' (J. P. François, E. Mathieu and M. Suberchicot), Ministry of Industry, 1980.

Stoffaës, C., *Le Grande menace industrielle* (2nd edition), Collection *Pluriel*, Paris, Livre de Poche, 1980.

Stoleru, L., *L'Impératif industriel*, Paris, Ed. du Seuil, 1969.

Stopford, J. M. and Wells, L., *Direction et gestion des entreprises multinationales*, Paris, Ed. CLM, Publi-Union, 1974.

Stopford, J. M., Dunning, H. and Harerich, K. O., *The World Directory of Multinational Enterprises*, London, Macmillan, 1980.

Tardy, G., 'L'industrie en Europe', *Futuribles*, December 1979.

Thuillier, J. P., 'Les Investissements directs européens aux Etats-Unis: investissements croisés et centralisation du capital', doctoral thesis, University of Paris-Dauphine, 1979.

Tugendhat, C., *The Multinationals*, London, Pelican Books, 1973.

UN, *Les sociétés multinationales et le développement mondial*, New York, 1973.

UN, *Les sociétés transnationales dans le développement mondial: un réexamen*, New York, 1978.

US Senate Committee of Finance, 'Implications of Multinational Firms for World trade and Investment and for US Trade and Labor', R. B. Long, Chairman (Ribicoff report), Washington D.C., 1973.

Vaitsos, C. V. and Saussay, Ph. de la, 'Le Second Elargissement de la CEE et les stratégies des firmes transnationales, commerce et implantation: quelques données générales', *Revue d'économie industrielle*, No. 12, 2nd quarter 1980.

Vaupel, J. and Curhan, J. P., 'The World's Multinational Enterprises, a Source Book of Tables', Graduate School of Business Administration, Harvard University, Boston, United States, 1973.

Vellas, F., 'Stratégie industrielle et pouvoir de négociation, le programme Ford Fiesta', supplementary thesis, University of Social Sciences, Toulouse, 1978.

Vernon, R., *Les Entreprises multinationales*, Paris, Ed. Calmann-Levy, 1973.

Vitry, G., *Les Données de la politique industrielle*, Fifth national meeting at Chantilly of ADEFI, September 1979, Paris, Ed. Economica, 1980.

Wilkins, M., *The Emergence of Multinational Enterprise*, Cambridge, Harvard University Press, 1970.

Bibliography to Supplement

Andreff, W., *Les multinationales hors la crise*, Paris, Ed. Le Sycomore, 1982.

Bandt, J. de and Judet, P., 'Le tissu industriel français face à la coopération technologique et industrielle avec le Tiers-Monde', preparatory report, Ministry of Industry; Conference 'Coopération technologique et industrielle France/Tiers Monde', Marseille, 26–7 September 1983.

Banville, E. de and Verilhac, J. *Saint-Etienne, Le capital redistribué, histoire industrielle 1970–1982*, Saint-Etienne, Ed. Cresal, 1983.

Bauer, M. and Cohen, J., *Qui gouverne les groupes industriels?*, Paris, Ed. Seuil, 1981.

Beaud, M., *Histoire du capitalisme 1500–1980*, Paris, Ed. Seuil, 1981.

Beaujolin, F., *Vouloir l'industrie, pratique syndicale et politique industrielle*, Paris, Les editions ouvrières, 1982.

Bellon, B. and Chevallier, J. M., *L'industrie en France—collection Enjeux pour demain*, Paris, Ed. Flammarion, 1983.

Benlahcen Tlemcani, 'L'industrie du ciment dans le monde: un exemple d'oligopole stable', postgraduate thesis, University of Social Sciences, Toulouse, 1983.

Berthelot, Y. and de Bandt, J., 'Impact des relations avec le Tiers Monde sur l'économie française', Report for the Ministry of Planning (one volume and 10 annexes), Paris, Documentation française, 1982.

Berthelot, Y., Pineye, D. and Sid Ahmed, A. K., 'Accompagner le développement industriel du Tiers-Monde', preparatory report, Ministry of Industry; Conference 'Coopération technologique et industrielle France/Tiers Monde', Marseille, 26–7 September 1983.

Bertrand, H., 'L'industrie automobile française aujourd'hui et dans les années 80', *Revue d'Economie Industrielle*, No. 19, 1st quarter 1982.

Bertrand, H., Mansuy, G. and Norotte, M., 'Vingt groupes industriels français et le redéploiement', *Economie et Prévision*, No. 51, 1981.

Bourguinat, H. (ed.), *Internationalisation et autonomie de décision: les choix français*, GRECO conference of CNRS, Bordeaux, June 1981, Paris, Ed. Economica, 1982.

Boussemart, B. and Rabier, J. C., *Le dossier Agache Willot*, Paris, Presses de la Fondation Nationale des Sciences Politiques, 1983.

Bouyssonnie, J. P., *Au coeur de la bataille électronique*, Paris, Jean Picollec, 1982.

Caire, G., 'Codes de conduite: multinationales et acteurs sociaux', *Revue d'Economie Industrielle*, No. 22, 1982.

Cardot, Z. and Dubarry, J. P., 'Les importateurs sont-ils aussi exportateurs?', *Economie et Statistiques*, No. 142, March 1982.

Cardot, Z., Dubarry, J. P. and Sabatte, D., 'Importateurs et exportateurs: les opérateurs du commerce extérieur en 1979', *Cahiers du commerce extérieur*, No. 5, March 1982.

CEPEII, *Economie mondiale: la montée des tensions*, Report by the Centre d'Etudes Prospectives et d'Informations Internationals, Paris, Ed. Economica, 1983.

Claude, H., *La 3éme course aux armements*, Paris, Ed. Sociales, 1982.

CNRS, *Les flux d'investissement direct entre la France et les pays industrialisés 1965-1974*, by P. A. Ameller, F. Marnata, C. Sarrazin, P. Gantès and Y. Laplume, Paris, Ed. du CNRS, 1980.

Conseil economique et social (Economic and Social Council), 'La place et l'importance des transferts techniques dans les échanges extérieurs', CES report by M. Saint Cricq, June 1982.

Cotta, A. and Ghertman, M. (eds), *Les multinationales en mutation*, Conference, November 1982, *Collection Perspective multinationale of IRM*, Paris, Ed. PUF, 1983.

Credit National, 'La compétitivité de l'entreprise et le redéploiement industriel', Conference, October 1981; *Bulletin du Crédit National*, No. 34, 1982.

Didier, M., 'Crise et concentration du secteur productif', *Economie et statistiques*, No. 144, May 1982.

Dunning, J. H., *International Production and the Multinational Enterprise*, London, George Allen and Unwin, 1981.

Dunning, J. H. and Cantwell, J. A., 'Investissements américains directs et compétitivité technologique européenne', *L'actualité Economique*, Montreal, July 1982.

Estevenin, G., 'La pénétration étrangère du système productif français: une analyse sectorielle (NAP 90) sur la période 1975-1980', doctoral thesis, University Aix Marseille II, April 1983.

Frank, I., *Multinationales et développement: entreprises étrangères dans les pays en développement*, Paris, Ed. Masson, 1981.

Freyssinet, J., *Politiques d'emploi des grands groupes français*, Grenoble, Ed. Presses Universitaires de Grenoble, 1982.

Frobel, F., Heinrichs, J. and Kreye, O., *The New International Division of Labour*, Cambridge, Cambridge University Press and Paris, Ed. de la maison des sciences de l'homme, 1981.

Galambert, P., *Les sept paradoxes de notre politique industrielle*, Paris, Ed. du Cerf, 1982.

Ghertman, M., *Les multinationales—Que sais-je?*, *Collection No. 2068*, Paris, Ed. PUF, 1982.

Gilly, J. P. and Savary, J., 'Les groupes étrangers dans l'industrie de Midi-Pyrénées: impact et stratégies', *Revue géographique des Pyrénées et du Sud Ouest*, Tome 54, fasc. 3, Toulouse, Autumn 1983.

Grou, P., *La structure financière du capitalisme multinational*, Paris, Ed. Presses de la Fondation Nationale des Sciences Politiques, 1983.

Guilloux, M. C., 'Contribution à l'étude des stratégies d'implantation à l'étranger: l'exemple des entreprises françaises en Espagne', DEA memorandum, University of Bordeaux I, 1982.

Guir, R., 'Logiques d'internationalisation et théorie de l'organisation industrielle: les cas des investissements industriels français en Amérique du Nord', *Revue d'Economie Industrielle*, No. 21, 1982.

Haudeville, B., 'Redéploiement industriel et emploi en France de 1974 à 1979', AFSE conference, Paris, June 1982.

Herzog, C. and Richemond, A., 'Néo-protectionnisme et investissement international: le cas de l'accès au marché nord-américain', *Revue Economique*, No. 6, Paris, 1982.

IREP Developpement, 'La semi-industrialisation', by Cl. Courlet, A. François and P. Judet, *Cahiers de l'IREP*, No. 1, Grenoble, 1981.

Jemain, A., *Michelin, un siècle de secret*, Paris, Ed. Calmann-Lévy, 1982.

Judet, P., 'Les nouveaux pays industriels', *Economie et Humanisme*, Paris, Les éditions ouvrières, 1981.

Jura, M., 'Les effets des investissements étrangers sur la croissance française', State doctorate thesis, University of Paris X, Nanterre, 1982.

Kaplan, M. C., 'Enquête sur le redéploiement industriel des entreprises françaises', *Bulletin du Crédit National*, No. 33, 1981.

Koffel, H., 'Les firmes multinationales françaises en Afrique noire francophone', DEA memorandum, University of Toulouse I, 1982.

Lamant, J., 'Un exemple d'assistance technique', *Revue d'Economie et Humanisme*, No. 266, 1982.

Lefranc, T., *L'imposture monétaire*, Paris, Ed. Anthropos, 1981.

Lemettre, J. F., 'Le secteur public élargi au coeur d'une autre politique', *Revue d'Economie Industrielle*, No. 17, 1981.

Lietaer, B., *Le grand jeu Europe—Amérique Latine*, *Collection Perspective multinationale of IRM*, Paris, Ed. PUF, 1981.

Madeuf, B., 'L'ordre technologique international, production et transferts', *Notes et Etudes Documentaires*, No. 4641-2, Documentation française, Paris, 1981.

Mautort, L. de, 'Concurrence internationale et norme de production dans l'industrie automobile', *Revue d'Economie Industrielle*, No. 19, Paris, 1982.

Maxy, G., *Les multinationales de l'automobile*, *Collection Perspective multinationales of IRM*, Paris, Ed. Puf, 1982.

Michalet, C. A., 'Une nouvelle approche de la spécialisation internationale', *Revue d'Economie Industrielle*, No. 17, Paris, 1981.

Michalet, C. A., Delapierre, M., Madeuf, B. and Ominami, C., *Nationalisations et internationalisation, stratégies des multinationales françaises dans la crise*, Paris, Ed. Maspero La Découverte, 1983.

Muchielli, J. L. and Thuillier, J. P., *Multinationales européennes et investissements croisés*, Paris, Ed. Economica, 1982.

OECD, *Tendances récentes des investissements directs internationaux*, Paris, OECD, 1981.

Padioleau, J. G., *Quand la France s'enferre*, Paris, Ed. PUF, 1981.

Parti Socialiste, 'Socialisme et industrie', Conference, October 1980, Club Socialiste du Livre, Paris, 1981.

Pean, P. and Serini, J. P., *Les émirs de la République, l'aventure du pétrole tricolore*, Paris, Ed. du Seuil, 1982.

Perrin, J., *Les transfers de technologie*, *Collection Repères*, Paris, Ed. Maspero la Découverte, 1983.

Prud'homme, R., 'Les investissements des multinationales de l'automobile dans le Tiers-Monde', AFSE conference, Paris, June 1983.

Rainelli, M., 'Structuration de l'appareil productif et spécialisation internationale', *Revue Economique*, No. 4, July 1982.

Reiffers, J. L. (ed.), *Economie et finance internationales*, 23 specialists collected by J. L. Reiffers, Articles dedicated to Doyen Marcy, Paris, Ed. Dunod, 1982.

Reiffers, J. L., Cartapanis, A., Experton, W. and Fuguet, J. L., *Sociétés transnationales et développement endogène, effets sur la culture, la communication, la science et la technologie*, Paris, Ed. Presses de l'Unesco, 1981.

Revue d'Economie Industrielle, 'Les politiques industrielles', Special number, No. 23, Paris, 1st quarter 1983.

Revue Economique, 'Les nationalisations', Special number, No. 3, Paris, May 1983.

Ruffini, P. B., *Les banques multinationales*, *Collection Perspective multinationale of IRM*, Paris, Ed. PUF, 1983.

Savary, J., 'Les effets des entreprises multinationales sur l'emploi: le cas de la France', Document de travail No. 24, International Labour Office, Geneva, 1983.

Savary, J., 'Les multinationales contre la crise?', *Revue d'Economie Industrielle*, No. 26, 4th quarter, 1983.

Savary, J., 'Impact des l'investissement étranger en France sur l'emploi industriel (1974-1983)', chronique-Annuaire 1983/1984, *Revue d'Economie Politique*, 1984.

STISI, 'Importations, exportations et filiales françaises de firmes multinationales', by J. P. François and J. Mathis, Ministry of Industry, Collection 'Traits fondamentaux du système industriel', No. 10, 1982.

STISI, 'Le secteur public dans l'industrie avant et après les nationalisations', Ministère de l'Industrie, Collection 'Traits fondamentaux du système industriel', No. 25, 1982.

Stoffaës, C., 'Objectifs économiques et critères de gestion du secteur public industriel', *Revue Economique*, No. 9, Paris, 1983.

Thollon Pommerol, V., 'Les groupes publics et privés', *Economie et Statistiques*, No. 147, Paris, 1982.

Index of Companies

Index